BATSFORD PSYCHOLOGY SERIES

Moral Learning and Development

Theory and Research

Moral Learning and Development

Theory and Research

Douglas Graham

Senior Lecturer in Psychology
University of Durham

B. T. BATSFORD LTD London

First published 1972
© Douglas Graham 1972
Printed in Great Britain by
Willmer Brothers Limited, Birkenhead
and bound by C. Tinling and Co. Ltd, Prescot
for the publishers B. T. Batsford Ltd
4 Fitzhardinge Street, London W.1

ISBN 0 7134 0981 9

Published in the United States of America by
Wiley & Sons, New York

Contents

Acknowledgments

I should like to express my thanks to Louise Simpson Hendry, who first stimulated my interest in this field; to the University of Durham for granting me a sabbatical term; to my colleagues in the University of Durham Department of Psychology, especially Neil Bolton, for doing my teaching during my absence; and to Lindsay Waller, Dorothy Graham and Miles Wenner for help with proofs and index. My greatest debts, however, are to my wife and to Barbara Atkinson, formerly of the University of Durham Department of Psychology; to Connie for her unfailing tolerance, sympathy and understanding at all times, and to Barbara for constant encouragement, reassurance and support over a number of years. My debt to both of them is greater than I can ever express.

Introduction

When we raise the question of moral development and learning, we have at once to recognize the need to define the three constituent terms, 'development', 'learning' and 'moral'. We shall consider development and learning first, leaving until last what we mean by 'moral', the most difficult of the three terms to define.

In psychology, the term 'development' refers to progressive change in individuals which takes place over time, particularly as the individual grows from infancy through childhood and adolescence to adulthood. There is physical development, sensory development, emotional development, intellectual development, social development and moral development. It is clear enough from the names of these areas of development, what each in general refers to. However, the reality which develops is the individual, and each area of development represents an abstraction from the whole process, which we make for convenience. Thus, it should not be thought that intellectual development, emotional development and so on proceed completely independently of each other. But it is convenient to divide development up into such areas and it is certainly true that, although development in one area is not independent of development in other areas, development does not by any means proceed at the same pace in all areas. For various reasons, we may be mainly interested in *one* area of development—as we are in moral development—and may devote our attention mainly to investigating the changes over time which take place in this area, even though changes in other areas may affect changes in this particular area, and in turn may be affected by such changes. The changes which take place in the course of development will depend partly on 'built in' or constitutional factors in the individual, largely determined by heredity, and partly by environmental factors and experience. In so far as development takes place as the result of such built in, constitutional factors, it is generally referred to as 'maturation'. Walking is a good example of the development of behaviour as a result of maturation. Hereditary factors may be of several kinds : (1) those which are common to men and animals; (2) those which are characteristic of men but not animals; (3) those which are peculiar to one sex or the other; (4) those which make each individual unique from the start of life. Deprivation of essential things in the environment, such as adequate nutrition, may of course prevent maturation from taking place, but here we have a *lack* of something specific which *prevents* natural growth from taking place rather than the presence of environmental factors which specifically promote development. The development of things like the capacity for mathematical thinking depend to a much greater extent upon experience of particular kinds of factors in the environment (training in numbers, in abstract thinking and the like), though it is clear that hereditary factors are also involved. When particular kinds of experience are of relatively great importance, and we feel justified in thinking that there has been some change in the individual as a result of such experience, we talk about *learning*. It will be clear that, just as no organism can survive without some dependence on its environment, environmental factors can only be significant if we have an organism to respond to them, and the effect of events in the environment will depend upon the characteristics of the organism as a responding and organizing system. In some cases, it may appear more important to pay attention to, or seek to understand, the maturational aspects, in others, more important to pay attention to the environmental factors which stimulate learning. Which aspect we concentrate upon will also depend upon what kind of initial view we may take about the fundamental psychological nature of the human organism. In a sense, all points of view are interactional in that, although we may adopt what is largely a maturational point of view, searching for developing capacities or built in trends in the human individual to explain changes in behaviour, we cannot *wholly* ignore the environment, though we may choose to treat it as given. Similarly, although we may concentrate upon trying to explain development in terms of the kinds of experience to which the individual has been subject, we cannot *wholly* ignore natural growth processes which change the nature of the individual organism and therefore its responsiveness to experience. But different approaches may nevertheless be concerned more with one aspect than the other. Exponents of the variety of modern psychological theory called 'learning theory' have concentrated mainly upon trying to explain development in terms of the history of events which have impinged upon the individual, and in this they have tended to view human beings as essentially responding organisms which react to processes like conditioning and reward and punishment. Piaget and others, on the other hand, have devoted more attention to what they believe to be essential aspects of the growing human organism in *dealing with* the environment, e.g. the human being's capacity for organizing experience and imposing meaning upon the environment.

The difference between the two points of view, predominantly environmentalist and predominantly maturational has been associated with another important difference. The environmentalists have been rather strongly committed to a view of development as a process of continuous change, as experience gradually accumulates and enables the individual to handle more complex events effectively. In so far as people show similar development, this is to be attributed largely to the fact that they have had similar experiences—otherwise they would have developed differently. Since experience is on this view continuous and development gradual, development has been viewed largely as a quantitative matter, or perhaps as a matter of increasing complexity. For example, as a child grows up, he gradually becomes more intelligent in the sense that he has more capacity for solving more complex problems. The predominantly maturational view has tended to be associated with some idea of qualitatively different stages of development. For example, as a child gets older, he passes through successive stages of intellectual growth, each stage emerging from the previous stage, but distinguished by characteristics which make it qualitatively different from every other stage. Now, the idea of stages might seem to imply a discontinuity in development, and suggest that an abrupt transition is made from one stage to the next. However, Piaget makes clear that in this view, the concept of stages of development does not require the assumption of discontinuity. Rather, development is a process by which children gradually begin to operate in terms of the next higher stage, increasingly use the mode of functioning characteristic of that stage, and gradually make less use of more 'primitive' modes of functioning, though these may still be retained and used on occasion. Thus, although discontinuity of development logically implies stages of development, stages of development do not necessarily imply discontinuity.

The term 'moral' may be used in three main senses. (1) It may be used to refer to 'resistance to temptation', or the inhibiting of behaviour which is regarded as 'wrong' though perhaps pleasurable or profitable. In this sense, an immoral person is one who does not inhibit such impulses but pursues the immediate satisfaction of his desires. However, one may refrain from socially disapproved actions because one is afraid of the consequences. In this case, whether an action is regarded as moral will depend entirely on the social definition of the behaviour as 'good' or 'bad'. (2) It may refer to the control of behaviour by reference to 'internalized' standards rather than by reference to the possible consequences of the behaviour for the actor. In this sense, one must have regard for the motives and intentions of the actor; actions carried out or not carried out because of fear of consequences are not moral—actions carried out or not carried out because of prescriptions or prohibitions accepted as compelling, are. However, in so far as these prescriptions and proscriptions have been *internalized,* they represent the acceptance of external authority. They are accepted as 'naturally' right without any genuine understanding of reasons for their acceptance. (3) It may indicate behaviour which is carried out by reference to rules or principles which are rationally accepted in the sense that reasons for accepting them are understood and felt to be legitimate. Immoral behaviour in this sense is behaviour which is carried out in the pursuance of ends, in spite of the fact that the behaviour or the ends conflict with the requirements of such rules or principles. In this sense, moral behaviour is behaviour consequent upon a moral decision, which itself entails a moral judgment as to what is the right thing to do. The main basis of such judgments is the golden rule that one should take full account of the rights of other people, and apply to one's own behaviour the rules of right and wrong which one holds to be applicable to others' behaviour. To be immoral is to fail in this sense to take full account of the rights of others, or to claim special privileges for oneself which one does not allow to others. Something like this last use of the term 'moral', indeed, is frequently regarded as the only proper use. It implies that, to be capable of a high level of morality, one must have sufficient intellectual capacity to understand the nature of moral rules or principles, and the capacity to analyse problems and dilemmas in terms of these rules or principles, and decide how they should properly be applied.

It is, however, arguable that 'morality' in the first two senses may be a pre-requisite for the development of the capacity for both moral judgment and moral behaviour in the third sense. We must get to know what things are called 'right' and what things are called 'wrong' before we can understand the *kind* of things to which these moral labels are commonly applied, and we must have an understanding of how these moral labels are used, and what they mean, before we can begin to ask questions about the basis of such labelliing, and in what terms and how far current practice in this respect can be justified. Before we pass judgment on people for pursuing the satisfaction of their own desires at the expense of others, we must 'know' that they are capable of inhibiting their behaviour, or not doing what impulse suggests. We have to learn to inhibit behaviour before we can justify such abstention in moral terms. We have to learn to accept and follow rules before we can understand the principles upon which they rest, and, perhaps, how far they are justified. 'Good habits' may well be the basis from which we can proceed to question the ultimate 'goodness' or 'rightness' of some of them. But Peters,[225] like Piaget, suggests that to encourage an acceptance of externally imposed discipline in fact discourages people from becoming moral in the third sense of the term. Perhaps we might resolve this by suggesting that, as soon as children develop understanding and a grasp of language, parents might leave their children in no doubt as to how they expect them to behave, but try to justify these expectations in such terms as the child can understand. The older and more intelligent the child, the more abstract and rational justifications he will, other things being equal, be able to follow and accept. But these justifications need not necessarily mean that other methods (reward and punishment) may not be used concomitantly. They may, indeed, be necessary. It is obviously also important for parents and others in authority to set an example of living up to their own standards. Thereby they set a double example—a behavioural example which their children may imitate, and an example of acting according to rule. If parents act at variance with their precepts, they may suggest that rules can be bent to suit personal convenience.

Following the three-fold division made by Aristotle, we may view human conduct as having three aspects or dimensions—the cognitive, the affective and the behavioural. The cognitive aspect refers to such processes as perceiving, judging, knowing and thinking. In the moral sphere, this includes such things as knowledge of moral rules, understanding of the nature and the 'why' of moral rules, and moral judgment, i.e., the capacity for deciding, in terms of general principle, whether a given action or course of action is good or bad, and for deciding which of alternative courses of action are most defensible in moral terms. It also includes the capacity for self-criticism by reference to principles, as distinct from feelings of remorse or guilt. The affective aspect refers to the kind of feelings we have in relation to actions which we consider right or wrong—in particular, to feelings like anticipatory anxiety, guilt, remorse and shame, which are experienced in relation to our temptations and transgressions. It also includes the positive feelings of satisfaction which we experience when, for example, we go out of our way to help someone, and the feelings of human sympathy which induce us to respond to others in need even at a cost to our own self-interest. It may further be extended to include feelings of moral indignation which we may experience when we believe that some kind of injustice appears to be flourishing. The behavioural aspect refers, as the term indicates, to overt behaviour—resistance to temptation, taking steps to put right, if we can, the wrongs to others which have resulted from our transgressions, confessing our guilt; and on the positive side, not merely the avoidance of what we consider to be wrong, but the performance of those actions which we believe to be right, for example helping others. In so far as we believe that the 'conscience' forms a single more or less organized and self-consistent system, and that it makes sense to talk of a general 'moral character', we should expect to find a fair degree of consistency both within each area and between areas. Those with the highest level of moral judgment, for example, should, in general, also be those who act in the most moral way. What are the grounds for supposing that this is indeed so?

Hartshorne and May[130] in their painstaking work more than 40 years ago included tests of honesty, cooperation and persistence, and other measures. Since they found only small correlations between their measures, they concluded that 'morality' was mainly a matter of responses specific to particular situations, and not a general matter at all. Moral development was therefore to be regarded as the learning of a large number of rather specific habits. However, Maller[193] and Burton[57] in later analyses of Hartshorne and May's material, found evidence that there was some degree of generality across situations, although it was not very great. Burton's finding that honesty was not entirely specific is confirmed by Nesbitt's[220] finding of a factor of honesty after a factor analysis of a number of 'moral' tests. (Incidentally, Nesbitt's honesty factor seemed to be strongly tinged with intelligence.) Likewise, Sears, Rau and Alpert[249] found that behavioural tests of resistance to temptation correlated on average about $+.26$, with some correlations substantially higher.

Allinsmith[4] found that the tendency to give 'guilt' responses in a story completion test varied considerably with the situation depicted in the stories; and we ourselves found little generality across stories in the giving of 'self-critical' responses. Grinder and McMichael[122] did find measures of remorse, confession and restitution related. But the use of story-completion techniques seems so unsatisfactory that we cannot have too much faith in 'measures' of this kind. As far as moral judgment is concerned, Durkin[72] found considerable variations between situations in the use of 'reciprocity' (see p. 218) as a basis of judgment, while Johnson[148] found low consistency across different kinds of question in a moral judgment test based on Piaget's ideas. Durkin also reported that the same kind of answers might be given for quite different reasons. We ourselves found some tendency for self-critical responses (story-completion) to be related to level of moral judgment.

Porteus and Johnson[229] report that cognitive measures of moral judgment were virtually unrelated to affective or 'feeling' measures. They also found that their cognitive measures were not significantly related to ratings on moral behaviour made by peers. Kohlberg,[166] however, found that students who cheated tended to make moral judgments on his material on a conventional basis rather than in terms of moral principles; and Ruma and Mosher[239] found moral judgment to be quite substantially correlated both with guilt as assessed by the Mosher guilt scale and a measure of guilt based on remorse and self-critical judgment. A number of investigations have used measures of resistance to temptation, in the form of amount of cheating or infringement of rules in experimental situations, and related these measures to moral judgment or to measures of guilt based upon projective techniques, but they have not shown clear agreement. Grinder[120] found resistance to temptation in his ray-gun game unrelated to measures of moral judgment, while Allinsmith[4] found that resistance to temptation was not directly related to guilt. Burton, Maccoby and Allinsmith[58] did, however, find that resistance to temptation was related to a tendency to use 'confession' responses in story completions, and this was confirmed by Rebelsky, Allinsmith and Grinder.[232] On the other hand, Grinder and McMichael[122] found resistance to temptation related to remorse but *not* to confession or restitution. Porteus and Johnson[229] report no relation between their measure of affective reaction, while Medinnus[199] likewise found no relation between resistance to temptation and a measure of 'external-internal orientation'. We ourselves, in our own investigation, found no relationship between the making of self-critical (sentence completion) responses and cheating.

These findings may, in general, seem to indicate that the

different 'aspects' of morality are more or less independent. However, several things must be borne in mind. First of all, the methods used are not very satisfactory. Projective techniques have often been used as measures of guilt, tendency to react by confessing, etc., but the *validity* of such measures has not been satisfactorily demonstrated. Responses may not in fact correspond to the real feelings or response tendencies of the children concerned. Secondly, studies which have used cheating and the like as measures of 'resistance to temptation' have in fact been using very limited situations indeed as if they had real importance. Thirdly, and most important, is the question of how far we should expect concrete behaviour to be consistent over a wide range of different situations, even if there are general moral tendencies or dispositions. It should surely be obvious that, generally speaking, we must allow for the specific characteristics of the situations, which mean that different children may view these situations in different ways. For example, a child may be given the opportunity to cheat in two different 'games'. But if he is intensely interested in one and keen to do well in it, then this situation means something very different to him from the *other* game-situation, and also something different from what it means to some other child who is not in the least interested in doing well. Moreover, cheating may seem immoral or *intrinsically* wrong (in contrast to being forbidden) only to some older children. Again, a high level of consistency in real life situations should only be expected either when the range of situations is, for one reason or another, very restricted, or when a high level of abstract thinking enables general principles to be applied over many and varied situations. Indeed, consistency in a genuinely *moral* sense is a mark of *highly* moral people, i.e. people who regulate their lives to a large extent by self-accepted ethical principles. Among lesser mortals, and especially among children, behavioural consistency is likely to reflect more the range of situations over which their training has extended, and in which they have been taught to conform to certain expectations. To the more conventional, in fact, some actions of the most highly moral people, fully consistent with their other behaviour in terms of their own principles, may appear inconsistent, because the more conventional cannot understand either the principles or the way in which they are being applied. It is just not reasonable to suppose that there is *no* relationship between moral judgment and behaviour, although it is obvious enough that people do not behave in accordance with their judgment all the time, and some people perhaps not so very often. In so far as laboratory studies fail to find any such relationship, this is likely to be because they are not the kind of studies which are likely to show up the relationship. Their value may lie primarily in demonstrating that judgment and action are not always related, if indeed any such demonstration is necessary. It seems, further, impossible to suppose that the feeling aspect is not also related to action, and to judgment, although again, it is clear that there is no simple correspondence. It may very well be that in many cases, it is the feeling aspect which mediates between judgment and action. If we feel the discomfort of remorse, we may be motivated to do something to relieve it. A recent study by Schwartz *et al*[245] is very much to the point here. They report the following findings. (1) Level of moral thought was associated with refraining from cheating. (2) Need for achievement *tended* to be related to refraining from cheating. (3) Level of moral thought tended to be related to helpfulness in the sense of sacrificing one's own interest for the sake of others (altruism). (4) Need for affiliation was associated with helpfulness. (5) Need for achievement was *not* related to helpfulness. The authors conclude, 'We hold that a lack of overt moral consistency, such as that observed here, results in part from the mitigation of the effects of morally relevant characteristics by other variables. If this is so, analyses of the cues present in different situations of moral conflict and of the important morally neutral dispositions they are likely to activate should permit one to predict when conduct will or will not be morally consistent' (p. 55). They further observe that there may be 'natural empirical clusterings of the conditions accompanying moral conflict for each moral domain' (*ibid.*)—for example, conflict about helpfulness may tend to arouse affiliative tendencies. This analysis is very much in keeping with the view expressed above.

Theories relevant to moral leaning and development

There have been three main theories which have influenced thinking about moral learning and development in recent years—
psychoanalytic theory, learning theory and cognitive developmental theory as expounded by Piaget and his followers and
successors, especially Lawrence Kohlberg. While it is true to say
that these have been the main theoretical influences, some investigators have taken an eclectic or empirical view, others have been
influenced by more than one of the three main theoretical
approaches, especially by psychoanalytic theory and learning
theory, while yet others have been influenced by role theory and
by an approach in terms of the kind of self-concept or self-picture
which human beings develop and how this comes about.

Generally speaking, psychoanalytic theory has emphasized the
feeling aspect, learning theory the behavioural aspect and cognitive developmental theory, as its name implies, the cognitive aspect,
although Piaget has insisted on the association of cognition with
action. However, both psychoanalytic theory and learning theory
may be said to have been based ultimately on the feeling aspect
in the sense that both assume that the satisfaction of certain 'needs'
produces feelings of pleasure. Both these theories have taken a
basically hedonistic view of men as motivated to maximize their
pleasure or satisfaction by reducing the 'tension' associated with
the internal stimulation which arises from 'instincts' or 'needs'.
Psychoanalytic theory has found a main source of what makes
experiences satisfying in a basically sexual 'instinct' (libido) which
may find direct or indirect satisfaction. Learning theory has tended
to view the basic sources of satisfaction as lying in the physical or
biological needs of man, and to regard other sources of satisfaction as derived from these needs by association. However, it is
true that some learning theorists, especially recently, have taken
a less restricted view, while some, like Skinner, have tended to avoid
the issue by not defining what the ultimate sources of satisfaction or
'reinforcement' may be, but proceeding in a pragmatic way by
starting from observations that some things *do* in fact seem to be
satisfying or reinforcing and using this fact to influence the course
of behaviour.

Learning theory, especially in its more extreme forms, has tended to view human behaviour as entirely causally determined in the sense that if only we knew enough about a person's constitution, his personal history and the situation in which he finds himself, we could predict his behaviour with a very high degree of confidence. In general, learning theory has also minimized the difference between socialization and moral development, and has argued that moral behaviour and values are acquired by the same kind of processes as any other behaviour is learned. One can learn to be 'bad' in precisely the same way as one learns to be 'good'. It all depends upon the kind of experiences one has—how one becomes conditioned, and what rewards and punishments one receives. Psychoanalytic theory has also tended to take a deterministic view, but in a somewhat different way. It has rather assumed that all human behaviour is purposive in the sense of being consciously or unconsciously directed towards the relief of tension or the satisfaction of impulses, and that a 'meaning' can be found for the most irrational, obscure or apparently trivial behaviour; it is deterministic in the sense that it assumes that behaviour for which the individual actor may be quite unable to account consciously, does not occur by chance, and that the individual is 'made' to behave as he does. Similarly, psychoanalytic theory has tended, though less obviously than learning theory, to obscure the distinction between socialization and moral development, by its emphasis on the process of 'introjection' of values, i.e. the process of taking over unthinkingly values given by parents and other authority figures. We use the term 'socialization' here to refer to the child's learning of the ways of his society and his adjustments to the social requirements imposed upon him. Moral development refers to the process by which the child becomes capable of making moral choices which may actually bring him into conflict with the norms of his society.

Cognitive developmental theory has tended to take 'basic motivation' for granted, and to concentrate upon the development of the human capacity for organizing experience into meaningful structures of increasing complexity and abstraction. Moral development requires not merely responsiveness to experience and training, nor internalization of given prescriptions and proscriptions, but an active organizing process by which things and the values attached to them come to be seen in a new light. Here, social experience, of course, occupies a crucial position, and Piaget, for example, indicates the importance of social exchange as providing the raw material necessary to stimulate moral development. Piaget claims, in fact, to take a specifically interactionist position, from which he views the individual as developing in a continuous process of 'assimilating' experience by interpreting it in terms which are currently meaningful to him, and 'accommodating' to new experience by reorganizing his own system of meanings to enable a more adequate level of functioning to be attained. As compared especially with learning theory, however, the outstanding feature of Piaget's approach, especially perhaps in relation to moral development, is the importance which he attaches to the natural process of development. Indeed, a primary task of cognitive developmental theory, according to Kohlberg, should be to establish 'genuine developmental dimensions' of moral judgment in the sense of types of judgment which increase with increasing age, more or less regardless of cultural differences (although cultural factors may affect both the specific content of judgment and the speed of development).

It is important to draw attention to one further kind of difference between the three types of theory. Psychoanalytic theory may be called a 'loose' theory. By a loose theory as compared with a logically 'tight' theory, we mean that the various concepts and propositions with which the theory is built are not closely related logically to one another in such a way that the theory constitutes a single integrated whole, each part of which occupies a necessary position in relation to every other part. For example, it is not altogether clear how the various kinds of identification of which Freud makes use are related to one another. Freud in fact never brought together all his exercises in theory in a systematic way. During the course of his life, he was continually not only developing but changing his views on different questions, and it is not always easy to reconcile discrepancies. Moreover, his ideas are, in general, difficult to test empirically by the usual methods of scientific investigation. For example, how would we test the truth of the proposition that every child has an Oedipus complex? Learning theory has, in general, been developed in a logically tighter way, with more regard for internal consistency and systematic coherence. It has also been developed in closer association with empirical studies designed to test propositions derived directly from the theoretical formulations. Cognitive developmental theory, although it has sometimes been accused of being vaguely formulated, has also been developed in closer association with empirical research than has psychoanalytic theory. Consequently, our treatment of the three types of theory differs somewhat. It seemed best to try to present the relevant parts of psychoanalytic theory historically as presented by Freud, in order to give some idea of how Freud came to formulate these aspects of his thinking, and to suggest implicitly why the theory is difficult to test empirically. Both learning theory and cognitive developmental theory are presented with more reference to relevant empirical research.

Freud's later concern with the nature and development of morality is foreshadowed in the *Studies in Hysteria*,[92] where the 'censorship' is referred to—a mechanism by which a new idea has to submit to approval by the ego before being allowed into consciousness (p. 269). In the case of Elizabeth von R., for example, Freud refers to an erotic desire 'whose acceptance into consciousness was resisted by her whole moral being' (p. 157). Whether the new idea is admitted to consciousness or not depends on the nature of the ideas already held by the ego. The 'censorship' also performs the function of selecting memories which can continue to be available. More specifically, mention is made of the 'repressing' of ideas which are incompatible with the ego. The term 'ego' here seems to be used not in its later sense as part of the tripartite division of the mind into id, ego and superego, but in a rather vague way to refer to the person as he is aware of himself. The idea of a censorship which keeps unwelcome ideas from consciousness is also used in *The Interpretation of Dreams*, for example, 'the state of sleep makes the formation of dreams possible because it reduces the power of the endopsychic censorship'[95] (p. 526). In the censor, we can recognize the forerunner of the superego, and it should be noted that from the start, Freud was referring to an *unconscious* process, since the ego was not thought of as deliberately *suppressing* the unwanted wish. Somewhat later, in his *Introductory Lectures on Psychoanalysis*,[104] Freud wrote, 'You know that there are dreams which can be recognized as the satisfaction of justified wishes and of pressing bodily needs. These, it is true, have no dream-distortion; but they have no need of it, for they can fulfil their function without insulting the ethical and aesthetic purposes of the ego' (p. 143). The degree of distortion of wishes which occurred in dreams was, Freud explained, proportional to the shocking nature of the wish and to the severity of the censorship. There were thus two problems involved in Freud's idea of repression—that of the nature of the unacceptable wishes or ideas, and that of the nature and source of the 'ethical tendencies of the ego'. In one sense, of course, unacceptable wishes or ideas may simply be those disapproved of by the society in which one lives; but Freud was concerned rather with basic and fundamental unacceptables, universal and characterizing human nature in all societies.

The nature of the unacceptable

In his early days, it appeared to Freud, influenced as he was by Charcot, that the cause of neurotic disturbance was always connected with sex and the unacceptable wishes therefore, in such cases, always sexual; and throughout his life, Freud was to emphasize the importance of sex, though he greatly widened the significance of the term. Somewhat later, he came to believe that the trouble lay in premature sexual experience such as seduction by an older person, i.e. in a repressed traumatic experience. He then realized, however, that it was not the experience as such that mattered, but the impact which such experience had had and the way it had been reacted to, whether the person had 'responded to them with "repression" or not'.[97] (p. 277) Later still, Freud came to believe that all patients could not have had *actual* premature sexual experiences of a traumatic kind, and concluded that what he believed himself to have observed were fantasies, reflecting wishes connected with forbidden sexual impulses. Thus he came to the view that there must be such sexual impulses from an early stage in childhood, and was led to formulate one of his central notions, that of the Oedipus complex. In his *Interpretation of Dreams,* he concludes, largely on the basis of analyses of dream material, that 'being in love with one parent and hating the other are among the essential constituents of the stock of the psychical impulses which is formed at that time' (i.e., early childhood)[95] (pp. 160–161), supporting his own observations with references to the Oedipus legend. It is clear that he had already widened his use of the term 'sexual' to include any cross-sex attachments, not merely experiences directly involving sex in its narrower connotation, and thus to include the cross-sex relations between parents and their children. It is also clear, however, that he regarded such childish attachments to parents of the opposite sex as being in an important way 'the same kind of thing' as more mature sexual attachments.

In *Three Essays on Sexuality*,[96] he develops his theory of the sexual instinct much further, arguing that the sexual instinct includes a complex of 'component instincts'. Freud defines an instinct as a stimulus arising from within the organism, a need which is abolished by satisfaction but cannot be escaped from by avoiding action, as could an external stimulus. 'By instinct is provisionally to be understood the psychical representative of an endosomatic, continuously flowing source of stimulation, as contrasted with a "stimulus", which is set up by single excitations coming from without. The concept of instinct is thus one of those lying on the frontier between the mental and the physical. The simplest and likeliest assumption as to the nature of instinct would seem to be that in itself an instinct is without quality, and, so far as mental life is concerned, is only to be regarded as a measure of the demand made upon the mind for work'[96] (p. 168). Although the *aim* of an instinct is to achieve satisfaction by abolishing the stimulation, there may be various ways of doing this, and some instincts may even be called 'aim-inhibited' when *some* satisfaction is achieved when the instinct is deflected from its original goal. Similarly, an instinct may find satisfaction by means of a wide range of different 'objects' which may continue to change during a person's lifetime. Instincts which find satisfaction in socially approved behaviour are said to be 'sublimated'. Some components of the sexual instincts are associated with the sensitive zones of the body known as 'erotogenic zones'—especially the mouth, anal region and genitals—which can readily be understood as sources of stimulation. The precise nature of other component instincts is not clear, for example, the desire for mastery (associated with sadism), the impulse to 'look' and so on. By the concept of erotogenic zones and component instincts, the pleasure got by the infant from sucking is assimilated to, though not identified with, the pleasure got from stimulation of the genitals and later from sexual experience proper. In fact, *all* forms of sensual pleasure are regarded as related, and as fundamentally connected with sexual pleasure.

Freudian stages of development

The idea of erotogenic zones and the basic continuity of all forms of sensory pleasure led Freud to another major idea, that development from birth proceeds through a series of four main stages, defined in terms of the zone which was the major source of libidinal (sensual) gratification at the time—the oral, anal, phallic and genital stages. At the earliest or oral stage, gratification is obtained mainly from the mouth by sucking and later by biting; at the anal stage, from defecating or retaining faeces; at the phallic stage, from manipulation of the sexual organs. These three stages are said to be followed by a 'latency period' when no further development takes place until sexual maturity. Proper satisfaction at the mature or genital stage involves genuine relationship with a member of the opposite sex, not just the kind of relationship in which the partner is used solely as a means of obtaining pleasure. Crucial to Freud's theory is his notion that if for any reason 'normal' satisfaction is not obtained at any stage, libido or sexual energy becomes 'fixated' at that stage and further satisfactory development cannot readily take place.

Freud attached considerable importance to fixation at these levels as a factor in the formation of later character. Fixation at the early oral level would predispose a person, he thought, to such traits as gullibility, fixation at the later (biting) oral level might lead to such later characteristics as sarcasm or disputatiousness. Fixation at the anal level caused by excessively strict toilet training might find later expression in such traits as stinginess or obsessive or sadistic tendencies. Since the phallic stage is associated with the Oedipus complex, in which the male child is said to have erotic feelings toward his mother associated with sensations arising from his genital organs, and since these feelings have to be violently repressed because of the fear of losing his sexual organs occasioned by parental prohibitions against playing with them and because of jealousy of his father as a rival for his mother's love, the phallic stage is especially important and may affect later personality in a variety of ways which may be highly relevant to the development of moral control and responsibility.

Another important associated idea is Freud's notion of 'reaction-formation' whereby repressed impulses (which may be connected with any stage of development) become transformed into characteristics with an *opposite* significance. Thus Anna Freud[91] (p. 16) refers to shame and disgust as reaction formations against exhibitionism and 'messiness' respectively, and in *Instincts and their Vicissitudes*[101] Freud himself mentions pity as a reaction formation against sadistic impulses. Reaction formations represent denials of or defences against stronger forbidden impulses. According to *Character and Anal Erotism,*[98] reaction formations are particularly likely to arise during the latency period, between the Oedipus stage and the beginning of maturity, though they may, and indeed frequently do, occur earlier. In psychoanalytic theory, they are an especially important factor in the development of character, including moral character, because they represent a permanent modification of the personality or character structure.

The nature and source of the ethical tendencies of the ego –
Narcissism and the ego-ideal.

The first major suggestion concerning the origin of the ethical tendencies of the ego is to be found in Freud's paper *On Narcissism.*[100] Here, Freud distinguishes object-libido (love directed toward other people) from ego-libido (love of oneself). A human being has originally two love-objects, 'himself and the women who nurses him' (p. 88). If one assumes the quality of libido or 'love-energy' to be given, then the more one loves oneself, the less one can love others. In childhood, apart from the love for 'the woman who nurses him', libido is largely ego-libido. But in the course of normal development, the child becomes interested in and attached to other people, i.e. a proportion of libido becomes object-libido. Another way of putting it is to say that the child forms object-cathexes or emotional attachments. When this happens, we have 'pictures' of the objects of attachment as of actual or potential sources of satisfaction (i.e. internalized images). In certain circumstances, for example, when we are ill, libido is withdrawn from objects—we become, as we say, preoccupied with ourselves. But although as a child grows up, more of his libido is normally absorbed by object-attachments, he is, as Freud says, 'not willing to forgo the narcissistic perfection of his childhood; and when, as he grows up, he is disturbed by the admonitions of others and by the awakening of his own critical judgment, so that he can no longer retain that perfection, he seeks to recover it, in the new form of an ego-ideal. What he projects before him as his ideal is the substitute for the lost narcissism of his childhood in which he was his own ideal', i.e. when it had not occurred to him that he was other than perfect (p. 94). Thus, the ego-ideal represents a kind of idea or fantasy of a perfect self as against the imperfect self which is the object of criticism. Criticism may be either in respect of things one has done and should not have done, or in respect of things one ought to have done and has not. Libidinal gratification in the form of self-approval is obtained when the ego-ideal is attained and discomfort is experienced when it is not. Thus Freud includes all forms of 'self-satisfaction' as depending on libido or basically sexual energy. The main source of the criticism which is the basis for the formation of the ego-ideal is the parents, although they are reinforced by all those who influence the child—'an indefinite number of fellow men' (p. 102). Once the ego-ideal has been formed, failure to meet its standards leads to a sense of guilt which was originally the fear of losing the parents' love. Freud specifically equates this 'special institution in the mind', as he calls the ego-ideal, with conscience. What is new is not the idea of the ego-ideal, but the context of narcissism and libido theory in which it is placed.

Identification with an abandoned love-object

A second suggestion concerning the nature of moral tendencies can be gleaned from Freud's paper *Mourning and Melancholia*.[102] In this paper, Freud is primarily concerned with the self-depreciation characteristic of depressed states. He observed that in such cases, the *grounds* on which a depressed patient criticized himself were often grounds which would have given more justification for criticizing some other person with whom the patient had had a close emotional relationship which had terminated for one reason or another. As Freud puts it, he felt that in such cases, an object relationship had been undermined and the libido which had sustained it was not used to form a fresh object relationship, but withdrawn into the ego, where it served 'to establish an *identification* of the ego with the abandoned object. Thus the shadow of the object fell upon the ego, so that the latter could henceforth be judged by a special agency, as though it were an object, the forsaken object. In this way an object loss was transformed into an ego loss, and the conflict between the ego and the loved person into a cleavage between the critical activity of the ego and the ego as altered by identification' (p. 249). The more narcissistic, i.e. the more selfish, the attachment to the love-object is, the more likely this kind of identification is to occur. It does not really seem quite clear *how* such an identification takes place. But according to Freud, what happens is that criticism and hostility, instead of being directed against the love-object or other person, is displaced against the self. Freud identifies the mental agency of this criticism as the ego-ideal, 'the agency commonly called "conscience" ' (p. 247).

Roger Brown[54] has taken up Freud's notion of identification with a lost or abandoned love-object, and suggested that if, as a result of the Oedipus situation, the little boy gives up his mother as a love-object, we might expect him to identify with his *mother,* and to internalize moral values via this identification, instead of via identification with his father. There seem to be two main difficulties about this. In the first place, Freud seems to assume that when identification with the lost love-object takes place, the critical faculty of the ego is already established, otherwise it could not play its criticizing role. In the second place, Freud assumes that it is the identified-with figure which is criticized in the guise of the ego, whereas if this kind of identification with the mother contributed to the development of the critical faculty, we would have expected the identified-with figure to have been the source rather than the recipient of criticism. Thus, although Freud makes ingenious *use* of the critical faculty of the ego in attempting to explain depression, it does not seem that the notion of identification with an abandoned love-object as here expounded is of very much help in explaining how this critical faculty arises. The most that can be said is that identification with the mother on this kind of basis might contribute something to psychoanalytic explanation of the 'incorporation' or taking-over of parental prohibitions and injunctions.

Identification and the Oedipus complex

This has generally been regarded as Freud's major contribution to the theory of moral development. His fullest account of identification is given in *Group Psychology and the Analysis of the Ego*.[106] Identification is, he says, 'the earliest expression of an emotional tie with another person. . . . A little boy will exhibit a special interest in his father; he would like to grow like him and be like him and take his place everywhere. We may simply say that he takes his father as his ideal. This behaviour . . . fits in very well with the Oedipus complex, for which it helps to prepare the way' (p. 105). It appears from this that identification with the father is not, or at least is not entirely, the result of the Oedipus complex, but exists prior to it. Freud clearly did not think that the Oedipus complex and its repression could provide the whole explanation of where the ego-ideal came from, but it is not quite clear how he thought that the prior or primary identification of the little boy with his father came about.

As Freud views it, however, at the same time as the boy is developing an identification with his father, he is also establishing an object relationship with his mother—he wishes, not to be like, but to possess his mother. It is again not clear just why Freud thought here that the relationship to the mother was an object-relationship rather than an identification, except perhaps on the grounds of 'built-in' factors of a fundamentally sexual nature. However that may be, Freud claims that the Oedipus complex results from these two processes, identification and object-relationship, coming together. When this happens, the boy becomes jealous of his father, and partly as a result of his castration fears which act to repress his longing for his mother, and partly no doubt because of his existing identification with his father, the object relationship to his mother is given up and the identification with his father rendered more powerful. Freud indicates that the idea of a parental threat to the little boy's sexual organs need not be taken too literally, and in the *Introductory Lectures* writes, 'We shall be satisfied by realizing that the child puts a threat of this kind together in his imagination on the basis of hints, helped out by a knowledge that auto-erotic satisfaction is forbidden and under the impression of his discovery of the female genitals'[104] (p. 369). No allowance seems to have been made here by Freud for the possibility that customs may change and autoerotic activities may not always be forbidden, or for the possibility that there may be many children who never see the organs of the opposite sex until they are a lot older than the age (about five years or so) at which the Oedipus complex is supposed to establish itself. The equivalent of the 'castration complex' for little girls is said by Freud to be 'penis envy', in which the little girl is supposed to feel that she has already been deprived, presumably by way of punishment. This 'fait accompli' is said by Freud to be less disturbing than the threat to the male child.

Later, in *The Ego and the Id*[107] Freud says of the primary identification with the father, 'perhaps it would be safer to say, "with the parents"; for before a child has arrived at definite knowledge of the difference between the sexes ... it does not distinguish in value between its father and its mother' (p. 3 n.). The development of an object-cathexis or object relationship to the mother must therefore mean that in so far as there was an identification with the mother, either this continues alongside the object-tie, or is replaced by it. A further complication is that, with the Oedipus complex, the boy is obliged to give up his object-tie to his mother. Freud says that the boy's identification with his father now takes on a hostile aspect, and the relationship with his father becomes an ambivalent one, involving both love and hate. The intensified identification with his father does enable the boy to retain *something* (at second hand) of the object-tie to his mother. A little girl will also, of course, establish primary identifications with both parents, but will form an object-tie to her father, and identify in a secondary way with her mother. She may, however, identify with her father as well; and, far from having a clear-cut identification of boy with father and girl with mother, the 'complete Oedipus complex' produces some degree of identification of both boy and girl with both parents, and some degree of ambivalence toward both parents. Freud's explanation, not a very convincing one, is that 'in both sexes the relative strength of the masculine and feminine sexual dispositions is what determines whether the outcome of the Oedipus situation shall be an identification with the father or with the mother[107] (p. 33). Presumably, if both identifications survive, it will be the relative strength of father or mother identification which is determined by the sexual disposition. Freud in fact allows that ambivalence toward both parents may be the result of bisexuality rather than of identification which arises through rivalry. The outcome of the combination of mother and father identifications is the formation of the superego, or internal source of prohibitions and demands, these being originally *external* prohibitions and demands coming from the parents. Freud did, however, believe that the superego had an essentially *masculine* quality, and therefore reflected mainly the identification with the father.

Id, ego and superego

Freud first introduced the division of 'the mind' into the three systems which he called the id, the ego and the superego, in *The Ego and the Id*.[107] While the id is wholly unconscious, both the ego and the superego have unconscious as well as conscious parts or aspects. The id consists of all the primitive inherited impulses. It functions in terms of the 'primary process'. As Hall and Lindzey say, 'It attempts to discharge tension by forming an image of an object that will remove the tension. For example, the primary process provides the hungry person with a mental picture of food'[126] (p. 33). The best example of primary process functioning is when people have wish-fulfilling dreams, and it was in *The Interpretation of Dreams*[95] that Freud first introduced the concept of primary process. A mental picture of food, however, does not satisfy hunger. A more complex system of response is required, and is provided by the secondary process functioning which characterizes the ego. The ego distinguishes between image and reality, is able to assess reality and therefore to indicate appropriate action by which id impulses may be satisfied. Another way of putting it which Freud also used is to say that the id operates in terms of the pleasure principle, the ego in terms of the reality principle. At the beginning of life, however, all is id, and the ego gradually becomes differentiated out of the id as the executive function of the personality, as it were. The *power* which runs the ego is derived from the id, whose impulses demand at least some satisfaction. The superego is the moral part or system of the personality and imposes restrictions on the ego in the matter of impulses which may be satisfied in action. The ego therefore has to achieve a balance between the demands of the id and those of the superego. Although more recently, a distinction has been drawn between the superego and the ego-ideal, the former term referring to the proscriptive, prohibiting or negative functions of conscience, and the latter to the prescriptive or positive functions (what one ought to do rather than what one must not do), Freud himself does not seem to have made this distinction, and in general, once he started to use the notion of superego, included the ego-ideal functions within those of the superego. He generally, however, *emphasises* the proscriptive functions. Schafer[242] suggests several possible reasons for this, including Freud's personal interest in the 'negative therapeutic reaction', in which patients seemed to 'cling to' their neuroses when improvement seemed possible, and in cases of melancholia. In the *New Introductory Lectures*,[113] Freud referred to the ego-ideal as made up of the superego's standards of perfection. Ernest Jones[150] takes this up and observes that the ego-ideal is the 'standard of individual perfection that invokes aspiration', largely if not wholly conscious, while he regards the superego as the 'unconscious conscience that criticises id impulses and gives power to the ego' whenever the ego is tempted to accept unacceptable impulses from the id. This formulation, however, is at variance with Freud's own and, particularly in its emphasis on the superego as *exclusively* unconscious, seems to be unnecessarily restrictive and out of line with the usage of most other psychoanalytic writers. In any event,

Freud seems to emphasize that it is primarily the forbidding and exhorting parents with whom the child indentifies.

In the *Outline of Psychoanalysis*[114] Freud follows a similar line, and goes on to say that *both id and superego* represent influences from the past, including both heredity and what is taken over from others (such as parents), whereas the *ego* depends mainly on personal experience, including all kinds of contingent events. Freud seems here to have meant that the ego is built up out of the child's experience in overcoming difficulties presented by the outside world. In the same work, Freud states that a 'superego must be presumed to be present whenever, as in the case of man, there is a long period of dependence in childhood' (p. 147) —presumably because the long dependence might be expected to create fear of loss of support. Freud's statement, however, seems to imply that wherever we have a long period of dependence we must also have the mental equipment necessary to develop a superego or conscience. This does not follow logically. In fact, the only creature to whom it seems that we can properly attribute a conscience is man, in whom also the period of childhood dependence is a long one. But, although it may be reasonable to assume that a relatively long period of dependence may be a prerequisite of conscience, it seems unwarranted to regard it as a sufficient condition.

In the *New Introductory Lectures*,[113] Freud refers specifically to the influence of the *parents,* emphasizing the importance of the threat of withdrawal of love, which various other writers have taken up since. 'The part which is later taken on by the superego is played to begin with by an external power, by parental authority. Parental influence governs the child by offering proofs of love and by threatening punishments which are signs to the child of loss of love, and are bound to be feared on their account. This realistic anxiety is the precursor of the later moral anxiety; so long as it is dominant there is no need to talk of a superego and a conscience' (p. 62). Freud continued to believe, however, that the superego was essentially 'masculine', owing its severity to the importance of the father in determining its quality. Thus, according to Freud, one should expect, other things being equal, that the stronger identification with the father would produce the stronger superego.

The ideal outcome of the Oedipus situation, according to *The Dissolution of the Oedipus Complex*,[109] is for the Oedipus complex not just to be repressed, but to be subjected to 'destruction and abolition' (p. 177). Identification with the parents means that 'the authority of the father or the parents is introjected into the ego and there it forms the kernel of the superego.' Thus is established the basis for normal guilt, as the feeling associated with failure to meet the demands of the superego. The libido involved in the Oedipal attachment is, Freud says, partly 'sublimated', i.e. becomes available as energy for other (socially approved) purposes, and is in part transformed into feelings of affection. In the case of little girls, Freud thinks that, since the castration threat or its equivalent must be much less severe than for boys, the formation of the superego must 'far more than in the boy . . . be the result of upbringing and of intimidation from outside which threatens her with a loss of love. The girl's Oedipus complex is far simpler. . . . In my experience it seldom goes beyond the taking of her (the mother's) place and the adopting of a feminine attitude towards her father' (p. 178). Thus, Freud believes that the superego in males is likely to be much more harsh and cruel than in females. It is interesting to note that Freud's observations on the importance of 'upbringing' and 'intimidation . . . which threatens . . . loss of love' in the case of the girl, at least opens the possibility that *boys too* might acquire a superego in this way. Freud himself clearly believed, however, on the basis of his clinical experience, in the much greater severity of the male superego, and consequently found this simpler formulation inadequate.

According to Freud, if the Oedipus complex is only *repressed*, without any sublimation or transformation of libido, this constitutes the real source of later neurotic abnormality. It may even provide the basis for an exorbitant level of guilt. In his paper *Criminals from a Sense of Guilt*,[103] for example, Freud argues that in some cases (especially, one imagines, in some apparently 'motiveless' crimes), guilt is present *before* the crime, and is the occasion of, rather than the consequence of the crime. The crime

B

would then represent the seeking of punishment for repressed, unrecognized but still active Oedipal impulses and the *real* guilt would be guilt associated with these Oedipal impulses. Freud refers again to his idea of crime from a sense of guilt in *The Ego and the Id*[107] when he indicates that the sense of guilt itself may be unconscious, the superego criticism being repressed by the ego. The idea of 'unconscious guilt' has met with considerable criticism from non-Freudians, however, and raises problems concerning the criteria by which it may be recognized. We may simply observe here that, whether the sense of guilt is regarded as potentially unconscious or not, it seems possible that some few compulsive crimes have a motivational source in obsessive guilt, and one must note that Freud certainly did not imply that this kind of interpretation could be applied to more than some special cases.

Repression and the superego

In *Moral Responsibility for the Control of Dreams,*[108] Freud writes, 'It is a remarkable fact that the more moral (a man) is the more sensitive is his conscience. It is just as though we could say that the healthier a man is, the more liable he is to contagions and to the effect of injuries. This is no doubt because conscience is itself a reaction-formation against the evil that is perceived in the id. The more strongly the latter is suppressed the more active is the conscience' (p. 134). The analogy of liability to contagion and the effects of injuries does not seem to be a happy one. But apart from this, Freud seems to mean that the greater the number of repressed impulses, the stronger must be the superego or conscience which represents defence against these prohibited impulses. But since the impulses are kept unconscious, the way in which his conscience manifests itself is in a relatively high level of guilt in response to all kinds of *minor* transgressions, failures to live up to one's ideals, even undesirable thoughts, and also in a tendency to blame oneself for unhappy fortuitous events. As Freud puts it, referring to the possessor of this kind of conscience, 'When misfortune befalls him, he searches his soul, acknowledges his sinfulness, heightens the demands of his conscience'[112] (p. 126). This can, of course, also be regarded as reflecting a need for punishment. Logically, one may ask whether Freud's way of putting the question, i.e. asking why the most moral men have the most sensitive consciences, is the only way, and whether one might not more sensibly reverse the question, asking why those with the most sensitive consciences are the most moral men. If put in this way, indeed, the question seems tautologous—those with the strongest consciences are most likely to avoid wrongdoing, and also to feel the most guilt when they do transgress. It seems most likely that Freud was impressed by clinical cases in which he observed or believed himself to have observed a quite *disproportionate* amount of guilt (conscious or unconscious), and that he formulated things as he did because of this apparent lack of 'balance'.

Aggression and conscience

In *Instincts and their Vicissitudes*,[101] Freud refers to the distinction between the sexual instincts (to which the general term 'libido' is applied) and the ego-instincts or self-preservative instincts, among which he included hunger and aggression. This distinction he regarded simply as a matter of convenience, but he assigned to the ego instincts the function of providing the basis for the control of the sexual instincts. In *Civilization and its Discontents*,[112] he revised his view of aggression and introduced a theory of mutually opposed Life and Death instincts, the latter being the ultimate basis of all aggressive and destructive tendencies, including self-destruction. This aspect of Freud's theorizing, however, has not generally been accepted by psychoanalysts, and we need not dwell upon it here. It will suffice to say that Freud saw aggression as an instinctive component of man's nature and an enduring threat to the stability of society. In *Civilization and its Discontents,* he asks the question, how does culture check aggressiveness? Aggressiveness he regards as inevitable. But its *outward* expression is controlled by the fact that it can also be directed *inwards,* against the ego and, 'in the form of conscience, is ready to put into action against the ego the same harsh aggressiveness that the ego would have liked to satisfy upon other, extraneous individuals' (p. 123). In *The Ego and the Id*,[107] Freud had indicated that the severity of the superego does not necessarily correspond to the actual severity of the parents. Indeed, children with relatively mild parents tend to have more rather than less severe superegos. The severity of the superego, Freud argued, was proportional to the intensity of the Oedipus complex and the amount of energy used in overcoming it. Now, he argues that when the parents originally frustrated gratification, this must have caused aggression which in turn had to be overcome or given up. What happens, Freud argues, is that this aggressiveness is directed inward rather than outward, and is added to the superego, increasing its severity. Thus, he now suggests that the severity of the superego depends partly on the amount of aggression felt by the child toward his parents, which itself depends partly on constitutional factors and partly on experience; and partly on the need to inhibit this aggression. In a footnote, Freud refers to Alexander's comment concerning excessive parental indulgence and excessive parental severity—that in excessive severity the child has insufficient grounds for repressing his hostility, though he may *suppress* deliberately its outward expression against the parents, and thus has insufficient grounds for adding the aggression to his superego, while in excessive indulgence, the child has insufficient justification for expressing *any* hostility against his parents and thus should tend to develop a more severe superego. 'Apart from a constitutional factor which may be supposed to be present,' says Freud, 'it can be said, therefore, that a severe conscience arises from the joint operation of two factors : the frustration of instinct which unleashes aggressiveness, and the experience of being loved, which turns the aggressiveness inwards and hands it over to the superego'[112] (p. 130 n.).

In the same work, Freud makes it clear that he regards the maintenance and progress of civilization as depending essentially upon limiting the satisfaction of *basic* impulses, including both libido and aggression. Since this renunciation will be accompanied by increasing severity of the superego, Freud thinks that civilization must impose an ever-increasing burden of guilt. In other words, increasing guilt is the individual price for civilization.

Parental superego and cultural superego

In *The Dissolution of the Oedipus Complex*,[109] as we have seen, Freud referred to the introjecting of 'the authority of the father or the parents'. In the *New Introductory Lectures*[113] he takes this one step further and states that the child's superego is based upon identification with the parental *superego* rather than with the parents as they are. 'The contents which fill it are the same and become the vehicle of tradition and of all the time-resisting judgments of value which have propagated themselves in this manner from generation to generation' (p. 67). This seems to mean that the child introjects, or takes into himself, the prohibitions, injunctions and values which his parents express toward him, rather than those by which they regulate their own conduct. These values will almost always be values generally accepted in the community to which the parents belong. Freud also allows that during childhood, the superego may be influenced by various persons who have 'taken the place of the parents' (people like teachers, for example), although it will retain the quality of the superego as originally established with the renunciation of the Oedipus complex and accompanying processes. These 'other persons' will, in general, tend to support the values acquired from the parents, although not necessarily always in every detail.

In *Civilization and its Discontents*,[112] Freud shows that he is not wholly insensitive to social processes and to historical development by referring to a 'community superego'. 'The superego of any epoch of civilization,' he writes, 'has an origin similar to that of an individual. It is based on the impression left behind by the personalities of great leaders—men of overwhelming force of mind, or men in whom one of the human impulsions has found its strongest and purest, therefore often its most one-sided expression' (p. 141). Clearly, one may identify also with such great personalities and 'improve' the 'level' of one's superego.

Freud's view of justice

In *Group Psychology and the Analysis of the Ego*,[106] Freud argues that all attachments in social groups are based upon the identification of the group members with the parent-figure or leader. But this must create envy and hostility among the members, since each member would really like to have the attentions of the leader all to himself. This envy and hostility, in turn, must be brought under control. Hence the members identify not only with the leader but with one another. Thus, rules are set up to ensure that no member gets more than any other, or at least, not more than his 'fair share'. This, Freud thinks, is the basis of the development of social justice. Justice is essentially, then, a reaction formation against envy and its accompanying hostility. Little need be said about this notion except that, as an explanation of how the sense of justice develops, it seems very one-sided and inadequate, and in fact, provides quite a good illustration of the kind of position Freud got into by trying to find an ultimate basis for all kinds of positive social attachments in libido theory.

Limits to conscience

In his preoccupation with the superego, Freud often seems to write as if he were describing processes which took place in every child, and as if everyone had a conscience or superego. It is true that Freud held that in virtually everybody, what he called the 'original prohibitions'—against incest, cannibalism and murder —are internalized. Beyond this, however, his view as clearly expressed was that the majority of people lacked either the constitutional capacity or the experiences to develop a high level of internalized control. In the *New Introductory Lectures*,[113] he writes, 'Following a well-known pronouncement of the philosopher Kant's which couples the conscience within with the starry Heavens, a pious man might well be tempted to honour these two things as the masterpieces of creation. The stars are indeed magnificent, but as regards conscience, God has done an uneven and careless piece of work, for a large majority of men have brought along with them only a modest amount of it or scarcely enough to be worth mentioning' (p. 61). Despite some degree of incompatibility with his view that civilization exacts an ever increasing toll in the form of guilt, Freud clearly seems to have felt that the majority of men must be restrained by force or by fear in one form or another, i.e. by external rather than internal sanctions, and that the few must act as the conscience of the many.

Comment

Freud has often been criticized for the use of anthropomorphic thinking. It is said that when he talks in his earlier writing about the censor and in his later writing about the superego, he is presenting a picture of a kind of homunculus within the mind of the person, exercising prohibitive or prescriptive functions. This criticism is, however, not entirely justified. Although Freud often writes in terms of such graphic analogies, he really uses the terms 'ego' and 'superego' to refer to two systems of organization within the psychological make-up of the individual. The superego refers to a hypothetical system of (mainly unconscious) internalized control by which unacceptable impulses, especially those connected with sex and aggression, are controlled. One aspect of the operation of this system with which Freud was particularly concerned was that revealed in what seemed to be *excessive* standards of behaviour and feelings of guilt and remorse which seemed *disproportionate* to the individual's actual present situation. To talk of the superego criticizing the ego is perhaps anthropomorphic use of language; but it is a use which reflects pretty faithfully, common experience, as when we speak of 'telling ourselves we ought to have known better' and the like. In fact, the superego language reflects experience much better than the language of conditioned responses. The experience is certainly that of having a conflict 'in one's mind'. If someone says, 'I know it's all right to do it, but I can't ever do it without feeling I shouldn't,' this reflects the irrational aspect of the impulse-control system as we experience it. In other cases, feeling that a person's behaviour might be comprehensible if feelings of discomfort had existed, when in fact no such feelings had been reported, Freud assumed that there might be unconscious guilt or superego activity.

It is clear that Freud's superego was not conceived as a collection of separate prohibitions and prescriptions related in a chance manner, but as a *system,* so that a person with a well-developed superego would have exacting standards (though he would not normally be fully aware of their basis), would tend to behave in a way consistent with these standards, and to feel guilt or remorse after infringing them. Thus, we should expect to find the superego operating in a consistent way. This does not mean that the operation of the superego should be logically consistent, but there is an implied consistency about the superego which can be recognized behind apparent inconsistencies. Freud certainly did not mean that moral behaviour need always be consistent. For different kinds of socially 'wrong' behaviour may have different meanings for the actor; he may be powerfully tempted in one situation and not in another. Indeed, it may be claimed that it should be an important task of psychoanalysis to reveal the inner meanings and motives. And while one would expect to find *some* relationship between tendency to feel guilt and inhibition of immoral impulses, it does not follow from psychoanalytic theory that this kind of consistency should be perfect. Some people may indeed be more ready to abstain, and feel less guilt, some may be more ready to transgress and feel more guilt. However, we should certainly expect people with a greater tendency to feel guilt also to be *more likely* to avoid what they regard as wrongdoing.

A fairer criticism of Freud's theory is that it is difficult to test in the sense that it is hard to deduce from it unambiguous empirical propositions or statements relating to observable facts which are capable of being supported or proved wrong by independent observation. This is partly because Freud's theory consists of a number of strands rather than a closely woven whole. Moreover, Freud formulated his theories in the first instance so that they would help him to understand the cases with which he dealt, and he may be said to have 'tested' his theories in the analytic situation as he experienced it, largely in terms of the extent to which he felt that the theories 'fitted' the total pattern of his observations of his patients and other observations which he felt to be relevant. Observations of patients included observations of overt behaviour, verbal communication, non-verbal cues, e.g. indications of anxiety, somatic symptoms and dreams and other fantasies reported by the patient. Freud did not keep detailed notes of his hours with his patients, believing that this impeded rather than improved therapy, and instead, wrote up summary notes at the end of the day on the cases he had seen that day. It is very possible that selective memory may have been at work and had a distorting effect. It is also possible that the complex interplay of patient's communication and therapist's interpretation affected the continual theoretical reconstructions which Freud felt to be necessary. It should, however, be said that Freud himself fully realized that everything beyond the noting of directly observable behavioural signs (including speech) *was* by way of interpretation or reconstruction.

It is particularly difficult to test Freud's general theory of libido and aggressive impulses and their relation to the superego on the theory's own terms, because, since the 'instincts' are subject to such complicated 'vicissitudes' and hypothesized processes such as reaction formation may mean that an instinct finds expression in behaviour which appears to represent the very opposite of its ordinary form of expression, it is extremely difficult to specify the conditions under which we should expect to find, and not to find, specified and observable behavioural signs, and thus to make testable predictions. Most of the confirmatory evidence comes from case reports by other analysts who have already largely accepted Freud's basic theories. The trouble is that many who are not analysts and look for independent objective evidence, do not feel that they can accept the evidence of psychoanalytic case studies.

Freudian theory posits the inevitability of the Oedipus complex for every male child and its equivalent for every female. As evidence in favour, fantasies, dreams, myths and interpretations of children's behaviour are produced. Most non-Freudian psychologists admit that there are strong emotional attachments of children to parents, and even that the attachment of boys to their mothers and of girls to their fathers may have an element in them reflecting the sex difference, but they feel unable to accept either the powerful libidinal or sexual basis for such attachments which Freud posited, or the crucial significance which he attached to the Oedipus complex and its repression or resolution. Freud himself, however, regarded his 'discovery' of the Oedipus complex as probably his most important contribution, and all Freudians, including such 'revisionists' as Melanie Klein and the ego-psychologists have followed him in accepting the Oedipus complex and its fundamental importance.

Freud's theory of the superego depends very largely upon the notion of identification with the parents. If we were to regard the Oedipus complex (and its equivalent) as *the* basis of identification, this would certainly give a relatively simple solution to the problem of how identification comes about. But Freud saw that in fact, this would not do. It is clear that he came to regard parental identifications as taking place *prior* to the Oedipus complex, although he regarded the Oedipus complex as a crucial contributory and intensifying factor, especially in boys. His purpose undoubtedly was to provide an ultimate basis for identification in libido theory, and our summary account of the views which Freud expressed at various times will indicate that he encountered considerable problems in doing so. His notions of primary identification with both parents, object-relationship to the parent of the opposite sex and the 'complete' Oedipus complex indicate the extent of strain imposed by the attempt to accommodate identification and superego development within the libido theory. Freud's valuable contribution in drawing attention to the irrational aspects of conscience, to the possible importance of the very early years and in particular to the importance of emotional relationships between parents and children should not blind us to the fact that his 'libido theory' of the development of conscience cannot really be regarded as adequate.

In both his earlier and his later work, Freud clearly emphasizes the importance of relations with the parents during the first six years or so of life. During these early years, the basic nature of the superego, according to Freud, is laid down. After the Oedipus period has been succeeded by the latency period, further development of the superego is largely a matter of elaboration or modification. Freud allows that further experience, e.g. the influence of teachers or other models, may be relevant to such elaboration or modification, but the *basis*—how far one has a superego and whether it is relatively tolerant or relatively severe and exacting— is established during the early years. It is important to realize that the crucial thing is not the prohibitions and injunctions which *are* internalized, but the development of the capacity for internalizing prohibitions and injunctions, and the way in which this is done.

Although Freud is so largely concerned with the superego, he does not deny that ego factors may also be important for conscience—for example, the ability to *postpone* the immediate satisfaction of desires. In the *New Introductory Lectures*[113] (p. 64), he refers to 'ego identifications' based on admiration and respect, which contribute to the development of character, though not to the superego. Likewise, he did not deny that rational elements could affect moral judgment and behaviour. It seems, indeed, that he tended to take this for granted. Was not the whole aim of psychoanalytic therapy to free the patient as far as possible from control by irrational forces emanating from both id and superego and enable him to make rational choices? The superego cannot be rational without the ego; but the ego cannot be moral without the superego. Because he did not specifically consider the more rational aspects of conscience and morality, Freud does not indicate how superego functions and ego functions might combine, nor what the balance between the two systems might be.

Freud emphasized the negative sanctions in relation to parents and parent figures rather than the prescriptive aspects. In his earlier statements about the ego ideal and his later statements about the superego, the emphasis is on criticism by parents. Although one tends to think mainly in terms of criticism relating to the prohibition of undesirable behaviour, this can easily be extended to include criticism for failing to live up to some stated or implied standard, i.e. criticism for *not* doing as well as for doing. It seems likely that the 'negative' aspect of the superego was related to Freud's view that basic social rules and prohibitions are restrictions upon man's instinctual drives which threaten society and therefore must be curbed, and these rules are therefore primarily proscriptive rather than prescriptive. It is interesting that those who favour the view of conscience as based essentially on conditioned anxiety also stress negative sanctions and fear, while Aronfreed, in his own version of learning theory, likewise stresses the importance of aversive training for the internalization of control of behaviour. Thus the importance which they attach to aversive training seems to reflect views on the need to inhibit the expression of 'natural' impulses or drives not far removed in essence from the views of Freud.

Melanie Klein and Ego Psychology

Melanie Klein and the early superego

Melanie Klein in her relevant writings emphasizes three main points, (1) that the superego originates at a very early age indeed; (2) that innate aggressiveness or destructivness plays a major part and (3) that early relations between mother and child are of crucial importance. She claims that 'the early stages of the Oedipus complex extend, roughly, from the middle of the first year to the third year of the child's life'[160] (p. 179). The earliest pleasure in sucking is succeeded by pleasure in biting, with the advent of the 'oral sadistic' stage. The infant is extremely sensitive to any kind of feeding frustration, which it finds terrifying, and in face of which it feels helpless. Because of innate aggressiveness, the reaction to frustration is not only one of helplessness, but also one of intense rage. This rage is dangerous, since it may threaten the source of satisfaction so that combined with the rage is further anxiety concerning the danger of the child's being destroyed by its own aggressiveness. This aggressiveness must therefore be in part repressed and this is the 'earliest measure of defence on the part of the ego'[158] (p. 268), and a first step in the formation of the superego.

The child's earliest major experiences are the physical ones of 'taking in' and 'putting out'. These then become, as it were, models for the two processes of *introjection* and *projection*. The child almost literally tries to incorporate the breast. In so far as it is satisfying, the breast becomes a 'good object', to be incorporated. In so far as it is frustrating, it becomes a 'bad object', to be expelled. What is 'good' then tends to be incorporated or 'introjected', what is bad expelled or 'projected'. Dangerous aggression is bad and therefore tends to be projected. The child's aggressive fantasies about biting and tearing the offending object are projected onto the parent, who thus becomes a kind of 'threatening monster'. This projected parental image is then re-incorporated and the child forms an image of a hostile, threatening parent. There is thus a kind of continuing dialectic process of projection and incorporation. According to Melanie Klein, the child also has fantasies about possessing the contents of the breast by scooping out, and at the anal sadistic stage, about sucking out and eating up the inside of the mother's body. Also, the child has fantasies about copulation as an act of oral incorporation, and about the mother being full of babies which the child wishes to eat up and destroy. These fantasies represent a kind of phylogenetic or 'instinctive' adumbration of later knowledge. Somewhat later, castration fears are induced by the child's own sadistic wishes, attributed to the parent and incorporated in the child's images of his parents.

Melanie Klein[160] thinks that the nature of the superego formation depends partly on whether libidinal fixation is predominantly at the oral-sucking stage or at the oral-sadistic stage (where biting is common). If the former, then *kindly* aspects of the mother-image are likely to be introjected, which leads to the introjection of a kindly father image as well, because of the equation of breast with penis.

Because of the very large amount of aggression, the early superego is especially severe. As the child progresses toward the genital stage, the introjected images become less frightening, partly because the most sadistic stages are left behind, partly because the cruel images resulting from the projection of aggressive fantasies are modified by actual experience of the parents, which the child becomes progressively more able to appreciate. The ego, Klein says, can now find support against the superego in positive relationships, and approval from parents becomes a 'cue' for superego approval. Anxiety thus becomes less overwhelming, and is transformed into guilt. If, however, guilt is too strong, it will again be experienced as anxiety. Klein takes up Freud's notion of 'criminals from a sense of guilt', generalizing far beyond Freud's statement. In her essay *On Criminality*,[159] she writes, 'Children who unconsciously were expecting to be cut to pieces, beheaded, devoured and so on, would feel compelled to be naughty and to get punished because the *real* punishment, however severe, was reassuring in comparison with the murderous attacks which were continuously expected from fanatically cruel parents' (p. 278). And again in *The Early Development of Conscience in the Child*, in the same volume, she writes, 'We must assume that it is the excessive severity and overpowering cruelty of the superego and not the weakness or want of it, as is usually supposed, which is responsible for the behaviour of asocial and criminal persons'[158] (p. 270). As a general proposition, there is no evidence whatever to support this, and certainly Freud would not have agreed with it.

Klein refers to the earlier stage, at which the infant attributes its own hostility to the 'bad' mother as the 'paranoid position' and the later stage, when the mother is seen as both 'good' and 'bad', when both good and bad aspects are introjected and hostility thus directed against the self, as the 'depressive position' (about 12 months of age). Elements of both 'positions' are incorporated in the sense of guilt. Money-Kyrle[207] suggests that two extreme types of conscience might be distinguished, (a) the persecutory conscience based on fear of punishment and (b) the depressive conscience, based on the fear of injuring or disappointing someone one loves. The former, he suggests, tends to respond to guilt by attempts at propitiation, the latter by attempts at reparation. These two types of conscience might perhaps be regarded as approximately corresponding to an authoritarian and to a humanistic attitude. This, however, is quite speculative.

Klein's theories are speculative in the extreme. Her views seem to imply that innate factors, especially aggressiveness, are so strong that any differences in child-rearing practices are likely to be of little importance in comparison with these innate factors, and that the role of parents is largely confined to lessening the effects of innate aggressiveness. This is a rather depressing position, and a recommendation of child-analysis for all is really scarcely a practicable suggestion! As Ruth Monroe[208] (ch. 5) points out, Klein's views are based on her observations of older children being analysed, especially by the play technique, and not on direct observation of infants. (Much the same criticism is, of course, made of Freud, whose theories of child development were based largely upon the analysis of adult cases.) The elaborate and complex system of impulses and fantasies, love, hatred, projection and introjection which Klein develops seems, in the absence of any direct confirmatory evidence, very tenuous. How can we really know what kind of 'fantasies' infants may be having? Indeed, have we grounds for believing that infants are capable of any such fantasies at all? In view of the initial implausibility, very convincing evidence would be required. It seems unlikely that we shall ever have it—or at least, not for a very long time to come.

Freud and the ego

In his *New Introductory Lectures*[113] (p. 38), Freud refers to the function of the ego as being to reconcile the claims of the id, the superego and the external world. It has thus got a kind of executive role, in the service of the id and superego. Freud also talks of 'ego identifications' with other people, such as well-known and admired figures, which take place during the course of one's life, subsequent to the period in which the superego is formed and therefore distinguished from *superego* identifications, although this distinction between ego and superego identification is not always clear. In the performance of its functions, the ego 'controls' the operations of movement, thinking, memory, sense of time, and in particular, the capacity for synthesizing and bringing mental contents together. 'It alone produces the high degree of organization which the ego needs for its best achievements. The ego develops from perceiving the instincts to controlling them; but this last is only achieved by the psychical representative of the instinct being allotted its proper place in a considerable assemblage by its being taken up into a coherent context. To adopt a popular mode of speaking, we might say that the ego stands for reason and good sense, while the id stands for the untamed passions' (p. 76). Freud seems to regard the ego as deriving its energy largely from the id, in the form of 'desexualized' libido, but he is not entirely clear about this, and does admit that the character of the ego functions (including perhaps the mechanisms of defence) is affected by constitutional factors. In *Analysis Terminable and Interminable,* he says it may well be the case that 'even before the ego has come into existence, the lines of development, trends and reactions which it will later exhibit are already laid down for it'[115] (p. 240). Although, however, according to many direct and indirect hints, Freud was well aware of the importance of the ego and its functions, he never developed his views on them very systematically, often giving the impression of taking them rather for granted.

Ego psychology after Freud

Hartmann[128] refers to the ego functions as ego 'apparatuses'. Unlike Freud, he believes, not that the ego is differentiated out of the id, but that the state of the new-born is 'undifferentiated' and that *both* id and ego are differentiated out of this original undifferentiated 'mass'. The newly born child is not *wholly* a creature of instincts or impulses, but has 'inborn apparatuses', e.g. perceptual mechanisms and protective reflexes, which represent the original basis of what becomes the ego. These bodily mechanisms have *primary autonomy* and function in their own rights, not on the basis of libido energy from the id. They do not function solely as a result of the impact of the external world on instinctual drives. Hartmann refers to the ego functions or ego apparatuses as constituting the 'conflict-free ego sphere'. He refers to 'that ensemble of functions which at any given time exert their effects outside the region of mental conflicts' (pp. 8–9), and more specifically writes, 'Learning to think and learning in general are independent biological functions which exist alongside, and in part independent of, instinctual drives and defences' (p. 14). The exercise of such conflict-free functions is in *itself* pleasurable not *merely* because these functions may be instrumental in satisfying instinctual needs, though of course they *do* become thus instrumental. The capacity for *anticipation* is also a crucially important ego function. In Hartmann's view, we need to determine the kind of things which go to make up a 'strong' ego, capable of exercising directed, integrated control, as distinct from a 'weak' ego, to a large extent at the mercy of passions or superego or requirements from without (e.g. demands from other people). A view of the ego such as Hartmann's, it would appear, might enable psychologists of various different theoretical persuasions to contribute to the elucidation of what makes a 'strong ego'. Some work, though not a great deal, has been done to this end.

Hartmann also refers to 'secondary autonomy' in the sense that patterns of behaviour may develop because they *are* instrumentally satisfying, i.e. they enable other satisfactions to be obtained, and then come to persist independently. For example, the habit of cleanliness may have been established in response to parental demands and fear of loss of love or approval, but may later be maintained 'on its own', perhaps even generalizing sufficiently to become an important part of the personality or character-structure of the person. It is said by Hartmann now to be maintained by 'neutralized' energy which has 'lost' its original libidinal aspect. This idea seems very similar to Allport's 'functional autonomy'.[6] Indeed, there are many points of similarity between Allport and the psychoanalytic ego psychologists.

Although Hartmann refers to the 'synthetic function' of the ego, he does not develop this idea in any detail. This synthetic or (perhaps more correctly) synthesizing function would seem to be highly relevant to the development of a sense of personal continuity and unity, and hence to the development of a sense of personal responsibility.

Hartmann specifically allows ego factors an important part in his discussions of morality. He thinks that 'knowledge' (including self-knowledge) and 'reason' cannot *supply us with* values, but can 'help us to recognize what is "really" our own hierarchy of values—that is, the actual structure and goals of our value-rational actions (i.e. actions carried out in the pursuit of some value) does not coincide with the value-system we had consciously considered our own' (p. 83). In *Psychoanalysis and Moral Values*,[129] he makes very plain his view of the importance of the ego. 'On the long way from the interiorization of parental demands after the Oedipal conflicts to the more elaborate codes of the adult, another factor becomes decisive. That is a process of generalization, of formalization and of integration of moral values. It would be difficult to attribute what I have in mind here to the superego itself. It rather corresponds to what we know of the functions of the ego. One can say, I think, that in what one may call the moral 'codes' the influence both of the superego and of the ego, particularly of the integrating and differentiating functions of the ego, are traceable' (pp. 30–31). Later in the same work, Hartmann comments in a way suggestive of Piaget on the persistence of what the latter would regard as a form of 'moral realism'. 'As to the psychological roots of the frequent incapacity to distinguish statements of fact from problems of moral validity, it seems plausible that the ways in which the primary imperatives are impressed upon the mind of the child have something to do with it. In the early years . . . these demands are brought to bear on the child in a way that makes them incontrovertible and absolute. They are often presented to the child not as demands from one person to another, but as objectively valid—at a developmental stage on which the child is not capable of distinguishing this kind of 'objectivity' from the one which he learns under the influence of the slowly maturing reality principle' (pp. 63–64). Hartmann's general approach and emphasis on 'autonomous' ego processes seems, in principle at least, to open up the possibility of some bridges between psychoanalytically oriented theory and both learning theory and developmental theory. The possibilities here are perhaps more strikingly suggested by Schafer when he writes, 'The child's development expands and crystallizes during the latency period when on the one hand, the environment provides schooling and teachers as secondary figures for object relations and identification and on the other hand, the child is able to engage himself with peers and adults in increasingly sophisticated ways'[239] (p. 138).

Anna Freud seems to take very much the same view as Hartmann when she says[91] (p. 172) that ego functions such as memory, reality testing, seeing the relation between cause and effect, reasoning, purposively directed muscular action and integrating capacity are prerequisites for socialization. Formalized systems of rules, she thinks, do not become internalized. The appreciation and acceptance of these *external* systems requires a well-developed ego. 'What a functioning superego is expected to ensure is not the individual's identification with the content of any specific laws but his acceptance and internalization of the existence of a governing norm in general.' That is, the superego sensitizes the individual to the necessity of *some* norms or principles with a clear 'must' about them. The unquestioning conformist is, in his attitude to *actual* laws, carrying on the attitude of the compliant child. But he may not feel any inner urgency, though he accepts that he and others 'should' obey the laws. The ability to criticize existing laws effectively requires ego rather than superego functioning, as Hartmann indicates. McKenzie[188] proposes that the role of the superego is to *make us stop and think*. In a morally mature person, the acceptance of an existing edict, or the decision as to what a situation calls for, should depend largely upon ego functions; but one should not underestimate the basic sensitizing function of the superego. Similarly, M. H. Stein[258] talks of an initial superego reaction 'followed by an ego appraisal of the situation'. He maintains (1) that 'self-observation is an essential element in the process of reality testing' and (2) that 'self-evaluation is inextricably linked and is intimately involved with superego functions. Therefore, the superego functions play an essential, if indirect, role in reality testing and reality adaptation' (p. 275). How does a child learn to cross the road safely? At first, he may be physically restrained, scolded or even punished, and this is, for him, the primary aspect of the situation. 'He can hardly ignore the fact that his parents are prohibiting and perhaps angry,' says Stein. 'No matter what words they use, their tone and gesture will carry *that* message more readily than the knowledge that the action may be inhibited for other reasons' (p. 287). The prohibition may become internalized, and, parallel to this, *other* reasons may be accepted for exercising care in one's kerb behaviour. Stein gives another instance of his point. Punitive factors, he holds, play a leading part in the process by which children learn to tell the truth. For the child, lies are forbidden, punished, 'bad', corresponding to his internalization of parental disapproving authority. It is *later* that he learns to recognize other grounds on which to regard lying with disapproval. This is, of course, Piaget's argument, except that Piaget does not go beyond the 'heteronomous' acceptance of authority, while Stein assigns it to 'superego' processes.

Anna Freud also emphasizes the importance of verbalization for superego and ego control. The ability to verbalize is, she thinks, essential for the replacement of primary process by secondary process functioning. The verbalization of perceptions of the external world precedes that of perceptions of the internal world, and the latter contributes to the development of reality testing and control of primitive impulses by the ego. Temper tantrums may sometimes represent a 'motor affective outlet for chaotic drive-derivatives',[91] (p. 111), i.e. a primitive mode of expression of impulses. In this case, they should disappear as soon as speech and other ego functions allow more effective expression and control. Lying may also represent the insufficiently developed capacity of the ego to distinguish between 'inner' and 'outer' worlds (although it may later be used by the ego in the service of material gain or the avoidance of punishment). Again stealing may be deliberate for gain, but may also represent an undeveloped capacity for distinguishing 'mine' from 'not mine', 'self' from 'object'. 'The ideas of "mine" and "not mine", which are indispensable concepts for the establishment of adult "honesty", develop very gradually, keeping step with the infant's gradual progress toward achievement of individual status. The notion of "being deprived of" or "stolen from" is understood by (the child) long before the opposite one, that other people's property has to be respected. Before the latter becomes meaningful the child has to extend and intensify his relationships to his fellow beings and to learn empathy with their attachment to their property' (p. 117). We may note Anna Freud's insistence that an adequate capacity for *empathy* is a necessary prerequisite for understanding and observing the property rights of others.

Edith Jacobson[145] makes the point that the development of realistic representations of both self and others depends increasingly on the development of perceptual functions. After the age of about one year, the normal child begins to be able to conceive of 'the future' as distinct from the immediate present. This development of an adequate time perspective is an important factor for moral growth. At this age, too, the child is able to distinguish singly features of his parents, to see differences between them and differences between himself and them. He thus builds up his 'idea' of himself on the basis of the perceptions of such differences. The first real awareness of the 'non-I' takes place, according to Spitz, at the age of about three months, the first real awareness of the 'I' at about two or two and a half years of age. Jacobson believes that self-perception is entirely an ego function while self-*evaluation* is shared by ego and superego.

Ego defence mechanisms

In 1894, Freud had referred to 'defence' in a short article entitled *The Neuropsychoses of Defence*.[93] Here he described certain cases of what he called 'defence hysteria'. He wrote, 'These patients . . . had enjoyed good mental health up to the moment at which an occurrence of incompatibility took place in their ideational life; that is to say, until their ego was faced with an experience, an idea or a feeling which aroused such a distressing affect that the subject decided to forget about it' (p. 47). There is in this article some suggestion that there are different possible methods of defence which the ego may use in such a case. In another rather longer article in 1896, Freud wrote that certain hysterical symptoms 'arise through the psychical mechanism of (unconscious) defence, that is, an attempt to repress an incompatible idea which had come into distressing opposition to the patient's ego'[94] (p. 162). Thus, he here equated 'defence' with 'repression'. After this, Freud abandoned the use of the term 'defence' until it occurs again in *Inhibitions, Symptoms and Anxiety* in 1926. Here, we find Freud writing, 'It is of advantage to distinguish the more general notation of "defence" from "repression". Repression is only one of the mechanisms which defence makes use of'[110] (p. 114). And again, 'It will be an undoubted advantage, I think, to revert to the old term "defence", provided we employ it explicitly as a general designation for all the techniques which the ego makes use of in conflicts which may lead to a neurosis, while we retain the word 'repression' for that special method of defence which the line of approach taken by our investigations made us better acquainted with in the first instance' (p. 163). According to Freud here, the immature ego of the child has its own particular notion of danger threatening both from the outside world and from its own impulses, and develops techniques for making the dangers tolerable. These techniques then tend to become firmly established in the personality as 'mechanisms of defence'. Anna Freud was the first, in 1936, to explore systematically the possible nature of these defensive processes.[90] This attention to defensive manoeuvres of the ego indicated a view of the ego no longer exclusively as the mediator between id (impulses), superego and the hard facts of the outside world, but as an active agent, working out a kind of 'compromise solution' to its problems which might be more or less viable, but might alternatively be excessively costly in terms of happiness and efficiency (severe neurosis). Of the superego, Anna Freud observes that 'its contents are for the most part conscious and so can be directly arrived at by endo-psychical perception' (p. 5)—i.e. by introspection. The superego, however, becomes perceptible only because of its effect on the ego as perceiver—for example, when disapproval from the superego evokes feelings of guilt. This is also of course true of the id, though much more of the contents of the id are not open to consciousness. But since it is through the ego that we first 'sight' the id and the superego, it follows that the ego must occupy a central position, and its activities, including its defensive tactics, must be of central interest. Anna Freud's view of the superego as 'for the most part conscious' is in particular contrast to that of Ernest Jones, who regards the superego as 'the unconscious conscience'[150] as distinct from the conscious ego ideal or 'standard of individual perfection that evokes aspiration'.

The main defence mechanisms to which Anna Freud refers are repression, projection, displacement, reaction formation, fixation and regression. Although the excessive use of any of these mechanisms is likely to interfere with adequate moral functioning, we have a more immediate interest in the particular form of defence mechanism which Anna Freud describes under the head of 'identification with the aggressor'. In this context, she refers to Aichhorn's report of a boy whose teacher complained that when he was reprimanded, he made grotesque faces which produced uproarious mirth among his fellow pupils. As Anna Freud recounts, 'observing the two (master and pupil) attentively, Archhorn saw that the boy's grimaces were simply a caricature of the

angry expression of the teacher and that, when he had to face
a scolding by the latter, he tried to master his anxiety by involun-
tarily imitating him. . . . Through his grimaces he was assimilating himself to or identifying himself with the dreaded object'
(p. 118). A little later, she goes on, 'In "identification with the
aggressor" we recognize a by no means uncommon stage in the
normal development of the superego.' Note that she says this is
by no means uncommon, not that it is a *necessary* aspect or stage
of superego development. She refers to children who 'identify with
the aggressor' as 'internalizing other people's criticisms of their
behaviour'. In *this* sense, 'identifying with the aggressor' would
seem to be virtually indistinguishable from the child's identifying with the authoritative, prohibiting parent, though 'identification with the aggressor' has been used in a more general way to
include identification of adults with their oppressors, for example,
rather than solely to refer to identification of children with their
parents. In any case, according to Anna Freud, such 'internalizing
of other people's criticisms' is not to be regarded as *ipso facto* the
same thing as self criticism. The first response to the internalized
criticism is to project it back upon the outside world (cf. Melanie
Klein). 'The moment the criticism is internalized, the offence is
externalized. This means that the mechanism of identification with
the aggressor is supplemented by another defensive measure,
namely, the projection of guilt' (p. 128). In this way, the ego or
person learns what is blameworthy without having to 'accept' self
criticism. Thus we have righteous indignation at the wrongdoing
of others as a precursor of genuine guilt feelings. 'This stage in the
development of the superego is a kind of preliminary phase of
morality. True morality begins when the internalized criticism,
now embodied in the standard exacted by the superego, coincides
with the ego's perception of its own fault. From that moment, the
severity of the superego is turned inwards instead of outwards
and the subject becomes less intolerant of other people' (p. 128).
Thus, *mere* internalization of criticism is not sufficient for the
proper development of the superego. There has to be a genuine
sense of having done wrong—the criticism has got to be accepted
as justified and to be wholly directed inwards against the self. 'It
is possible,' says Anna Freud, 'that a number of people remain

arrested at the intermediate stage in the development of the super-ego and never quite complete the internalization of the critical process. Although perceiving their own guilt, they continue to be peculiarly aggressive in their attitude to other people' (p. 129). The emphasis upon the full acceptance of *oneself* as at fault is extremely important. It reminds one of Kohlberg's definition of guilt in terms of awareness of having failed to live up to *self-accepted standards*. It is also worth noting that this use of introjection plus projection may remind us of Melanie Klein's use of the idea of a kind of dialectic of introjection and projection in very young children. Two points, however, in Anna Freud's exposition, do not seem very clear. In the first place, it is not clear how the ego *comes* to accept the full impact of self criticism. Secondly, although as we have noted, Anna Freud refers to the kind of manoeuvre she describes as 'by no means uncommon' in the development of the superego, she writes as if it were an essential stage.—'True morality begins when the internalized criticism . . . coincides with the ego's perception of its own fault.'

There is one further idea of Anna Freud's, outlined in *The Ego and the Mechanisms of Defence* which seems worth drawing attention to—her use of the mechanism of projection to account for 'a form of altruism'. Referring to the case of a young woman patient who, when small, had had fantasies of having beautiful clothes and children, Anna Freud says, 'The repudiation of her own sexuality did not prevent her from taking an affectionate interest in the love-life of her women friends and colleagues. She was an enthusiastic matchmaker and many love affairs were confided to her. Although she took no trouble about her own dress, she displayed a lively interest in her friends' clothes' (p. 135). Just as, in the projection of 'unaccepted' though internalized criticism we have people being disproportionately *severe* to others, in this case we have the patient, with a strong superego herself, being particularly *tolerant* to those onto whom she projected her wishes. So also, we find cases of a girl devoting herself to promoting the affairs of her sister when at bottom she would really like to be the active one herself. As a classic example of this kind of 'altruistic surrender', as she calls it, Anna Freud instances the case of Cyrano de Bergerac. According to her, then, the mechanism of projection, which tends to be disruptive of human relations when it is our aggression which we project, may work in a positive way, promoting the formation of satisfying and socially valuable relationships. The difficulty here is to specify in more than an *ad hoc* way, the conditions in which projection should work in one way and those in which it should work in the other.

The theoretical framework of E. H. Erikson

E. H. Erikson[74, 75] lays particular emphasis on the synthesizing function of the ego in developing a stable system of ideas and attitudes, to self and to others, and in achieving successful solutions to 'crises'. For Erikson, the id corresponds to our animal nature. It is 'everything which would make us mere creatures.' The ego is a conscious controlling system, which enables past experience to be brought to bear on present experience. The superego is constituted on the basis of experience with significant others in one's life. Play, speech and thought become the major ego processes. Erikson does, however, like Freud, stress the crucial role of experience during the first few years of life for the development of a healthy person. Like Piaget, he believes that there are irreversible organismic laws of development, so that development follows a definite sequence of stages or phases, although cultural factors may facilitate or impede development and give it its particular content. Each stage or phase is thought of in terms of a particular 'developmental task' appropriate to that stage. The 'developmental task' at each stage is resolved in a way which is more or less productive and successful, or more or less unproductive and unsuccessful. Successful resolution at any stage enables the child to proceed to the next stage 'well-armed'. Inadequate resolution at any stage prejudices the child's ability to cope successfully with the next stage, and consequently the child's whole development, including his moral development. Erikson posits eight stages or phases, the first five of which cover infancy, childhood and adolescence, the last three being adult phases. Each stage can be viewed in terms of a bipolar continuum representing the degrees of success or lack of success in handling the developmental task appropriate to the stage.

(*1*) *Basic trust versus basic mistrust* (*infancy*). If the infant's needs are adequately met, if his environment is rewarding and dependable, he will develop a 'sense of basic trust' which will tend to produce a feeling of confidence. If he is unsatisfied and frustrated, his 'basic mistrust' will lead to an apprehensive attitude towards the world. Although the infant does participate in social exchanges, especially with his mother, he is nevertheless, at this stage essentially egocentric. A dependable relationship with his mother, however, does provide the basis for later identification with her, and for her continuing importance as an influence in his life.

(*2*) *Sense of autonomy versus sense of doubt and shame* (*18 months to four years*). The establishment of early trust tends to lead to the development of a sense of autonomy—that one's behaviour is one's *own*. But the *limitations* to autonomy, and continuing dependence also produce doubt concerning the autonomy, and a degree of shame. Play provides the secure exploratory world in which doubt and shame can be overcome. The parents' (ideal) role is the difficult one of providing security and firmness and yet allowing sufficient freedom for the development of autonomy to be possible. While in the first phase, the mother was the crucial figure, in the second phase the father and indeed other members of the family become of increasing significance.

(*3*) *Sense of initiative versus sense of guilt* (*four to seven years*). For Erikson, this is a particularly important stage for *moral* development. In his own words, 'It is at this stage of initiative that the great governor of initiative, namely *conscience,* becomes firmly established. Only as a dependent does man develop conscience, that dependence on himself which makes him, in turn, dependable; and only when thoroughly dependable with regard to a number of fundamental values can he become independent and teach and develop tradition'[75] (p. 80). The sense of initiative arises in the acquiring of new skills. Initiative becomes associated with responsibility. Guilt arises because the child's autonomy may be restricted by the actions of parents and others. This is especially so if he finds himself no longer able to rely so fully on those on whom he has been dependent. Such guilt may lead to a reduction of initiative; but the child may *also* feel guilt if he *rejects* the opportunities provided by the environment, i.e. if he neglects opportunities for *self-fulfilment*. It is important for ego development during this period that the child's increased mobility brings wider environmental opportunities. This is also the period when superego development begins, on the basis of the internalizing of the voices of the parents. Like Freud, Erikson believes that the superego is based largely on the superego of the parents, but he emphasizes the socio-cultural beliefs and norms which are manifested by the parents in other ways than simply by what they tell the child. Erikson also draws attention to what he thinks may happen when adults fail to 'live up to' their precepts and are 'found out' by the child. 'These transgressions,' he writes, 'often are the natural outcome of the existing inequality between parents and child. Often, however, they represent a thoughtless exploitation of such inequality, with the result that the child comes to feel that the whole matter is not one of universal goodness but of arbitrary power. The suspiciousness and evasiveness which is thus mixed in with the all-or-nothing quality of the superego, that organ of tradition, makes moralistic man a great potential danger to himself and to his fellow men. It is as if morality, to him, became synonymous with vindictiveness and with the suppression of others' (*ibid.*).

This stage is also the stage of the Oedipus complex (for Erikson, like the more orthodox followers of Freud, accepts the Oedipus complex as a major fact of development). Although *all* children are dependent upon the mother, a boy *also* becomes attached to his mother at this stage as the only 'available' female, while a girl similarly becomes attached to her father as the only 'available' male. At the same time, boy and girl are encouraged to *identify* with the same-sex parents, so that the boy has to shift his identification to his father, while the girl retains hers with her mother. However, an increasingly realistic attitude leads to the gradual lessening of the parental attachments in favour of increasing attachments to peers and to other adults, although identifications with the parents, especially with the like-sex parent continue, particularly as the main basis for the development of the superego. This, it will be seen, is a somewhat modified version of the Oedipus complex as conceived by Freud.

(4) Sense of industry versus sense of inferiority (seven to eleven years). The sense of industry corresponds to new tasks successfully undertaken, the sense of inferiority arises out of failure to prove one's ability. During this stage, the child's social activities with other children expand, especially with other children of the same sex. A more realistic attitude to parents develops, and relationships with other adults also increase. The successful development of a proper 'sense of industry' and of competence is of great importance for future attitudes, especially to work.

(5) Sense of identity versus sense of identity diffusion (adolescence). The sense of identity involves a sense of personal stability, purpose and integration. Identity diffusion means a sense of instability and uncertainty in the face of felt needs and impulses and the demands of the environment. The rapid physical maturation and the accompanying change in social status render the problem of sense of identity more acute. Erikson suggests that delinquency may sometimes represent 'a desperate attempt' to find a kind of identity by setting oneself *against* the expectations of society. He believes that the identity crisis may involve any or all of seven areas, each again defined in terms of an antithesis. (a) Time perspective versus time diffusion. A good time perspective, looking both forwards and backwards, is the ideal. It may be relevant here to note that criminals frequently show an inadequate time perspective. (b) Role experimentations versus negative identity. One should be ready to experiment with new roles rather than avoiding them. (c) Anticipation of achievement versus work paralysis. One should have realistic standards of achievement which one can look forward to achieving. (d) Sexual identity versus bisexual diffusion. One should have a picture of oneself as clearly belonging to one sex or the other. (e) Leadership polarization versus authority diffusion. The adolescent must learn to recognize legitimate authority and accept authority if this is required of him. (f) Ideological polarization versus diffusion of ideals. One must choose some kind of ideals and principles, from

the range open to one within one's society, which can then serve to integrate, guide and direct one's thought and action. Adolescent rebelliousness is part of the process, and should ideally lead to the acceptance of positive ideals of one's own. To fulfill *all* these requirements must surely be regarded as an ideal, since it would appear that very few people are likely to meet all of these demands.

Erikson's developmental scheme does not stop here, although the first five stages are of most interest to us here. The remaining stages are stages of adulthood.

(6) *Sense of intimacy and solidarity versus sense of isolation (early adulthood)*. This involves the two areas of work and relations with the opposite sex, particularly in the responsibilities of marriage.

(7) *Sense of generativity versus sense of self-absorption (adulthood)*. Generativity refers to one's attitude to the next generation and one's responsibilities towards it, in the widest sense. Self-absorption cuts one off from this vital function, and estranges one from the community which in its totality must accept this responsibility.

(8) *Sense of integrity versus sense of despair (mature age)*. The sense of integrity involves an acceptance of one's own life and death in relation to the whole recurring cycle of life and death, as opposed to a 'self-centred' feeling of despair and futility.

This is a very condensed version of Erikson's developmental scheme which, in particular, omits his concept of 'organic modes' of relating to the environment appropriate to each stage or phase of development (such as the 'incorporative' mode of the earliest phase), which form the physical 'model' for the corresponding 'psychological' modes of relatedness. It should, however, be clear that Erikson regards each stage as essentially constituting a *challenge* to the individual to resolve the particular conflicts and problems associated with that stage in a way which enables his energies to be used for a corresponding fruitful resolution of the problems of the succeeding stage, leading to the development of a mature and genuinely 'moral' *person*. As Ruth Monroe writes of

Erikson's scheme, 'Each solution is based upon the earlier ones. Mature integrity depends upon the basic development of trust, autonomy, initiative, etc. in the phases of growth characteristic for the organism. They must be supported by sound cultural institutions—at first primarily by the parents but ultimately extending to all the opportunities and restrictions of society'[208] (p. 224).

Fascinating as it is, and despite resemblances in some ways to Piaget's ideas, it must be said that Erikson's scheme is largely speculative, and the support for it subject to much the same kind of reservations as must be made over more orthodox psycho-analytic formulations. Support is largely in the form of individual and cultural 'instances' which the scheme seems to 'fit'. Direct confirmation of detail would, in general, be extremely difficult to come by.

The term 'identification' has been used by Freud and others in a number of different senses, and it is not easy to decide just what it should mean, let alone to assess its value. First of all, let us look at the different though (sometimes vaguely) related ways in which Freud himself used the term.

(1) In *Totem and Tabu*,[99] he uses it to refer to the 'magical' aspects of the act of *physical incorporation* when the sons in the primitive horde killed and *ate* their father. 'In devouring him they accomplished their identification with him, and each one of them acquired a portion of his strength' (p. 142). The motive behind this identification would then be one of envy or jealousy. Identification in this sense, which one might term the 'primordial' sense, is not really very important in relation to superego development nor the development of morality, except in so far as Freud himself seems to have thought that some phylogenetic basis was necessary to help to explain why the Oedipus complex was so crucial, and why human beings should have such a ready capacity for identifying with parents.

(2) In *Mourning and Melancholia*,[102] he uses the term to refer to the 'introjection' of a 'lost' love object. In this form of identification, a person responds to himself *as if* he were the 'lost object'. This sense seems more relevant to identification with a parent of the opposite sex than to identification with the same-sex parent.

(3) In *Group Psychology and the Analysis of the Ego*[106] he refers to 'primary identification'. A boy will, according to the view expressed here, have a primary identification with his father (and a girl with her mother), as a model and as the source of the ego-ideal. In *The Ego and the Id*,[107] Freud modified his position here

somewhat, suggesting that the primary identification was with the *parents,* presumably for both boy and girl. The idea of primary identification helps Freud to get round an objection to the notion of the superego as based upon identification resulting from the Oedipus complex—that children may show 'signs of superego' at a comparatively early age.

(4) In *The Ego and the Id,* he uses the word to refer to the *outcome* of the Oedipus complex, the normal outcome being that the boy identifies mainly with his father when the 'object-cathexis' to the mother is given up; while the girl identifies mainly with her mother. As we have seen, however, Freud admits that identification with *both* father and mother is likely to result from what he regards as 'the more complete Oedipus complex'. In *The Passing of the Oedipus Complex*[109] he emphasizes that it is the *authority* of the father or parents which is introjected. That is, the child is able to respond to symbolic representations of the authority of the parents without their having to be present. The Oedipus complex may be regarded as leading to intensification of identifications with the parents, rather than as the original basis for them.

(5) Again in *Group Psychology,* Freud says that a person may identify with another person when they both have some desire in common, without there being any libidinal attachment *between* them. The example which he gives here is of a girl in a boarding school who has a letter from a secret lover, as a result of which she has a fit of hysterics. Other girls who know of her affair may then also have fits of hysterics, indicating that they also would like to have a lover. This usage seems to refer to a form of vicarious satisfaction.

(6) In *Totem and Tabu,* Freud refers to the mother who identifies with her children as a means of achieving escape from boredom and frustration in an unsatisfactory or prematurely ended marriage. There is also a measure of the same thing in the pleasure which a child may take in its parents' achievements.

(7) In *Group Psychology,* he talks of the members of a 'group' (organized social grouping) identifying with one another so as to be able to *share* the satisfaction of relationship to the leader.

Senses (5), (6) and (7) all refer to processes by which satisfactions of others may be experienced as personally gratifying. Sense

(7) can readily be extended to cover 'identification' with the 'group' as such. It would seem that identification in this sense might be relevant to the making of more 'moral' decisions regarding conduct, in so far as it represents a general capacity for 'putting oneself in another's place'. Vicarious satisfaction may also form a basis for the development of such generalized empathy.

(8) In his *New Introductory Lectures*,[113] Freud mentions later 'ego identifications' with more realistic parental images as contributing to character formation and not as being taken into the superego. These ego identifications are probably of greatest importance in later adolescence; and they may be with figures other than parents. In so far as such identifications are based upon the achievements of the model, parental or otherwise, they might perhaps be regarded as forms of role-identification, lacking the strong element of one-sided personal authority of the earlier superego identifications.

Throughout, Freud views identification in all its forms as largely if not wholly unconscious. This is true also of Anna Freud's 'identification with the aggressor'. As far as this use of the term is concerned, much has been made of reports that prisoners in concentration camps frequently appeared to identify with their oppressors to the extent of wearing bits of old uniforms which had belonged to guards, insisting on rigid observance of rules, bullying other prisoners and so on. It seems doubtful how far it is necessary to posit identification with the aggressor to explain this kind of behaviour. Under catastrophic conditions, it might be that people adopt the only kind of value system available to them which seems to make some sense of their predicament. Baldwin[21] (p. 366) thinks that the evidence for identification with the aggressor is quite good. Others have been much more doubtful.

We can see from the brief review above of Freud's uses of the term 'identification', that these are by no means clear or wholly consistent. Stoke[260] has argued that Freud does not distinguish between 'emotional acceptance and attempts to duplicate behaviour'. Freud did argue[100] that a high ego ideal was not necessarily associated with a high level of conduct, implying that 'emotional acceptance' and 'attempts to duplicate behaviour' are not the same thing. Whether he is entirely justified in his

C

criticism of Freud, or not, Stoke has, I think, a point, in the sense that one 'kind of identification' might lead to duplication of behaviour, while another 'kind of identification' might lead to quite different behaviour. A case referred to by Grinker[122] may be relevant. A middle-aged man who had attained a success in business which had never been enjoyed by his passive father, identified with his father in many 'behavioural' ways such as wearing the same colour of shirts, following the same baseball team and the like. But as far as his *drive* was concerned, he had 'identified with' his dominant mother. Stoke himself refers to the case of a man who appeared to identify emotionally with his puritanical father but whose *conduct* was the opposite of puritanical. Similarly, again, we may find young people whose political affiliation is the opposite of their parents', but whose attitude to their political beliefs is precisely the same. Sometimes, mere similarity between parents and their children has been taken as an index of identification. This may be misleading, since such similarity may arise for a number of reasons which need not require us to assume any 'identification'. To mention an extreme case, similarity could arise on the basis of similar physical constitution or as the result of the operation of heredity.

Confusion has also arisen over whether identification is to be regarded as a *process* or as a *product*. Freud himself is not clear about this, and seems sometimes to imply the one, sometimes the other. His usage is not clarified by the fact that he does not discriminate clearly between identification and introjection. However, it is clear that introjection is a process, and there would be a case for regarding introjection as the process by which identification is established. Heilbrun[133] and Grinker[123] both think that identification should be regarded as a product. Sanford[241] and Mussen,[215] on the other hand, regard identification as a process. Sanford proposes that the term 'identification' be used to refer to the *mechanism* by which an individual unconsciously responds to the behaviour of others by 'initiating in fantasy or in reality the same behaviour himself. This is identification of the self with the object: it is different from empathy . . . and the like . . . properly called identification of the object with the self'[241] (p. 109). Mussen defines identification as 'a hypothesized process, accounting for the child's imitation of a model's complex, integrated patterns of behaviour—rather than discrete reactions or simple responses—emitted spontaneously without specific training or direct reward for emulation'[21] (p. 81).

The distinction between identification and imitation is not always clear. 'Imitation' has sometimes been regarded (e.g. by Mussen and by Lazowick[173]) as referring to the reproducing of specific actions of the model often consciously or deliberately, while identification has been taken to be a 'global' process enduring over time, in which the 'whole personality' is involved, and which may be unconscious or unintended. Mussen regards identification as requiring (a) relatively stable and enduring responses, and (b) a close personal attachment to the model; while Bronfenbrenner[51] considers Freud's thinking to imply two clear features (a) a motive in the child to become like the parent, and (b) the functioning of this motive in a 'whole pattern'.

Perhaps the best criterion of identification as distinct from 'mere' imitation would be the degree of involvement of the child in the process of identification, or the process by which an identification becomes established, and correspondingly, the degree to which the result is of emotional significance to the child. The greater degree of involvement would allow for the operation of unconscious factors. Kagan and Phillips,[153] in fact, have suggested that identification might be definable as 'vicarious involvement', and that physiological measures, such as the heart rate, might be used. This is an interesting suggestion, but its practical application would seem to be limited beyond laboratory situations. It would certainly be very difficult to apply anything like this idea to moral development or learning. Similarly, if we regard identification as requiring a greater degree of 'involvement' than imitation, it is very difficult to define *what* degree of involvement constitutes identification, and hence to distinguish clearly between identification and imitation.

A number of writers have taken the view that nothing is in fact gained by positing two different 'kinds of thing' and have suggested that the concept of imitation covers all that is needed, while that of identification is too vague to be of value and should therefore be dropped. Bandura and Walters,[27] for example, write, 'Both concepts . . . encompass the same behavioural phenomenon, namely, the tendency for a person to reproduce the actions, attitudes or emotional responses exhibited by real-life or symbolized models. Numerous distinctions have been proposed, of course, at one time or another. . . . However, one might question whether it is meaningful to do so, since essentially the same learning process is involved. . . . Therefore, it is in the interest of clarity, precision and parsimony to employ the single term, imitation, to refer to the occurrence of matching responses' (pp. 89–90). The assumption that 'the same learning process is involved' is precisely what the defenders of identification would object to.

Mowrer,[211] following an unpublished study by W. S. Lair in 1949, distinguishes between 'developmental' identification and 'defensive' identification. The former is a form of introjection of the lost love-object, e.g. when a child's mother is absent, he is able to make good the loss by having her symbolically present. For instance, the child may address himself in the terms of affection used by his mother, or cough like her. Defensive identification corresponds quite well to Anna Freud's 'identification with the aggressor'. The child *accepts* parental standards and the restrictions they impose. Mowrer believes that developmental identification has its basis in fear of loss of love, or in a sense of helplessness, defensive identification in fear of punishment. However, if fear of loss of love is equivalent to fear of having love withdrawn, then this may operate very much as a punishment, and the distinction tends to break down. Bronfenbrenner[51] makes very much the same distinction as Mowrer, but calls his two types of identification 'anaclitic' and 'defensive' respectively. Not unnaturally, theorists such as Sears[246] who have tended to take a more 'developmental' or 'anaclitic' view, have tended to think in terms of identification with the more *rewarding* parent, while those with a psychoanalytic bias have tended to stress identification with the more *frustrating* parent.

For Sanford,[241] identification is essentially an *unrealistic* process, to bolster up feelings of insecurity. It is 'evoked by a crisis, the crisis passes or is mastered, and we are able to observe no persisting effects' (p. 112). Thus, so far from being relatively stable and enduring, identification here appears as essentially *transitory*.

Sanford believes that identification must not be regarded as the basis of, and indeed must be distinguished from, the gradual adoption of parental standards. He differentiates between 'identification' in the sense of 'initiating in fantasy or reality the same behaviour' as the model, or 'identification of the self with the object', and 'introjection' which is the process by which prohibitions and standards are assimilated.

Kagan[151, 152] assumes that a kind of 'envy' is at the basis of identification. If the child (or other subject) sees that his parent (or other model) is able to have things which he would like but can't have, then he is likely to want to 'be like' his parents—he assumes, in other words, that the more *like* his parent he is, the more likely he will be to get the things which his parent has and he would like. What is said to him, also, tends to 'lead the child to the expectation that to be similar to the model is equivalent to possessing his positive and desirable attributes'[151] (p. 299). Presumably, similarity in respect of the parent's punishing role is included. Thus, perception of similarity comes to be satisfying for the child. Direct encouragement and rewarding of similar behaviour will further the process, but is not *sufficient* to account for it. Kagan states, 'Some degree of identification should be maintained as long as S. (the subject) perceives that the M. (model) commands desired goals. When the S. no longer perceives the M. in this fashion, then both the motivation for the identification and the intensity of the positive reinforcement should decrease' (p. 300). On the basis of his argument, Kagan suggests (a) that the strength of identification should decrease with age because the ability to satisfy one's needs by one's own behaviour should increase with age, and (b) that identification with a model who is in direct contact with the subject should be stronger than with a model not in direct contact, since perceived similarity should be stronger when the subject can actually see. However, there are many possible reasons why the strength of identification should decrease with increasing age, and presumably the nature of goals commanded will be an important factor. We might expect, for example, that boys would progressively identify more with their fathers even though they may interact more with their mothers, if their fathers are seen to command the kind of goals which are appropriate for males. In a later publication, Kagan[152] proposes that there are two basic causal sequences in identification. (a) If a child believes that he and his 'model' share significant attributes, he will experience the reactions and emotions of his model vicariously. This sequence defines the *feeling* of identification. (b) If the child *wants* the attributes and goals of his model, he will tend to adopt these attributes and the appropriate behaviour. According to Kagan, perceived similarity, which is still crucial, may arise either from adoption of the model's attributes, or from other people who *tell* him that he is like his model. Note Kagan's use of the concept of 'perceived similarity' to provide a kind of 'internal' reinforcement, and thus to reconcile the Freudian-derived notion of identification with a basically 'reinforcement' point of view. The difficulty with the idea of 'perceived similarity' from the point of view of learning theory is that we have no independent signs by which we can recognize perceived similarity when we see it, and no adequate means of knowing whether it operates as a reinforcer or not.

Kagan's idea of the appeal of models who command desired goals is very similar to the 'status envy' theory advanced by Whiting.[274] Whiting defines identification as 'the general process by which a person learns the role of another by interacting with him' (p. 113), thus emphasizing the two-person situation. He goes on to define 'status-envy' as following upon *seeing* the enjoyment of 'resources' (anything the child might want) by parents or others. He argues that during early infancy, the child will have no reason to 'envy' anyone else, and hence will identify with himself. (This is reminiscent of Freud's 'primitive narcissism'.) For Kagan, the situation only becomes significant when the child begins to feel that his parent is withholding resources, i.e. not giving him all he wants. This leads to *envy* of the parent's control of resources and to 'fantasy identification' with the parent. It is not, however, explained *how* this identification comes about. If a boy's mother controls most of the resources, then he will be likely to identify more strongly with her, *but* the behaviour socially expected of him will be that associated more with his father. This will tend to cause some degree of conflict. Moreover, the attention which mother pays to father (and possibly vice-versa) may be regarded as a 'resource' of father, and thus tend to encourage identification with father. The 'resource mediation' most likely to lead to learning by identification, according to Whiting, is the withholding of resources (including affection) when the child is naughty, and the supplying of resources when he is good. This leads, he thinks, to learning of the adult role by covert practice. The child should then respond to 'naughtiness' in others as his parents have responded; and he will then tend to respond to his *own* naughtiness in the same way. When he does so, he has 'internalized' the parental point of view.

The theory advanced by Mussen and Distler[216] is quite similar to Whiting's, but instead of assuming that the attractive feature of the parents' position is their ability to enjoy desirable resources, they think that the crucial factor is the parents' ability to control or dispense resources. This has been called the 'social power' theory; and indeed, some element of social power as well as consumption of resources seems to be involved in Whiting's statement. If, however, we distinguish between 'consumption of resources' as the criterion of the status envy theory and 'control of resources' as the criterion of the social power theory, we may ask whether, if these are alternative interpretations, there is any evidence in favour of one or the other. In fact, there is little evidence, but one laboratory study by Bandura, Ross and Ross[28] in which status envy and social power conditions were created experimentally, indicated that the social power paradigm was more successful in inducing imitative behaviour. However, there is no need for these two theories necessarily to be alternatives. In real life, both might well be involved. And there must be some reservations as to how far a short period laboratory experiment can be taken as an adequate test. The study by Bandura, Ross and Ross, however unsatisfying it may be, is the only attempt to deal with one particular difficulty which seems to affect all these three theories (Kagan's, Whiting's and Mussen and Distler's), that they posit processes which *could* plausibly facilitate identification, but offer no evidence for the existence of these hypothetical processes, nor suggest how one could confirm that they were actually going on in children in the way suggested.

Although in a sense, all theories of identification are concerned with 'role taking', some writers lay special emphasis on it. According to Bronfenbrenner,[53] Talcott Parsons thinks that what the child internalizes is a sequence of role-relationships, each depending on the nature of the relationship between the actors or participants at the time. Thus we have (a) identification with the mother as the source of care, when the relationship is one of oral dependence of child on mother, (b) internalization of the mother as the giver of love and of the self as the loved object, when the relationship is one of love-dependence. Mother's love becomes rewarding in itself and is conditional, for example, on bowel control. Parsons and Bales[223] say of this stage, '. . . in so far as the orally dependent child has internalized the mother as nurturant, he has also internalized 'secondarily' her concept of himself as object of nurturance. He can thus take her role towards himself or towards an alter' (p. 74). (c) Internalization of one or other parent in the adoption of a sex-role. The child first becomes aware of the distinction between male and female. He is then motivated to do things for both father and mother, and receives mother's love. Thus affection is attached to the father. The child then differentiates between the male father and the female mother, and adopts one or other sex role. He has now internalized a four-member system in which there is father role, mother role, son role and daughter role. What become internalized, it seems, are 'schemata' of systems of interpersonal relationships. Parsons and Bales say, 'identification should designate the process of internalization of any common collective "we-categorization" and with it the common values of the requisite collectivity' (p. 93). Here we have an attempt to adapt Freudian theory to a theory of role-relationships. It does not, however, seem very clear why a concept of 'identification' in addition to one of 'internalization' is necessary for such a role theory.

Winch[277] defines identification as 'the more or less lasting influence one person exerts on the behaviour of another' (p. 146). Thus for him, unlike Sanford, the influence must be more or less lasting, though the identification *process* need not necessarily be so. Winch distinguishes between 'personal' and 'positional' identification. Positional identification is very much a matter of role taking. It refers to behaviour when both the 'model' and the 'identifier' are occupants of related social positions and enacting reciprocal roles. Winch restricts the behaviour here to behaviour which is *relevant* to the role relationship. Positional identification may be of (relatively) long or short duration. The identifier, according to Winch, has strong feelings of respect and admiration for the model's *role behaviour* but need not feel drawn to the model as a *person*, but positional identification may well lead to personal identification. Indeed, quite a body of research and theory (see Newcomb, Turner and Converse[221] and other varieties of 'consistency theory' in social psychology) suggests that it would be quite normal for this kind of thing to happen. For Winch, Freud's primary identification with the *mother* is a case of 'the reciprocal interaction of the dependent infant and the nurturing mother' (p. 13). It is therefore a case of identification which is *both* positional and reciprocal. As a child grows older, he will be required or expected to occupy various positions and to enact the roles associated with these positions. The nature of the roles, and of other related roles, will of course depend upon the structure of the social system. 'The significance of structural variables,' says Winch, 'is that they determine the roles with whose occupants the child has an opportunity to interact, to observe, to admire or to dislike, to be rewarded by, to learn from, to identify' (p. 37). Clearly, children brought up in an extended family system or in an Israeli 'Kibbutz' will meet with different role taking demands and opportunities from a child brought up in a restricted family system. Winch refers to the cross-cultural study by Murdock and Whiting,[214] who reported that the presence of grandparents in the household makes for sterner imposition of the 'basic moral rules of society'. Winch's view of positional identification puts him quite close to the viewpoint of Parsons and Bales.

Winch goes on to suggest that normally, identification will tend to be mainly with the more 'functional' parent, i.e. the parent with whom a child has the greater amount of interaction which matters. Similarly, the more 'functional' the family, the more identification there is likely to be within the family. It would seem to be implied that the *less* functional the family, the more diffuse will be the child's role interactions, and the less the amount of identification in general. The argument that the more functional the parents and the family, the more will the child identify with parents is rather similar to Whiting's idea of status envy and Mussen and Distler's of social power. All three imply that the greater the amount of resources to which the parents (family) have access, the greater should be the identification of children with parents. Winch therefore argues that there should be more identification in upper class families than in working class families. This finds some indirect support from observations that upper class children are more likely to be governed by internalized standards, but direct evidence that identification with parents is greater among children of the upper class is slight. There may be various reasons why upper class children should be more subject to control by internalized standards. And the crucial factor might be the *relative* rather than the *absolute* amount of control of resources.

Hollander[143] also emphasizes both role taking and the functional aspect of the parents. Identification as 'taking the role of the other', however, he regards primarily as enabling possible 'acquisition of resources' to take place or 'deprivation of resources' to be avoided. The child learns, in other words, to 'predict' the parental reaction to 'good' and 'bad' behaviour, to 'try out' possible lines of behaviour covertly, and to modify his behaviour accordingly. Hollander suggests that perhaps it is the 'power to nurture' (to supply and to deprive of resources) which elicits identification. This is again very similar to Whiting's view. On this view, it is hard to see how any 'global' or strongly emotionally toned identification would be necessary. Identification would be reduced to anticipating parental reactions, and it is difficult to see how a 'moral' as distinct from a purely 'utilitarian' attitude could develop on this basis alone.

Howe[144] has developed a theory of identification relating different types of identification to different forms of communication. She distinguishes four forms of communication, developing sequentially. (1) The kind of communication which takes place between a mother and her baby, which is unconscious, and in which each responds automatically to the other. (2) The kind of communication in which a child *talks to himself* and unconsciously responds to his own words. (3) Communication involving awareness and intention, in which the child can anticipate the other's response and adapt accordingly. (4) Communication as in (3), but able to accommodate the more generalized attitudes of the community (George Mead's 'generalized other') rather than simply the attitude of a specific other. She thinks that we should distinguish two types of identification, one corresponding to forms of communication (1) and (2), the other corresponding to form (3) and (4). In type (1) identification, the parent 'becomes incorporated into the child's self as one party to a relationship of dependence which involves both parties, one at the active end of the relationship and one at the passive end' (p. 68). It is essentially a relationship with two 'actors' which is internalized. By being internalized is meant that the child can, in fantasy, take the role of *either* actor in the relationship and can, e.g., be the one who scolds or the one who is scolded, and consequent upon this, the one who scolds himself. The relationship is essentially one of dependence—of one who is powerless upon one who has power, and Howe talks of type 1 identification as 'power-identification'. It is not quite clear from this, however, why the child *should* take the role of 'scolder' or 'scolder of self', even though he has internalized the relationship to the extent of being able to do so.

Type 2 identification is referred to by Howe as 'functional identification' in which there is conscious role taking. Howe's view of the processes involved in the development from type 1 to type 2 identification is that type 1, 'power identifications' with the parents enable the child to develop his capacities and to gain a sense of his own identity. 'The superego is a personification of the powerful parents, while an essential part of the ego is the individual's image of himself' (p. 68). The sense of his own identity enables the child to *participate* in a real sense with other children and to begin to 'put himself in their place'. He can then, by such taking of the role of others, learn the 'rules of the game' as these apply to himself and others and involve reciprocal obligations. However, Howe assumes that at the time when the child is learning these 'rules of the game', the Oedipus complex becomes most intense. When the child has begun to see himself more objectively through his growing capacity to take the role of the other, he starts to become aware of inconsistencies in his own feelings, and tries to resolve his ambivalent feelings by directing his love to one parent and his hostility to the other. Identification of boy with father would then be not only in respect of his power, but to assume the role of husband in the family role system. The practical inability of the child to do this, which his awareness enables him to grasp, then heightens his self awareness and his critical awareness of the world around him, thus strengthening further the development of his ego. Howe makes an interesting attempt to bring together in a way clearly influenced by role theory, the views of Freud and those of Piaget and others who have emphasized the relations of children with their peers as distinct from a largely exclusive attention to relations with parents and parent-figures on the part of psychoanalysts. Despite Howe's efforts, however, the Oedipus complex does not seem to fit very well into this scheme, and one has the impression that it is brought in because its importance is regarded as already unquestionably established and therefore its inclusion inescapable. The main structure of Howe's admittedly speculative account could quite well stand without the Oedipus complex. Martin,[194] who also emphasizes unconscious communication between child and parent, thinks that the Oedipus complex need not be assumed to be essential. 'We can hypothesise,' he says, 'that identification takes place when a clearly-defined and appropriate model is available and to which the child becomes related in a rather unique way. . . . There is a unique interpersonal relationship established between father and son. Johnny develops the feeling of being the kind of person who plays a particular part in this relationship. The essence of the part seems to be its feeling of oneness with his father' (p. 213). This feeling of oneness, it would seem, results from the unconscious process of communication of feeling and attitude which such a relationship involves. Presumably also, the 'feeling of oneness' is the basis for the child's internalization of parental prohibitions and values, although it is not clear how this comes about. In fact, it is not very clear precisely what is meant by a 'feeling of oneness', nor how one could demonstrate its presence. Howe's explanation that it is the 'power' aspect of the relationship which is in the first instance crucial seems rather less open to objection on these grounds. However, there does not seem to be any evidence that increasing parental power is associated with increasing identification or an increasingly 'internalized' conscience.

On the whole, we may have a good deal of sympathy with Bronfenbrenner[51] (p. 38), when he comments on theories of identification that 'they offer elaborate and intricate explanations for phenomena presumed to be common if not universal; yet the evidence for the prevalence or even the sheer existence of these phenomena is extremely sparse.' The term has certainly been used in a most confusing variety of senses. We may indeed doubt whether it elucidates more than it obscures. Perhaps we might now try to see whether we can find some kind of analysis relevant to moral development without having to posit a *specific* process (or product) called 'identification'. The suggestion here is that we may, if we like, go on using the term 'identification' in an everyday kind of way, as a loose descriptive term, and perhaps when we are talking specifically about psychoanalytic theory, but that we should for more exact purposes, stop talking of identification and instead, use separate terms to refer to the different kinds of things which have been included under the general umbrella of identification.

(1) Taking the role of the other may refer to the purely utilitarian ability to predict what the reactions of the other are likely to be to one's own behaviour, and thus to know what to expect. By a slight extension, this usage can also cover the ability to rehearse some action *covertly*, i.e. in fantasy or without overt 'rehearsing behaviour', to anticipate the reaction of the other (e.g. the parent), and to adapt or adjust one's own behaviour accordingly. If we like, we might say that this involves symbolic representation of the parent in the form, particularly, of auditory imagery or 'internal conversation'. The child can imagine his parent saying 'Naughty!', perhaps repeating the word. But, while he may, for example, thus come to *inhibit* behaviour that is likely to be punished, this does not explain why he should *accept* the parent's valuation and make it his own. Modification of behaviour in this way may be a purely utilitarian matter, facilitating the gaining of 'goods' (including approval) and the avoiding of 'bads' (including disapproval). The importance of this as a form of socialization, however, should not be underestimated. Values *tend* to be

consistent with behaviour, although this is clearly not always the case.

(2) Similar behaviour which cannot be attributed mainly to a common preceding factor such as heredity or common environmental stimulation, but which requires direct or indirect observation of a 'model' can best be labelled 'imitation'. It may frequently be conscious and deliberate, but may be unconscious and unintentional as well. Nothing is gained by talking of this as 'identification'. While imitation is *relevant to* the learning of moral behaviour (including the overt *expression* of values), it does not explain the *acceptance* of values as one's own.

(3) Pretending to *be* one's parent (or other model, e.g. the postman) not only allows imitation, but enables the child to *devise* and try out behaviours which he may regard as appropriate to the 'picture' he has of the model's role. In so far as they are reinforced by parents, by other adults or by other children, both the imitating of parents and the devising of role behaviours are likely to be strengthened. While pretending to *be* another, a child also has the opportunity to take the role of the other in relation to this 'model other', thus extending his self understanding and his understanding of the complexities of role relationships.

(4) Learning of the appropriate sex role behaviours and attitudes may be understood in terms of *attending* (as a result of encouragement both direct and indirect—e.g. being supplied with 'male' toys) to the differentiating features of the appropriate sex role, and subsequent reinforcement for 'right' and 'wrong' behaviour, including reinforcement in various forms from peers as well as adults. A male child, for example, who does not learn the appropriate sex role very well may have learned the 'wrong' sex role, or numerous aspects of the wrong sex role, or, in less extreme cases, may simply not have learned to discriminate sufficiently between behaviour appropriate to the masculine role and behaviour appropriate to the feminine role, and thus appear *relatively* feminine.

(5) Emotional 'empathy' may be *relevant* to moral development in enabling us to be more sensitive to the consequences of our behaviour for others. It seems likely that this kind of empathy will depend to a large extent on the degree to which a child has been

encouraged by precept and example to *discriminate* signs by which the feelings of others can be recognized, and the degree to which he has been encouraged to act and reinforced for acting, accordingly.

(6) Vicarious satisfaction got from the achievement or pleasure of one or more other people may provide powerful motivation for altruistic action (*see* Chapter 9). This kind of vicarious satisfaction is particularly understandable in the case of parents who find satisfaction in the achievement of their children, and, to a lesser extent, perhaps, of children who find satisfaction in the achievement of their parents. But we seem able to derive vicarious satisfaction from the satisfaction of anyone to whom we are strongly attached. Sometimes we may be able symbolically to 'identify' with persons with whom we are not on terms of intimacy, perhaps because they appear as representatives of a 'community' of which we feel ourselves to be part, perhaps on the basis of common motivation, as when a boy follows with bated breath the fortunes of his favourite golf star, whose motivation he shares because he also would like to be an expert at the game. In so far as such 'heroes' are morally worthy characters, their influence may promote worthy aims in their followers, but this need not always or even generally be the case. It is also possible to make heroes in this sense out of historical characters, when the whole process is symbolic.

(7) *Acceptance* of the values of parents (and later, or under different circumstance, other models) might come about as follows. The child learns to distinguish between 'good' and 'bad' actions in terms of consequences, and from this develops the capacity to evaluate actions, including his own, as 'good' or 'bad'. The reactions of others, especially of parents (because they are of primary importance to the child) clearly indicate to him that many situations *call for* evaluation. The child is likely to accept, in the first instance, the parents' evaluations, including prohibitions, partly because they are the only basis which he has on which to 'judge', and partly because, since he is emotionally attached to (or likes) his parents, he is likely to be attached to their values also (basic principle of consistency theory). Thus, parental commands, prohibitions, preferences and values are early accepted

uncritically. Values manifested by others, including both adults and peers, may also be accepted uncritically if those others are sufficiently important to the child, and if he does not have other values already which are relevant to the same situations. It is only as the child's experience widens and his own capacity for critical evaluation develops that he becomes able to question the *basis* of the commands and prohibitions which he has accepted, and to realize that other kinds of evaluation are possible. The emotional attachment to his parents *facilitates* the acceptance of their values, and the nature of the parents and the way they treat the child will contribute to the way in which the child applies the values he has taken up; for example, whether in a particularly severe, self-critical way. It is perfectly reasonable to suppose that at least some early-acquired value-attitudes persist in a relatively primitive sort of way, whether we think of this in terms of 'super-ego' or not. It is also reasonable to suppose that these early acquisitions of value may 'set the tone' of later valuing acts and attitudes, and predispose children to particular modes or styles of moral attitude. The greater the degree of affectivity associated with early conforming and acceptance of values, perhaps, the greater may be the influence of such early experience in 'setting the tone'. Early-acquired attitudes often tend to be self-perpetuating, but there is also good reason to believe that later experiences may nevertheless have a transforming influence. We can, of course, refer to a child's acceptance of his parents' values as 'identification' or 'introjection'; but the present case is that by introducing complex, unclearly delimited terms like 'identification', we simply complicate a complex situation still further, casting little light upon it, and lumping together a number of different processes which are more likely to be understood if kept separate.

5

The Meaning of Guilt

In *Totem and Tabu*[99] Freud explains that guilt originated when the sons of the primitive horde slew their father because he was preempting the women, and were then overcome by remorse, because of the attitude of love which they also held toward him. When we remember that for Freud, the identification of the sons with their slain father was the original identification, we see that identification and guilt were for Freud closely associated. At the end of *Totem and Tabu,* Freud suggests that, even if his pre-history is wrong, the fact that these early men had impulses of desire for the women and desire for the death of the father would be a sufficient basis for guilt, provided that they also loved him. Thus, Freud seems to be saying that human beings have a built-in capacity for guilt corresponding to their built-in capacity for experiencing love and hate and complex combinations of both. This is a very stimulating suggestion.

In his paper *On Narcissism*,[100] Freud attributes the ontogenetic or individual basis of guilt to a fear of punishment by the parents, or more correctly, the dread of losing their love, this fear being later extended to 'an indefinite number of fellow-men', or 'dread of the community'. In *Criminality from a Sense of Guilt,*[103] Freud specifically relates feelings of guilt to the Oedipus complex. He is concerned with cases of people who, he believes, commit crimes because the unconscious sense of guilt occasioned by their unconscious wishes for the death of their father is so great, and is relieved by punishment for relatively minor offences.

In *Mourning and Melancholia*[102] he develops the idea that guilt is occasioned by the direction of criticism (aggression) against the 'introjected' object—in other words, by the turning of aggression inwards. The idea of aggression being turned inward to produce guilt is likewise found in *The Ego and the Id,* where we also find reference to feelings of guilt or self-depreciation as a reaction formation against unconscious aggression. The work where Freud devotes most attention to guilt, however, is *Civilization and its Discontents.*[112] Here, he specifically declares that guilt is occasioned by tension between the ego and the superego (without, however, revising his views about the sources of this tension). He again emphasizes that because of the process of internalizing involved in the development of the superego, guilt may now be occasioned by the mere *impulse* to offend without the actual deed, and that such impulses may be unconscious. But there are three relevant fresh points made in *Civilization and its Discontents.* (1) When the outward expression of aggression is inhibited, the unexpressed aggression is added to the superego, thus increasing the severity of guilt feelings. Thus, the amount of guilt will depend partly on the degree of suppression, and partly on the amount of aggression, which in turn, will depend partly on constitutional factors, partly on aggression-producing experiences (frustrations). (2) Since culture depends upon the restriction of both sexual freedom and the outward expression of aggression, especially the latter, it follows that the greater the level of cultural development, the higher the burden of guilt to be borne by those living in that culture. The price of cultural development is a high—and increasing—level of guilt. (3) Personal happiness is opposed to social unity. Social unity is based upon the giving up of individual instinctual gratifications; and in the case of aggression, this must mean turning from outward to inward expression. Similar arguments are repeated in the *New Introductory Lectures,*[113] where, for example, the 'unconscious need for punishment' is referred to as 'a piece of aggressiveness which has been internalized and taken over by the superego' (p. 109). These arguments, it need scarcely be said, depend upon the assumption of an amount of aggression which has to find expression somehow.

Finally, reference may be made to Freud's *Symptoms, Inhibitions and Anxiety,*[111] in which he regards guilt as a kind of moral *anxiety* in which there is fear of the superego. If guilt is a form of anxiety, it is a very special form since, as

Sandler[240] points out, it is distinguished in common usage by the lowering of self-esteem. The important point, however, is that Freud stressed the *similarity* between guilt and anxiety, a view also shared by many learning theorists.

John Rickman[235] also emphasizes the important role of aggression and ambivalence in determining feelings of guilt, but lays less stress on the fear or anxiety aspect. He writes, 'We feel guilt when, and only when, we do or intend an injury to a loved object (person or thing or abstraction such as Truth); and if we had no aggressive impulses we would never feel guilt; if we had no love within us, love and a desire to cherish, we would never feel guilt' (p. 77). Rickman thinks that the first stirrings of guilt may occur very early indeed—in connection with the infant's ambivalent attitude to the breast—but suggests that it might be a good idea to keep the word 'guilt' for the more highly-developed form, and to use the term 'proto-guilt' for the earliest and most primitive forms. This suggestion does not seem to have been taken up to any extent. Rickman sees very well that we may feel guilty after, for example, telling a lie. But it seems rather far-fetched to regard such a lie as an 'injury intended to a loved object'.

Like Rickman, Melanie Klein[160] thinks that the origin of guilt can be traced very early—to the primitive oral destructive impulses and the anxiety they arouse. Later, as the child's 'introjected images' become less frightening and more friendly, anxiety is more readily overcome. Anxiety tends to become guilt, which can then (with limits) be dealt with by restitutive or reparative measures. However, if guilt is too strong, it is again experienced as anxiety. Thus, for Klein, guilt is very closely related to anxiety.

D. W. Winnicott[278] also regards guilt as depending on the opposing feelings of love and hate. But Winnicott believes that the capacity to be concerned about others, and the consequent capacity for guilt require some degree of ego development and understanding. Guilt *originates* from anxiety, which can be experienced at a very early age. But the sense of guilt itself is gradually built up in relation to the mother, and is facilitated by opportunities for making reparation for wrongs done. 'When the capacity for concern is established, the individual begins to be in a position to experience the Oedipus complex and to tolerate the ambivalence that is inherent at the later stage, in which the child, if mature, is involved in triangular relationships as between whole human beings' (p. 26). The child really begins to feel guilty when wrongdoing and one's responsibility for it are accepted. This seems to imply conscious rather than, or in addition to, unconscious processes.

Erikson[74, 75] takes a different view again. He relates guilt to his third stage of development, characterized as 'initiative versus guilt'. While the child is extending the range of his own activity (autonomy), he comes up against a major restriction. 'This general readiness for initiative,' writes Erikson, 'meets its arch-enemy in the necessity of delaying and displacing its sexual core; for this sexual core is both biologically incomplete and culturally opposed by incest taboos. The Oedipal wishes (so simply and so trustingly expressed in the boy's assurance that he will marry his mother and make her proud of him, and in the girl's that she will marry her father and take much better care of him) leads to vague fantasies bordering on murder and rape. The consequence is a deep sense of guilt—a strange sense, for it forever seems to imply that the individual has committed a crime which, after all, was not only not committed, but would have been biologically quite impossible'[74] (p. 84). Thus Erikson, for all his cultural emphasis, accepts the Oedipus situation as the original source of guilt.

We have mentioned Winnicott's belief that guilt requires some measure of ego development. This is more strongly emphasized by Ausubel,[19] who believes that guilt arises not as a result of unconscious processes, but on the basis of ego processes oriented toward reality, including social reality. Guilt feelings develop from failure to meet expectations of 'powerful' parents on whom the child is dependent and to whom he is strongly attached. Ausubel defines guilt as a 'self-reaction to an injured conscience', requiring three conditions. (a) The person must accept certain standards as his own. (b) He must accept the obligation to regulate his behaviour according to these standards, and must feel responsible for his failure to do so. (c) He must have enough self-critical ability to recognize discrepancies between his standards and his behaviour. This is clearly a more cognitively oriented point of view, and is rather similar to that of Kohlberg (see below), though Ausubel and Kohlberg differ considerably in their general position.

The notion of unconscious guilt certainly raises difficulties. Normal usage associates guilt with a state of feeling of which the person concerned is well aware. If guilt is unconscious, then either the person must be *completely* unaware of it, or it must be experienced as other than a feeling of guilt—for example, as a feeling of vague unease. In either case it might, as Freud suggested, find expression in behaviour without any consciousness of guilt or of the real motive for the behaviour—for example, wrongdoing to provoke punishment. However, it is possible that in a case of 'seeking punishment', the person really does feel (consciously) a sense of guilt, but does not connect this with his behaviour, thus being unconscious not of his unworthiness, but of the real motive for what he does. This poses less of a problem than the thoroughgoing 'unconscious guilt' hypothesis. The difficulty is that case histories are reported of people who supposedly seek punishment, in which there seems to be no evidence that they really experience any special feelings of guilt or unworthiness. The justification for the idea of unconscious guilt then lies partly in the claim that only by hypothesizing something of this kind can any understanding of the case be obtained, and partly in the claim that such a notion fits in well with other data in the case history, in other words, with revelations of deeds or thoughts possibly explicable in terms of unconscious guilt. Whether we accept this or not will depend mainly on three factors, (1) how far we feel that any alternative explanation—for example, in terms of conditioning—equally well fits the facts of the case; (2) how far we feel that psychoanalytic theory in general is sufficiently satisfactory for us to prefer this kind of explanation to any other; (3) how far we feel that 'unconscious guilt' is so unsatisfactory an explanation that we prefer to leave the case unexplained until a more plausible explanation can be advanced. Kohlberg,[161] for one, is not attracted to the idea of unconscious guilt, and, from the cognitive point of view, considers that the term 'guilt' may be usefully employed when an individual makes a conscious self-critical judgment because he has failed to live up to some standard, but that Freudian notions of unconscious guilt are altogether too vague. Perhaps to some extent we might avoid the difficulty by keeping the term 'guilt' for consciously experienced feelings of remorse and self-criticism, and using the term 'unconscious need for punishment' for the hypothesized unconscious variety (as, indeed, Freud himself suggested[112]).

For the more radical exponents of learning theory (e.g. Eysenck), guilt seems to be equated with anxiety which results from the association of aversive stimulation (punishment) with the ending of a sequence of action. Thus guilt is basically little different from anticipatory fear of consequences, except that the consequences are extremely vaguely defined. However, it is certainly possible to feel both fear of consequences and guilt at the same time, and to be able to distinguish quite clearly between them. To regard guilt simply as a conditioned emotional response is to ignore the specific meaning of guilt which gives it its peculiar quality and enables us to distinguish it from other emotionally laden reactions like fear, shame or simply regret for something one has done. It is interesting that a learning theorist like Mowrer, for whom emotional conditioning is so important, should nevertheless regard feelings of guilt as generally *justified*, and as removable only by open confession, acceptance of punishment and thus a righting of the 'balance'.[213] Mowrer's view in this respect seems quite close to that of Ausubel.[19]

Shame and guilt

Although shame and guilt have been regarded as two different kinds of experience, and although we can often recognize in a commonsense way what is shame and what is guilt in other people, and can often distinguish when we ourselves feel ashamed and when we feel guilty, it is not so easy to define precisely where the difference lies and where one ends and the other begins. They are quite closely related, despite the tendency of some writers (such as Ruth Benedict) to regard them almost as alternatives and mutually exclusive.

Freud seems to have regarded shame as fear of others knowing about the kind of thing one would feel guilty about. In *Further remarks on the neuro-psychoses of defence*,[94] he writes that self-reproach for sexual activity in childhood 'can easily turn into *shame* (in case someone else should find out about it)' (p. 171). Elsewhere, he suggests that shame may result from genital inadequacy. In *An infantile neurosis*[105] (p. 92 n.) he comments that involuntary urination much more frequently causes shame than loss of bowel control; and Fenichel[81] (p. 69) says that shame begins in bladder training rather than in bowel training because in bladder training parents more frequently use shaming methods, in bowel training physical methods. It would appear doubtful whether this is still true, if indeed it ever was. Piers and Singer[228] remark that for Freud, shame was also a form of defence against exhibitionism, a kind of reaction-formation. According to Edith Jacobson[145] shame is originally a reaction to the exposure to others of loss of instinctual control, physical defects or failures, but normally quite soon becomes associated with internal conflict, for example, when we are aware of something disgraceful in ourselves. She thinks that shame refers more to fear of visual exposure, while guilt has more to do with verbal prohibitions, criticisms and requirements. Freud himself, of course, emphasized the importance of auditory communication in the formation of the superego and the consequent guilt. Jacobson also thinks that 'feelings of both shame and inferiority manifest a person's conflicts with standards that regulate self-esteem in terms of pride and superiority rather than moral behaviour in relation to others' (p. 146). Shame reactions tend to be related to dependency and to have a marked narcissistic quality; guilt reactions tend to be related to aggression.

Piers[228] regards shame as arising from tension between the ego and the ego ideal rather than between the ego and the punitive, prohibitive aspects of the superego as with guilt, and thinks that it occurs when there is failure to reach a goal. He also thinks that the 'unconscious sanction' in shame is fear of being abandoned, whereas the unconscious sanction in guilt is fear of being mutilated (castrated). Singer[228] supports this view. It is very hard to see how the view of Piers and Singer that shame arises from failure to live up to positive expectations while guilt arises from an infringement of prohibitions, can be maintained. Consider, for example, the case of a man who, as a result of a business failure, cannot properly maintain his family. May he not feel *guilt*, because he might have been able to fulfil positive expectations in regard to his family had he acted differently?

It has also been suggested that guilt involves intentional action, shame involuntary action. But if, with the best intentions, I fail my comrades, may I not feel guilty for my failure? Yet another suggestion is that shame has to do with intrinsic qualities, guilt with action or potential action. For example, if this were so, I should feel ashamed of my ugliness, but not guilty because of it, whereas I may feel guilty if I dawdle on the way to meet my wife. But may I not also feel ashamed of dawdling? What seems to be the case here is that I may feel ashamed as well as guilty about something for which I feel responsible, but cannot feel guilty for some quality as such, for which I cannot hold myself responsible. Another closely related distinction which would seem to be valid is that guilt always implies some moral factor, whereas shame *may* have to do with either moral or non-moral, though evaluated, factors such as physical appearance or being unable to sing in tune.

If we restrict ourselves purely to a consideration of guilt and shame in relation to moral questions, it is clear that the kind of things we are likely to feel guilty about, are also the things we are likely to feel ashamed about, and our feelings after doing something wrong may represent any blend of guilt and shame, in which it may be very difficult to distinguish the relative balance of the ingredients. On the other hand, there are situations in which we may feel guilty on one count and ashamed on another. A man, for example, who tries to seduce a young girl, may feel guilty about trying to seduce her, ashamed of having been impotent or of having otherwise failed in his purpose. Thus, in many ways, the relations between guilt and shame are quite complex.

Ruth Benedict[31] and others have suggested that cultures can be divided into 'guilt cultures' and 'shame cultures' according to whether the dominant moral sanction appears to be guilt or shame, the balance depending upon methods of child-training. The implication of this distinction is that guilt is an 'internal' and shame an 'external' sanction. However, there are difficulties in this position. (1) If values are not internalized, at least to some extent, why do the shamers go on shaming? (2) There are, as Singer[228] points out, 'inner' forms of shame as well as of guilt. We can feel ashamed and accept that we have something to feel ashamed about when there is little or no chance of our fault becoming public. (3) On the other side, it seems likely that the power of any internal sanction owes at least something to the fact that it is reinforced from without—even in the case of being supported by imaginary figures.

There is also the question of the relation of both guilt and shame to fear. Frequently, what we refer to as guilt or shame may have a powerful admixture of fear of consequences of one kind or another. Aronfreed[14] makes a useful distinction between the three terms, fear, guilt and shame, in terms of the 'cognitive orientation' of the actor. He suggests that what we feel after a transgression should be called 'fear' 'to the extent that its qualitatve experience is determined by a cognitive orientation toward an external source of aversive consequences for the transgressor' (p. 244)—in other words, if one's experience is 'expecting to be punished'. It should be called 'guilt' 'to the extent that the quality of the transgressor's affective experience is determined by moral evaluation of the transgression' (p. 245). 'Moral evaluation' is evaluation which 'makes reference to the consequences of an act for others' (ibid.). As Aronfreed says, 'we apply our moral judgment very readily to certain classes of behaviour, such as acts of aggression, whose consequences for others tend to be highly visible (ibid.). We have seen that psychoanalytic writers tend to view guilt as deriving from aggresssion. However, if we accept Aronfreed's definition of guilt, it need not always be associated with aggression. Suppose, for instance, that I drive my car at a fast speed because I am late for an appointment, and I have an accident in which someone is killed. I am likely to feel guilty, although only in a very peculiar sense could I be said to have been aggressive. In so far as our feeling 'is determined by a cognitive orientation toward the visibility of the transgression' (p. 249), then it should be called shame. In other words, if we are concerned in case something is shown which should not be shown, then we are experiencing shame. As Aronfreed points out, we may feel shame even when no-one has seen or is likely to see us, and we may feel guilt although our concern for consequences for others depends upon our fear that these consequences for others may have unpleasant repercussions for us. Although shame is *more* associated with an externally oriented attitude and guilt is *more* associated with an internally oriented attitude, the distinction between shame and guilt does not correspond wholly to that between external and internal orientation. Both shame and guilt may include varying degrees of each orientation. Similarly, some measure of guilt will be allied to fear if a child fears punishment *because* his action has been harmful to others.

Aronfreed's definition of guilt and shame indicates a useful criterion for distinguishing two kinds of experience. The only difficulty here is whether the definition of guilt in terms of moral evaluation of 'the consequences of an act for others' is not too narrow. Is it impossible to feel guilt in respect of an action which has no consequences for others? Is a child's concern over auto-erotic activities, for example, to be described simply in terms of fear or shame or regret, without any element of guilt? We have so long been used to thinking of such childish or adolescent feelings as 'guilt' that we may find it hard to accept a definition of guilt which virtually excludes them. Nevertheless, from the point of view of clarity, there is much to be said for Aronfreed's definition, and it does have the advantage of linking guilt firmly to concern for the interests of others, generally regarded as the basis of genuinely moral principles. As we shall see, Aronfreed's definition does not prevent him from attempting some analysis of the conditions under which guilt is likely to develop. It is clear that his commitment to a cognitive view means acceptance of guilt as a conscious phenomenon, dependent on moral judgment and the person's orientation or attitude to his offence and its consequences. Aronfreed is almost certainly right in his insistence on the need to give full consideration to the cognitive aspect of the experience. It is the cognitive or 'meaning' aspect which gives guilt the peculiar quality which we normally associate with the term.

6

Learning Theories I
Skinner, Mowrer, Eysenck

Skinner

The work of B. F. Skinner may be regarded as a classic example of a more extreme form of learning or 'behaviour' theory. The relevance of Skinner's views to moral learning may be gleaned especially from the book called *Science and Human Behaviour*,[253] but possible social implications are shown in his novel *Walden Two*,[252] which is about a kind of Utopian community based on Skinnerian principles.

Lana[172] points out two important assumptions of Skinner's approach. (1) Human activity or 'behaviour' (all human activity, including thinking, being regarded as 'behaviour') is *determined* 'by variables which are potentially discoverable. There is no such thing as spontaneous human activity, with the possible exception of non-directed bodily movements such as are found in infants' (p. 58). (2) The most profitable approach to the study of behaviour is in terms of relationships between events in the environment (independent variables) and behavioural responses of the organism (dependent variables) to such environmental events or stimuli. This is clearly an extreme form of empiricism in the Lockean tradition. It involves a functional 'input-output' view of the behaving organism, with little or no attention being paid to the nature of events going on *within* the organism. A corollary of this is that the most important factors influencing behaviour are (a) the nature of the immediate environment, (b) the history of the experience of the organism, i.e. the history of *past* environmental events and the organism's response to them.

Skinner himself refers to the kind of *responses* in which he is primarily interested as *operants*. He says, 'It is customary to refer to any movement of the organism as a "response". The word is borrowed from the field of reflex action and implies an act which, so to speak, answers a prior event—the stimulus. But we may make an event contingent upon behaviour without identifying . . . a prior stimulus'[253] (p. 64). For example, if a pigeon raises its head, or presses a bar, this need not be in response to any specific *eliciting* stimulus which has been administered to produce the response. The response may take place as a consequence of some unidentified stimulation. The important thing is that, when the behaviour is 'emitted', it can be 'reinforced' or rewarded. As Skinner remarks, behaviour which has already occurred cannot be predicted or controlled. 'We can only predict that *similar* responses will occur in the future. The unit of predictive science is, there- fore, not a response but a class of responses. The word "operant" will be used to describe this class. The term emphasizes the fact that the behaviour *operates* upon the environment to generate consequences' (pp. 64–65). A 'reinforcer' is an event which, when it follows upon some operant, makes the future occurrence of that operant more probable. In this way, Skinner avoids a *specifically and overtly* hedonistic position, but in fact, the basis of his whole approach is essentially a hedonistic one. For what makes a rein- forcer reinforcing? According to Skinner, some events (or stimuli) —such as food to a hungry animal—seem 'naturally' to act as reinforcers. Stimuli which 'start off' by *having* such reinforcement value are called *primary* reinforcers. Skinner is not really much bothered about what makes a primary reinforcer reinforcing. He refers rather vaguely to biological evolutionary factors, but in fact adopts a pragmatic criterion—it 'works'. 'Reinforcement' refers to the process of reinforcing, 'reinforcer' is used to refer to the reinforcing event. According to Skinner, there are two kinds of reinforcers, positive reinforcers and negative reinforcers. (1) A positive reinforcer, e.g. food, approval, success—is a stimulus which, when presented or given, *increases* the probability of the preceding operant behaviour occurring in the future. (2) A nega- tive reinforcer is a stimulus which, when *withdrawn,* increases the probability of recurrence of the preceding operant. A negative reinforcer, for example, would be a loud noise, or continued disapproval. The *cessation* of such 'unpleasant' or 'aversive' stimulation would reinforce any behaviour immediately preceding such cessation.

A crucial factor for Skinner is the 'schedule' of reinforcement. Reinforcement may be either 'continuous' (occurring on every occasion on which the operant occurs) or 'partial' (intermittent, occurring only on some of these occasions). If it occurs on only some occasions, then it may either occur at certain intervals of time, regardless of the number of occasions, in which case there is said to be an *interval* reinforcement schedule; or it may occur on every 'nth' occasion, say every tenth time, in which case there is said to be a *ratio* reinforcement schedule. If the interval of time is fixed, the reinforcement schedule is called a *fixed interval* schedule; if the time interval is variable, we have a *variable interval* schedule. If the ratio of reinforced to non-reinforced responses remains constant, we have a *fixed ratio* schedule, and if it is variable, we have a *variable ratio* schedule. There are also more complex kinds of *combined* schedules. As shown by experiments mainly with rats and pigeons, each type of schedule has rather different effects. In particular, partial reinforcement, especially ratio reinforcement, produces behaviour which is highly resistant to *extinction,* i.e. which will go on recurring for a long time after it has ceased to be reinforced.

A stimulus (or experienced event) which is *not* originally reinforcing may become so by being repeatedly associated with one which is. Thus, if a light comes on immediately before food is presented when, say, an animal presses a bar, then the light will come to act as a *secondary* reinforcer, and will then be capable of reinforcing other behaviour than the original bar-pressing. Secondary reinforcers, however, may *lose* their reinforcing power, or become extinguished, if they do not at least occasionally continue to be paired with primary reinforcers. Stimuli may also come to act as generalized reinforcers by being associated with many *different* reinforcers. The most obvious generalized reinforcer for human beings is money, but other important generalized reinforcers would be such things as attention, affection, approval and the like. Eventually, generalized reinforcers may become *independent* of their association with other reinforcers, a notion which strongly recalls Gordon Allport's[6] view of the 'functional autonomy of motives'.

If we want, then, to encourage any kind of behaviour and to establish 'good' habits, we must reward or reinforce that behaviour. If we wish to *develop* any kind of behaviour, then this may sometimes be done by 'shaping', i.e. by first of all reinforcing any of the behaviour *which occurs* and which seems to be a *step* in the right direction. We then proceed to *approach* the desired behaviour by progressive *selective* reinforcement of behaviour which gradually approximates to that which we want to achieve. *All* change in behaviour (including covert behaviour like thinking, when this is manifested in any observable way) is a gradual and continuous process controlled by reinforcement. Skinner distinguishes between social reinforcement and non-social reinforcement simply in that the former is mediated by the *social* environment, i.e. by other people. 'When a mother feeds her child,' Skinner writes, 'the food, as a primary reinforcer, is not social, but the mother's behaviour in presenting it is. . . . In the field of social behaviour special emphasis is laid upon reinforcement with attention, approval, affection and submission. These important generalized reinforcers are social because the process of generalization usually requires the mediation of another organism'[253] (p. 299). Social reinforcement is a special *kind* of reinforcement and has certain characteristics which distinguish it from non-social reinforcement. 'Social reinforcement varies from moment to moment, depending upon the condition of the reinforcing agent. Different responses may therefore achieve the same effect, and one response may achieve different effects, depending upon the occasion. As a result, social behaviour is more extensive than comparable behaviour in a non-social environment. It is also more flexible, in the sense that the organism may shift more readily from one response to another when its behaviour is not effective' (*ibid.*). Moreover, social reinforcement is generally not independent of the behaviour being reinforced. For example, Skinner mentions, an indulgent but ambitious parent 'who withholds reinforcement when his child is behaving energetically, either to demonstrate the child's ability or to make the most efficient use of available reinforcers but who reinforces an early response when the child begins to show extinction' (p. 300). Reinforcement from the natural world is rarely of this kind. For example reinforcement in the form of fish caught, of the fisherman's casting of his flies will not be adjusted to his behaviour in such a way that he catches a fish when his enthusiasm for casting begins to flag.

As *Walden Two* and *Science and Human Behaviour* clearly indicate, Skinner was much concerned with the question of *controlling* behaviour. 'When we discover an independent variable which can be controlled, we discover a means of controlling the behaviour which is a function of it'[253] (p. 227). What we require is (1) to know what independent variables (reinforcements etc.) important kinds of behaviour depend upon; (2) to have the power to control these independent variables; (3) to decide in what direction they are to be controlled. The first two problems are practical problems. 'Self-control', to which Skinner devotes a chapter in *Science and Human Behaviour* is a special case of control. 'When a man controls himself, chooses a course of action, thinks out the solution to a problem, or strives toward an increase in self-knowledge, he is *behaving*. He controls himself precisely as he would control the behaviour of anyone else—through the manipulation of variables of which behaviour is a function. His behaviour in so doing is a proper object of analysis, and eventually it must be accounted for with variables lying outside the individual himself' (pp. 228–229). Skinner remarks that the individual often controls *part* of his own behaviour when a response has conflicting consequences and leads to both pleasant and unpleasant results. The example he gives is that of drinking alcohol—it 'bucks us up', makes us forget our troubles and so on, and is thus positively reinforcing. But it also produces the discomforts or 'aversive stimulation' of the hangover, and possible unpleasant consequences of being seen 'under the influence' and so on. On the next occasion of temptation, the situation itself, or cues arising from the *early* stages of drinking 'will generate conditioned aversive stimuli and emotional responses to them which we speak of as shame or guilt. The emotional responses may have some deterrent effect in weakening behaviour—as by "spoiling the mood". A more important effect, however, is that any behaviour which weakens the behaviour of drinking is automatically reinforced by the resulting reduction in aversive stimulation. . . . We call such behaviour self-control' (p. 230). Thus, we have two 'sets' of responses or behaviour—the *controlling* responses and the *controlled* responses. There are various techniques of 'self-control' which an individual may use—for example, he may remove himself from temptation, or he may concentrate upon doing something else, i.e. carrying out behaviour incompatible with that which he wishes to control. But why do we want to put such controlling responses into action at all? Skinner's answer is simple. 'It appears . . . that society is responsible for the larger part of the behaviour of self-control' (p. 240); and society is responsible because *members* of society, by approval and disapproval ('generalized reinforcers') and by other means, provide appropriate reinforcers. By 'anticipating' such approval, disapproval and so on, the individual is able to control his behaviour himself. But in the last resort, the motive power is social reinforcement, though *how* this operates for any particular individual will depend upon his particular history of social (and other) reinforcement.

As far as punishment, i.e. the use of aversive stimulation to 'get rid of' unwanted behaviour is concerned, Skinner does not regard this as the *opposite* of reward. When behaviour continues to take place *without* being reinforced, it normally becomes 'extinguished', i.e. it drops out of the organism's repertory of behaviour. Now, various studies, notably that of Estes[76] with animals, report that punishment, while it may *suppress* the behaviour while the punishment is 'expected', does not reduce the total amount of the behaviour which the organism will produce when punishment is stopped. Continued non-reinforcement, on the other hand, *does* tend to lead to extinction of the behaviour. This fits quite well with observations of human behaviour. Moreover, punishment tends to arouse an emotional state which may tend to suppress not only the unwanted behaviour, but other and legitimate behaviour. However, Skinner suggests that punishment may be useful under the following conditions. (1) It may be useful to hold a response at a low level; but it will have to be continued indefinitely, as it doesn't *eliminate* the response. (2) Suppression of undesirable behaviour may enable an alternative response to be reinforced. (3) Punishment should always be given in the presence of discriminate cues for the response, i.e. in the presence of stimuli to which the unwanted behaviour was the response. This means that if punishment is delayed, it is likely to be ineffective because the stimuli which led to the unwanted response are likely no longer to be present. In any event, Skinner is a strong advocate of the use of positive reinforcement whenever this is possible. As far as 'moral' behaviour is concerned, he confines himself largely to indicating ways in which one can increase the *probability* of individuals behaving according to the requirements of any given socio-ethical system. It is never made explicit, in *Walden Two*, for example, what criteria should be used to decide what the *aims* of the society should be. The impression is given that it is a pragmatic matter, and that 'good' will arise out of the practical adjustment to the situation with which the society is faced. One might almost say that 'good' and 'bad' are ignored.

Similarly, Skinner's view of responsibility is essentially that the whole idea is, at least for psychology, misguided. 'An analysis which appeals to external variables makes the assumption of an inner originating and determining agent unnecessary,' he writes. 'The scientific advantages of such an analysis are many, but the practical advantages may well be more important. The traditional conception of what is happening when an individual controls himself has never been successful as an educational device. It is of little help to tell a man to use his "will-power" or his "self-control".... An alternative analysis of the *behaviour* of control should make it possible to teach relevant techniques as easily as any other technical repertoire. It should also improve the procedures through which society maintains self-controlling behaviour in strength.... The point has been reached where a sweeping revision of the concept of responsibility is required, not only in a theoretical analysis of behaviour, but for its practical consequences as well'[253] (p. 241). If we are to make the necessary revision, what view of responsibility are we to take? Skinner is quite explicit in his definition of responsibility in terms of the association of reward and punishments with different forms of behaviour. 'To say that a person is "held responsible" for an act is simply to say that he is usually punished for it' (p. 343). Skinner resolves in this way the problem, which has been a major one in law, of

D

determining whether a person is or is not 'responsible' by virtually denying the usefulness of such a concept of responsibility at all. When we regard a person as 'insane', what we mean is that we cannot *control* his actions in the more usual ways, and 'diminished responsibility' which is not insanity simply represents a lesser degree of uncontrollability. The conclusion is clear. People, though 'reasonable', are manipulable organisms rather than 'responsible' beings. Skinner concedes that 'it is necessary to endow the individual with a "knowledge of consequences" or some sort of "expectation" to bridge the gap between the past and the future. But we are always dealing with a *prior* history of reinforcement and punishment. . . . The "reasons" or "grounds" for an "end-seeking action" are simply some of the variables of which behaviour is a function' (*ibid*.).

Man is conceived, therefore, not as a being with the power of 'realizing' purposes or 'endeavouring' to achieve ends or 'trying to live up to' ideals or 'practising the principles' of justice or equity, but as a responding organism controlled by his past history and the nature of the situation in which he finds himself. To be 'moral' is to conform to certain kinds of expectations of reinforcement which may very well be symbolically mediated by the individual himself but which have their ultimate origins in reinforcement from others. We can speak in everyday usage, of man having a 'purpose', but in fact, he has this purpose simply as a function of his past experience, and therefore we must look to this experience, rather than to the purpose for the explanation of his behaviour. Frequently we can 'guess' at this experience without actually *knowing,* as when we attribute a person's behaviour to common social motives, i.e. to a common history of reinforcement which has made the behaviour in question reinforcing for many people. Very often we will simply not know enough of the relevant history to be able to account for or predict a person's behaviour, but if only we did know, then we would have the answer.

There is undoubtedly an appeal about such a simple, empirical approach. However, much of Skinner's argument is by way of analogy and extension from animal experiments. Moreover, as Lana points out[172] (p. 63), Skinner himself specifically allows[253] (p. 451) that all human behaviour 'is subject to Kantian *a priori*'s in the sense that man as a behaving system has inescapable characteristics and limitations.' Such characteristics as man's capacity for evaluation in terms of 'right' and 'wrong' may well be such 'built in' characteristics. It seems very doubtful if what we mean by 'right' and 'wrong' can properly be re-defined as, for example, what is approved and what is punished, since, along with other problems, this leaves the question of how they came to be approved and punished; just as it seems doubtful whether the peculiar quality of *guilt* can be got rid of by talking of 'aversive stimuli and emotional responses . . . which we speak of as shame and guilt', or of 'conditioned anticipatory anxiety'. As Lana says, 'It may be that what is very important in understanding the nature of a thinking, social being lies in an understanding of the nature of these *a priori* qualities. If this is the case then by his own admission Skinner's behavioural operants may be totally irrelevant in explaining some aspects of thinking and many aspects of social activity'[172] (p. 63). If Lana is right, and there seem to be grounds for supposing that he is, then a legitimate criticism of Skinner's and all allied positions would be, not that they regard man as a conditionable or as a controllable responding organism, but that they regard him as *essentially* and exclusively such. Conditioning and experience of rewards and punishments may be of considerable importance, without telling anything like the whole story.

Mowrer

Like Bandrua and Walters[27] and Aronfreed,[14] O. H. Mowrer is interested in the mechanisms underlying the process of imitation, which he regards as a crucial factor in the child's social and moral development. The child may imitate an adult because the adult's behaviour has been accompanied by some kind of reward which the adult gives the child, so that the adult's behaviour, and by generalization, behaviour of the child which resembles that of the adult, comes to have secondary reward value for the child. But in addition, Mowrer argues that if an observer sees a model behaving, and sees the signs that the model is pleased with the results of his behaviour, he, the observer, will be likely to imitate the model 'in anticipation' of experiencing the same desirable outcome. Mowrer writes, 'Suppose that organism A not only provides the "model" but *also* experiences the reinforcement. If an observing organism, B, experiences some of the same immediate sensory consequences of A's behaviour as A experiences it and also "intuits" A's satisfactions (or dissatisfactions), then we may suppose that B will be rendered more or less likely to repeat A's behaviour, although, to what is involved in simple imitation, is here added the element of *empathy*. The extent to which this "higher-order" vicarious learning occurs in animals is perhaps open to debate, but it occurs very commonly at the human level'[212] (p. 115). This is undoubtedly largely because of the mediation of symbolic processes (language). This kind of process is referred to by Bandura and Walters as 'vicarious reinforcement'.

But such processes, though important, are not sufficient to explain how children learn to inhibit behaviour in the absence of direct, externally administered rewards and punishments. This also depends upon conditioned fear. According to Mowrer, because of 'aversive states' (punishment) associated with 'undesirable' behaviour, an emotional response (fear) becomes conditioned to certain stimuli immediately preceding the punishment. He distinguishes between 'active avoidance' and 'passive avoidance'. In active avoidance fear is conditioned to 'environmentally presented, independent stimuli', and leads to flight from the region in which these stimuli are experienced. If a child, for example, is frightened by a dog, he may take active steps to reduce his fear by taking a roundabout way to avoid the dangerous corner where he has encountered the dog. In passive avoidance, fear is conditioned to 'certain response-correlated stimuli' which depend on the person or animal *doing* something. For example, a child is punished just after stealing jam. If conditioned fear or anxiety becomes attached to the stimuli which arise from his approach to the pot, then this will be reduced by desisting in future from such projected transgression. Thus, the child learns to *inhibit* his behaviour as a result of a process of classical conditioning which attaches fear to stimuli occurring relatively early in the forbidden sequence of behaviour, and the rewarding effect of the reduction in unpleasant stimulation. In earlier work, Mowrer emphasized the proprioceptive stimulation arising from the actions actually being performed, but later he allowed that the unpleasant affect accompanying the punishment was more likely in humans to be attached to, or mediated by, verbal or cognitive aspects of the situation. In emphasizing the factor of *timing* of punishment, Mowrer refers[212] to a 'preliminary report' on work by R. L. Solomon and his associates on puppies. Solomon refers to their impression that puppies punished just as they approached a plate of meat tended to show high 'resistance to temptation' when afterwards given the opportunity to eat the 'taboo' food, but little 'emotional upset' when they did succumb and eat the meat, whereas puppies punished during eating tended to show lower resistance to temptation but more emotional upset after eating the prohibited food. This impression is confirmed in a later article by Solomon, Turner and Lessac.[255] In the training sessions, punishment for eating the meat was given (a) *immediately* on touching the meat, or (b) five seconds after touching it, or (c) 15 seconds after touching, according to the group to which the animal had been assigned. Though there were no differences between the dogs in each experimental treatment in the *acquisition* of 'meat avoidance', the group with immediate punishment were highly resistant to temptation when otherwise starved, the group whose punishment had been delayed by 15 seconds were very much less resistant.

But why does acquisition of meat avoidance not reflect the effect of delay of punishment, i.e. why did the groups of dogs not differ in the number of trials taken to reach the criterion period of abstention from meat-eating which was set for the dogs before they were subjected to the 'test' of prolonged starvation? The authors' answer is a very interesting one. The dogs, they say, all *knew* which food resulted in punishment by the experimenter. But when the experimenter was no longer there, there was a change in the controlling stimulus situation—the hungry animals weren't sure any longer about the punishment. At *this* point, the conditioned emotional responses came into the picture. 'If emotional conditioned responses take mediational control of behaviour under conditions of cognitive uncertainty, the temporal characteristics of Pavlovian emotional conditioning will manifest themselves. This is why delay of punishment is a powerful determinant of (subsequent) resistance to temptation and the emotional concomitants of taboo violations' (p. 238).

It should follow that the greater the difference between the training situation and the temptation situation, the *less* resistance should be shown by the dogs trained under long delay. This explanation is interesting in two ways. In the first place, the authors have felt it necessary to introduce a cognitive factor into their explanation, despite the difficulties of such terms for a behaviouristic theory, especially with animals. Secondly, their results suggest that, for human beings, the stronger the 'cognitive assessment' of the situation, the *less* likely behaviour is to depend upon the factor of emotional conditioning.

Despite his concern with imitation and conditioning, however, Mowrer does retain the term 'identification'[211] (ch. 21). He seems to regard as 'imitation', reproduction of a model's behaviour in the presence of the model, and as 'identification', reproduction of a model's behaviour in the model's absence. He distinguishes between what he calls 'developmental' identification and 'defensive' identification. In developmental identification, the parent especially the mother, comes to have secondary reward value for the child because of association with the satisfaction of primary needs like food, and the child is frustrated by the parent's absence. Thus, he may reproduce, overtly or in fantasy, aspects of the parent's behaviour especially when the parent is absent. In defensive identification, the child finds the parent's presence rather than absence frustrating, and reproduces the parent's commands in order to avoid punishment. Mowrer says, 'The first of these includes much of what has previously been referred to by the term "imitation", and the second is synonymous with Anna Freud's expression "identification with the aggressor" (p. 615). He thinks that ambivalence develops when defensive identification is added to the earlier development identification, and suggests that developmental identification is associated with the learning of skills, defensive identification with the development of character. This is presumably because defensive identification refers to the 'internalizing' of prohibitions. It does not really seem to be the case that Mowrer's 'defensive identification' is the same thing as Anna Freud's 'identification with the aggressor', for Anna Freud surely did not mean this form of identification to refer to a technique for anticipating and avoiding punishment. Further, it would seem much simpler to assume that ambivalence arises because the parents play the dual role of nurturing *and* punishing the child. Finally, since 'developmental identification' seems to refer very largely to imitation on the basis of secondary reward value, and 'defensive identification' to refer to symbolic anticipation and avoidance of punishment, it would seem very questionable whether the additional concept of identification is necessary to Mowrer at all.

Eysenck

H. J. Eysenck[77, 78] has developed Mowrer's theory of conditioned anxiety in several publications, and argues that 'socialized behaviour rests essentially on a basis of conditioning which is applied during a person's childhood by his parents, teachers and peers, and that his conduct in later years is determined very much by the quality of the conditioning received at that time, and also by the degree of conditionability which he himself shows'[78] (pp. 99–100). He stresses that frequently punishment may follow so long after the misdeed that the conditioning of anxiety cannot take place. Indeed, for conditioning to occur, the punishment must be closely contiguous with the offence. Moreover, in everyday life, rewards frequently follow wrongdoing *before* punishment catches up with the offender, so that the reinforcing effects are greater than any deterrent effect the punishment might have. This would particularly be the case when the performance of the forbidden behaviour is itself rewarding. According to Eysenck, then, emotional conditioning, mediated by the autonomic nervous system rather than by the central nervous system, is the vital factor, and what we call 'conscience' is in fact no more than a system of generalized conditioned anxiety responses. Such anxiety responses are, as experiments show, likely to be very persistent indeed, and to require counter-conditioning to get rid of them, i.e. they do not readily 'wear off', but require a positive emotional response to be conditioned to the same stimuli, which will tend to lessen and ultimately to remove the anxiety response. Conditioned emotional responses are particularly likely to be persistent when they have been acquired under very unpleasant or stressful conditions. In human beings, moreover, the generalization of conditioned anxiety responses to stimuli other than those to which they were originally conditioned but in some way similar, is greatly facilitated and extended in range by the process of linguistic 'labelling'.

According to Eysenck, punishment which does not follow wrongdoing sufficiently closely to have inhibiting effects is likely, if anything, to have the effect of producing a higher level of drive or activation, and, as experimental studies indicate, beyond a certain point, this makes it harder to act at variance with old habits; thus punishment may be expected frequently to have the opposite effect from that intended.

The statement from Eysenck which we have quoted above refers both to the 'quality of conditioning' (and presumably the quantity) received in childhood, and to an individual's 'degree of condition-ability'. To take the second point first, Eysenck argues in favour of differences in conditionability, related to constitutional differences in both emotionality and introversion-extraversion. In an experimental investigation with rats, Eysenck took two strains of 'emotional' and 'unemotional' rats. All the animals were taught to go to a food trough whenever a buzzer sounded. The buzzer went on for two seconds, and as soon as it ended, food fell into the trough. However, if the unfortunate animal took the food within three seconds, it got an electric shock. Thus, the animal had to learn to delay feeding as a result of the conditioning of avoidance to the response of feeding whenever the food appeared. Eysenck reported that the 'unemotional' rats readily learned to delay their response and eat *after* the three seconds had passed, thus avoiding the shock and getting the food. The emotional rats much more frequently tended *either* (a) to eat straight away, regardless of the shock, *or* (b) to withdraw and not to eat at all, thus avoiding the shock, but only at the cost of remaining hungry. Eysenck argues that in the emotional animals, the drive level or arousal would be higher, so that *both* the desire to eat and the deterrent effect of conditioned fear would tend to be higher. But the animals who eat anyway would not have become highly conditioned with the number of conditioning trials given, while those who withdraw altogether would have been so strongly conditioned that they would be unable to make the required discrimination in the matter of time. Eysenck describes the three types of reaction as paradigms of normal, psychopathic and dysthymic (anxiety) behaviour in human beings—normal people are adequately conditioned, psychopaths hardly condition at all (thus being devoid of anticipatory anxiety and feelings of guilt), and dysthymics over-condition, not being able to allow themselves indulgences which would generally be considered quite normal and permissible. Now, according to Eysenck, the introverts among us condition more readily than the extraverts. Extraverts tend to build up inhibition faster, i.e. they become non-responsive quicker than introverts, and also experience stimulation less intensely than introverts; thus, conditioning should have less effect on extraverts than on introverts. Extraverts of high emotionality, then will tend to be more impulsive, take more risks, and so on. Eysenck's prediction therefore is that, other things being equal, more extraverts should be criminals, more introverts dysthymics (anxiety neurotics). Eysenck also relates his theory to body build, following the typology of Kretschmer. Introverts tend, he believes, to be people of asthenic build (tall and slim), while extraverts tend to be of the athletic type (powerful and muscular) or pyknic type (short, broad and inclined to fat).

But of course, we are not simply *either* readily conditionable *or* conditionable only with difficulty. There is a range of constitutionally determined conditionability, from the extremely conditionable to the extremely unconditionable. The *outcome* will depend partly on what constitution one starts with and partly on the efficiency of the conditioning which one receives as a child. Thus, more efficient conditioning with a less conditionable child may produce better results than poorer conditioning with a more conditionable child. Moreover, from the point of view of society, one may be conditioned to feel that the 'wrong' things are right and the 'right' things wrong. If we are justified in assuming that middle class parents are likely to accept the values of society more readily, and to condition their children more firmly in accordance with these values, then we would expect to find that middle class criminals are, on average, significantly less conditionable, significantly more extraverted, than working class criminals.

Eysenck's theory is a simple and straightforward one, and he produces evidence in support of at least some of it. For example, Fine,[87] in America, found extraverts to be guilty of more accidents and traffic violations than introverts, and S. B. G. Eysenck[80] in England found that unmarried mothers tended to be high in both emotionality and extraversion. However, these findings would seem to suggest that extraverts tend to be more impulsive, especially when also relatively high in emotionality, but not necessarily that they have less 'conscience'. Syed, in an unpublished study reported by Eysenck, found 100 women prisoners in London to be high in emotionality and extraversion, and this is perhaps the most positive support for Eysenck. Warburton (reported by Eysenck) in Chicago, found emotionality and extraversion characteristic of 'recalcitrant' prisoners, and Andry[7] reports recidivists to show a high level of emotional disturbance and tough, extrapunitive behaviour, which Eysenck regards as indicating extraversion. Lykken[181] in America and Tong (reported by Eysenck) in England both found psychopaths to be difficult to condition. Bandura and Walters comment[27] that although Lykken's psychopaths took longer to learn to avoid punishment, they nevertheless did learn, whereas we should have expected that real psychopaths would not. The five findings to which we have just referred all deal with a special *class* of criminal, the psychopathic and (in Andry's case), the recidivist. Perhaps it is not unreasonable to suppose that Andry's recidivists contained a significant proportion of psychopaths. The association would thus seem to be rather between psychopathy and extraversion or low conditionability. Argyle[10] in fact claims that *no* British studies using Eysenck's own Maudsley Personality Inventory have found delinquents to be outstandingly high in extraversion. Eysenck also reports the finding of West[272] that most prisoners come of respectable parents, and that most of their brothers are respectable too. This, he thinks, lends support to the importance of constitutional factors rather than experience. However, this is a doubtful corollary, because of the very great possible variety of individual experiences and their possible effects, especially when one allows for the *cumulative* effect of experience as a result of the continuous interpretation of experience in terms of past experience. Again, Eysenck does not explain why there should be so many non-recidivists. Many cases would seem to suggest that the individual does learn from experience. Eysenck also hypothesises that the difference in the rates of crime between England and America may be due to differences in social conditioning. He does not appear to consider that the conditions of life facing people in the two countries may be very different, and that the current situation may be as relevant as, or more relevant than, social conditioning to differences in the crime rates.

Eysenck's view of conscience is that it consists of all these *unreasoning* (sometimes unreasonable, sometimes not) feelings of discomfort which we may experience when we do or contemplate doing something with which our uncomfortable conditioned emotional responses have been associated by past experience and generalization. For example, Eysenck says that he himself still never feels quite happy about cutting potatoes with a knife, because of the strong conditioning against doing so which he received as a boy. He does not seem to distinguish between *this* kind of twinge and the kind of guilty feeling one has when one makes a self-critical judgment that one has failed to live up to self-accepted standards. Perhaps it might be said that by 'self-accepted standards' we simply mean a rather complex assortment, or even system, of verbal mediators, whereby our conditioned responses acquire a very high degree of generality. Or it might perhaps be said that such standards are but rationalizations of our feelings. However, when we talk about 'self-accepted standards', we imply that we really do understand the nature of, and the reasons for, such standards. If Eysenck simply means that early aversive conditioning may be important as a basis for further development, we can go a long way with him, although, as he himself admits,[79] he has rather ignored the role of positive rewards and 'operant' learning. But, as Derek Wright points out, a weakness with this kind of theory is that it does not provide an adequate basis for distinguishing between 'punishment and reward mediated by human agents' and 'those which are the impersonal consequences of behaviour'[280] (p. 615). Moreover, man is a rational as well as a conditionable animal, and even his conscience may surely have rational as well as conditioned emotional elements.

7

Learning Theories II
Bandura and Walters, Gewirtz,
Aronfreed, Dissonance Theory

Bandura and Walters

Albert Bandura and his associates, particularly R. H. Walters, are
reinforcement theorists who nevertheless regard both classical
conditioning and operant learning concepts as insufficient,
although important, for the explanation of social and moral learning. They take the view that behaviour, *once acquired or learned*,
is maintained or modified by the pattern of reinforcement—both
reward and punishment—to which it is subjected. But they feel
that reinforcement *by itself* is not enough to explain how new
behaviour and attitudes may be learned in the first place. They
criticize Skinner's idea of 'shaping' on the grounds that some
forms of behaviour—sometimes quite complex—may suddenly
appear in a child, under such conditions that one cannot reasonably suppose that they have been gradually built up by a process
of reinforcement of successive approximations; and they claim that
it is necessary to introduce the idea of 'observational learning' or
'modelling'—essentially a modern version of the old idea of
imitation. Thus Bandura and Walters write, 'We shall attempt
to explain the development of all forms of social behaviour in
terms of antecedent social stimulus events such as the behavioural
characteristics of the social models to which a child has been
exposed, the reinforcement contingencies of his learning history,
and the methods of training that have been used to develop and
modify his social behaviour'[27] (p. 44). Bandura and Walters do
not deny the importance of constitutional factors, but choose to
concentrate upon what they call 'social learning influences'
because they feel that in the present state of our knowledge, this

is the more profitable strategy to follow. They point out that the principles of social learning are 'ethically neutral' in the sense that they will be equally applicable to the learning of all kinds of behaviour or attitudes, however positively or negatively these may be valued—one learns good habits and bad habits, approved attitudes and disapproved attitudes in the same way, and according to the same principles. In relation to reinforcement, Bandura and Walters emphasize in particular that in human beings, a great deal of reinforcement is of the variable kind, frequently with both ratio and interval varying. For example, if a child is *sometimes* (perhaps to save his mother embarrassment) given sweets to keep him quiet, then it is not to be wondered at if he shows persistent fits of crying or temper tantrums when he wants sweets. Again, parents cannot watch their children all the time, and it is likely that unwanted behaviour is at least occasionally rewarding without being punished. This may well be one of the reasons for undesirable behaviour the persistence of which may continue to puzzle parents and others.

Generalization, or the association of an act with stimuli similar to but other than those with which it was originally, or first became, associated, is clearly an economical and indispensable process, but it may sometimes be either too wide or inappropriate. It is too wide if, for example, fear induced by a fright from a dog is extended to all animals; it is inappropriate if it is based on an irrelevant quality, for example, if a child is frightened by a woman with a blue hat, and is then afraid of anyone with a blue hat, or even of anything blue. Successful social and moral learning depends very much upon the ability to make appropriate discriminations, i.e. to respond or not to respond with a particular kind of behaviour according to the differences between situations, rather than responding in the same way to all because of their similarities. One learns, for example, when it is socially appropriate, and even *morally* appropriate to tell a lie.

Bandura and Walters then refer to the importance of learning to inhibit behaviour, i.e. learning not to do things we want to do. It is possible, as animal experiments have shown, to influence the occurrence of behaviour by selective reinforcement, i.e. by rewarding desired behaviour and not rewarding undesired. But this is apt to be a long, cumbersome and difficult process, and apart from this, we are left with two possibilities—punishment, or the administration of some painful or unpleasant stimulus, and the withholding of a positive reward. In relation to punishment, Bandura and Walters note Mowrer's distinction between passive avoidance depending on proprioceptive or 'internal' stimulation associated with the response, and active avoidance depending upon the provocation of fear by external stimuli, but comment that 'in social learning both external cues, particularly those associated with the presence of the socializing agents, and internal cues contribute to response inhibition. Conditioned emotional responses may, in fact, be elicited simply by the presence of an adult who has been the agent of punishment; in such cases, the external cue may result in response inhibition without the child's making any preparatory neuromuscular or postural adjustments associated with the commission of the act' (p. 13). Bandura and Walters agree that the 'withholding of reinforcers' may be very like punishment from the child's point of view, but argue that this is most likely to be the case with 'active confiscation of privileges', which is likely to be accompanied by either physical punishment or verbal reproof. In this case it may lead to suppression of the behaviour only when punishment is likely, and may perhaps also lead to undesirable escape behaviour such as avoiding parents or lying. On the other hand, withholding of rewards *should* be more like simple non-reinforcement in its effects, and more likely to lead to behaviour designed to bring about the restoration of the lost rewards. From the point of view of social learning theory, it would obviously be important to know about the kind of conditions which are likely to make the withholding of rewards appear as a form of punishment, but there do not seem to be any really relevant studies here. In any event, there is no doubt that punishment *can* be highly effective in modifying behaviour, especially if suppression of unwanted behaviour increases the probability of alternative behaviour which can then be rewarded. This is a point stressed by Skinner, as we may remember. Simple as this procedure sounds, however, it may be much harder to put into practice than at first might appear.

The emphasis which Bandura and his associates put upon

'imitation', 'modelling' or 'observational learning' and upon 'vicarious reinforcement' is probably the most important aspect of their work. In their emphasis on imitation, they deal summarily with the concept of identification. Admitting that imitation and identification have been distinguished on various grounds by different authors, they point to the confusion and lack of agreement, and write, 'It is possible to draw distinctions between these and other related terms—for example, introjection and incorporation. . . . However, one might question whether it is meaningful to do so, since essentially the same learning process is involved regardless of the content of what is learned, the object from whom it is learned, or the stimulus situations in which the relevant behaviour is emitted. Therefore, it is in the interest of clarity, precision and parsimony to employ the single term, imitation, to refer to the occurrence of matching responses' (pp. 89–90). Similarly, Bandura writes, 'In social learning theory an identificatory event is defined as the occurrence of similarity between the behaviour of a model and another person under conditions where the model's behaviour has served as the determinative cue for the matching response'[22] (p. 217). No allowance is apparently made for cases in which there may be 'identification' with some aspect of a parent's attitude or emotional style, while overt behaviour is quite different, but this is not really a difficulty, since the child may be said to be imitating these aspects only. The real difficulty is in explaining why certain aspects of parental behaviour (in the widest sense) should be imitated and adopted while others are not.

According to Bandura,[22] there are two kinds of process which mediate imitation or modelling, an *imaginal* system and a verbal system. Images of the model's behaviour are formed by sensory conditioning based on contiguity. When an observer watches someone else, he has a series of perceptual responses. If the experience is repeated a number of times, any item or part of the series of stimulation will acquire, by temporal contiguity, the capacity to evoke images of the other events of the series, although they are no longer present. But if the behaviour of the model can be 'verbally coded', as a great deal of human observed behaviour is, observational learning is likely to be very much quicker and to be capable of being retained over a long period of time. In this case, the sequence of behaviour is represented in a set of verbal instructions, which can then guide behaviour when an appropriate cue occurs. Obviously, attention to relevant behaviour of the model is necessary, and motivation facilitating attention must be an important factor. Thus, a child will be more likely to observe and learn from some models than others, and especially from members of his own family, and to observe some forms of behaviour (including verbal behaviour) rather than others. Bandura's idea of imaginal and verbal mediation here is very similar to Aronfreed's[14] (ch. 4) notion of a 'cognitive template'. As far as long-term retention of the results of observational learning are concerned, overt practice may be important, but so also may covert rehearsal, where practice is symbolic rather than overt. This may be particularly important in relation to 'moral learning', i.e. the acquisition by imitation, of verbal precepts and prohibitions.

Imitation or modelling or observational learning does not imply that the observer's performance must copy in detail that of the model. In particular, the intervention of verbal mediators enables the observer's behaviour even to be of a different kind, though based on the model in crucial ways. For example, a child who observes a model carrying out some motor task may, when he comes to perform the same task, actually use a different hand. In some cases, quite a wide range of specific behaviours may all meet the requirements of the verbal formulation. This freedom should be particularly significant in regard to attitudinal and evaluative learning.

Among the factors affecting the probability of modelling is nurturance, or affectionate treatment by one's parents (or others). According to Mowrer[212] the behaviour of nurturant parents acquires secondary reward value because of its association with feeding and other primary satisfactions, and, by generalization, behaviour resembling the parents' will also be rewarding. The view of Sears[242] is similar, except that he postulates that the child learns to depend upon his parents but that, in order to encourage independence, they withhold affection and nurturance, and the frustration of the child's dependency need leads to imitation of parental behaviours as a kind of 'replacement'. Bandura and Walters[27] and Bandura[22] refer to various studies supporting the view that, in general, children more frequently model nurturant parents. However, as Bandura points out, there may be reasons in addition to or other than the secondary reward value of parent-imitative behaviour. Affectionate parents are likely to spend more time with their children and thus give them more opportunities to observe their parents and learn to behave like them. This fits in quite well with the view that attachment in young children may be based largely upon familiarity rather than secondary reward value. And children who model their parents are perhaps likely to increase their parents' interest and approval, and thus there may be a circular process. This is perhaps of more importance in its negative form—when children who do not model or are otherwise recalcitrant provoke their parents to reduce their nurturance and attention. But analysis in terms of nurturance and the positive reward value of imitative behaviour do not really deal with the problem of why children should imitate the *punishing* behaviour of their parents as by applying critical remarks to themselves. It does not seem very convincing to suppose that positive reward value should have generalized to aversive behaviour to a sufficient extent to overcome the aversive quality of the behaviour.

'Vicarious reinforcement' refers to the 'second-hand' effect which reinforcement of the model's behaviour may have on the behaviour of the observer, and Bandura and his associates lay considerable stress on this kind of 'reinforcement at second hand'. In addition to their role in observational learning, they propose that models may have three important functions—disinhibiting, inhibiting and eliciting. Disinhibitory effects occur when observation of a model's behaviour serves to release behaviour which is already in the child's repertory but the actual performance of which would otherwise have been inhibited. The disinhibitory effect is likely when the behaviour of the model might have been expected to result in unpleasant consequences but do not. Eliciting effects are rather similar to disinhibitory effects, but occur when the behaviour is not likely to have incurred punishment, e.g. in the case of following an example in volunteering one's services. Inhibitory effects are most likely when the behaviour has had unpleasant consequences for the model, but may also be seen in the tendency for children to show the same fears as their mothers.

Once a particular kind of imitative behaviour has occurred, it will, of course, be subject to the effects of direct reinforcement. If it is rewarded, it is more likely to recur. Thus, for example, in the acquisition of sex-typed behaviour, we have the combined effects of observational learning and direct reinforcement. The child who behaves like his father will generally (though by no means always) be rewarded for doing so. But if a range of imitative behaviour is consistently rewarded then we may have a generalized habit of imitation established. This is very much the view of Gewirtz (see p. 116), though Gewirtz does not admit the possibility of observational learning in the first place. Baer and Sherman[20] suggest that this habit of imitating may then be maintained in the absence of further reward from outside agencies, because of the secondary reward value of 'likeness to the model'. This is virtually the same view as that of Kagan[156] who talked of 'perceived similarity' to the model as the reinforcing factor. If *some* imitative behaviour is *not* reinforced, but is punished (such as smoking by a child), then in addition to generalization, the child must also learn the appropriate discriminations in respect of what and when to imitate. Bandura is doubtful about the explanation of generalized imitation in terms of the secondary reward value of similarity to the model, parent or otherwise, and suggests another possibility—that generalized imitation is due to inability to discriminate between the kind of imitative behaviour which is rewarded and the kind of imitative behaviour which is not rewarded. The better the ability to make this discrimination, the more likely it is that a child will continue to imitate in ways which are rewarded, but will stop unrewarded imitation. This is very close to the interpretations of Gewirtz, for whom generalized imitation as a habit is central to the explanation of 'identification'.

Bandura and Walters refer to various experimental studies confirming their views. Bandura, Ross and Ross[28] and Kuhn, Madsen and Becker[171] showed that seeing aggressive models either 'live' or in films increased the amount of aggression displayed by young children. Walters and Amoroso[270] found that observers would imitate a model even in the absence of reinforcement of either observer or model. They also found that such imitation was especially likely in circumstances where the observers did not know how they were expected to behave and were provided with no standards other than that supplied by the model. This is, of course, the position of the young child, and is an extremely important factor. Bandura and McDonald[24] found that observation of models had more effect in altering children's moral judgments in the direction of greater 'objectivity' or greater 'subjectivity' than direct reinforcement. Bandura[22] (p. 317) concludes that the findings of this experiment 'are somewhat analogous to evidence from informal observation that children often persist in their efforts to reproduce through imitation child-prohibited adult role activities that are observed to be highly rewarding to parental models'. This seems to suggest that the most likely explanation of children's tendency to reproduce parental critical comments is that they learn that the situation is one calling for evaluation, and they have only one model for such evaluation.

Bandura makes out a good case—if one be required to be made —for the importance of a child's model for his social and moral learning. The relevant experiments show that such processes as he hypothesizes *can* take place as hypothesized. However, to re-name the old 'imitation' as 'modelling' or 'observational learning', does not contribute much to showing *how* imitation is possible or how it actually operates; while to provide experimental paradigms can only suggest that real-life social and moral learning might take place as the paradigm indicates. The experiments, although suggestive, are not *really* tests of the theory as a theory of how social and moral learning in general takes place.

Gewirtz

J. L. Gewirtz,[116] like Skinner represents a more extreme version of behaviouristic learning theory. Although he shares Bandura's emphasis on the importance of reinforcement for the maintenance of behaviour once acquired, he differs from him in not accepting that 'imitative behaviours' may be acquired by 'observational learning' without direct reward and/or punishment. 'It is my thesis, then,' writes Gewirtz, 'that matching or imitation learning

is only a special case of instrumental learning, and that it is illusory
to hold that . . . generalized imitation and identification takes
place without the direct instrumental training from socializing
agents that defines the first type' [direct tuition] (p. 141). He is
even more outspoken in his criticisms of writers like Kohlberg[164]
and Aronfreed[14, 15] for their emphasis upon intervening cognitive processes such as Aronfreed's 'cognitive template'. Gewirtz
writes, 'It appears that intra-psychic, cognitive-act euphemisms
phrased in common-sense or immediate-experience language are
often employed to characterize heuristically the bases for a subject's behaviour in a given context. However . . . it is far from
obvious whether the locus of such heuristic terms is meant to be
the head of the subject or (the theory) of the scientist, or the
immediate experience of the subject or of the scientist as if he
were the subject. Thus, the distinction between the statement of a
problem and its explanation can be obscured, and empirical questions can lose their importance or appear to be solved simply
by the application of cognitive labels to them' (p. 134). Of the
'cognitive template', he remarks that it 'Seems to offer an explanation for the acquisition of identification behaviours only insofar
as we are told that the acquisition of one is the basis for the
acquisition of the other.' Of Aronfreed's 'affective value' and
Kohlberg's 'motives for mastery and interesting consequences', he
observes, 'As they have no independent operational status in the
imitation context, these concepts as presently formulated can
only be inferred from the very imitative behaviours they have
been devised to explain' (p. 145). The trouble, in other words, is
that we have no way of confirming the existence of a 'cognitive
template' independently of the behaviour it is supposed to be
explaining. It is confusing, misleading, unparsimonious and
unnecessary. The crucial objection is that it is unnecessary. How,
then, does Gewirtz get on without such 'intervening cognitive
processes'?

He argues that all the kinds of behaviour which go under the
head of 'identification' are essentially simply a form of imitation,
and that imitation is simply a form of instrumental (reward-
gaining) behaviour. First, he maintains that the first imitative
responses 'must' occur by chance or by specific tuition by parents,

for example. (But of course, they only 'must' occur by chance or by tuition because the particular kind of theory requires it.) When once these responses *have* occurred, they are rewarded directly by the parents. After a number of imitative behaviours have been rewarded and acquired, a class of behaviours is established, which may include a range of quite diverse behaviours which are, however, functionally equivalent in the sense that they are all *imitative* behaviours. Gewirtz refers to 'generalized imitation', which is defined as existing 'when many different responses of a model are copied in diverse situations often in the absence of extrinsic reinforcement'. Examples of imitative behaviour are then likely sometimes to be reinforced, sometimes not, and so the response class of 'imitative behaviour' will be intermittently reinforced. In so far as reinforced and non-reinforced imitative responses cannot be distinguished, even imitative responses which are themselves *never* rewarded, will nevertheless tend to persist as members of the (functional) response class. If *some* kinds of imitative behaviour are frequently reinforced and others are not, or are punished, then we are likely to have discrimination of rewarded and non-rewarded imitative behaviour, the latter *not* being maintained. But in so far as a response class of 'imitative behaviour' is maintained, there must be, in Gewirtz's view, at least occasional *external* reinforcement of a range of behaviours belonging to the response class. Under the general label of behaviour, of course, Gewirtz includes 'behaviours implied in such general dispositions as are often termed motives, values, or attitudes' (p. 154). He later comments further, 'Identification with the model at the level of abstract values may require finer discriminations by the child but ... should follow the same principles as generalized imitation' (p. 157). There is no difficulty about the fact that in young children, imitation may be restricted to imitation of one or a few models. This will simply reflect the pattern of external reinforcement. Gewirtz believes that the kinds of thing which have been included under the term 'identification' can in fact be explained in terms of instrumental learning. In other words, while a term like 'identification' may have some value as a descriptive label, it is superfluous from the point of view of explanation, and even its value for description may be illusory. Gewirtz and Stingle[117] (p.

390), indeed, suggest that the main difference between 'identification' and 'imitation' is that the former is simply a more vaguely
defined, more complex, more inclusive and hence less satisfactory
substitute for the latter. Gewirtz himself continues to use the term
'identification' to refer to the kinds of thing included by others
under this heading—perhaps a confusing thing to do. In the light
of Aronfreed's insistence on the crucial role of anxiety, it is interesting that Gewirtz does not deal in any detail with fear anxiety,
but indicates like other reinforcement theorists, that it may be
significant in that its removal or avoidance should be rewarding
as representing the removal or avoidance of an aversive or
unpleasant stimulus.

A view which seems essentially similar to that of Gewirtz is
expressed by Mischel,[204] writing of the acquisition of *self-control*
and the ability to *delay* responses. For him, the probability of
any behaviour is a function of the 'subjective expectancy' that it
will lead to particular consequences in a given situation *and* of
the reinforcement value of these consequences. This 'subjective
expectancy' is not an arbitrary notion, but is directly dependent
upon direct and vicarious experience. 'Manipulable social stimulus
events,' says Mischel, are 'the critical determinants of self-controlling behaviour' (p. 108). Bandura and Mischel[25] report that
watching models could affect delay of response, but they refer to
the need for newly-acquired 'self-control' to be supported by
intermittent reinforcement from without.

One point of which Gewirtz makes no mention is the reproducing of *aversive* behaviour of the model, which has been directed
against the subject, e.g. when a child 'punishes' or scolds himself.
Mischel and Grusec[205] found that whether the model was *rewarding* or not did not affect the extent to which children 'rehearsed'
the model's aversive behaviour, but the amount of power or
control exercised by the model did—high control was associated
with more imitative rehearsal of the aversive behaviour. It is not
hard to see how Gewirtz might explain this in terms of his concepts—it is likely that powerful models will have rewarded a child
for applying to himself the model's punishments or criticisms. For
example, he may end signs of disapproval or restore signs of
affection. This is less likely in the case of a model who is rewarding

but has little power. Thus a response disposition may be established to imitate even the aversive behaviour of powerful models.

Gewirtz's approach has the same kind of appeal on grounds of simplicity as Skinner's, and is subject to the same kind of limitations.

Aronfreed

Justin Aronfreed lays considerable emphasis upon aversive stimulation and anxiety, and upon cognitive mediating processes in the 'internalization' of control of behaviour. Aronfreed and Reber[16] define conduct as 'internally controlled' 'if it can be reliably elicited in the absence of socializing agents, after having been acquired under the control of either direct response outcomes which were mediated by the agents or the display of similar conduct by the agents' (p. 4). This definition includes conduct which consists in the 'negative' suppression of undesirable behaviour and in the 'positive' performance of desirable behaviour. It also allows for initial learning by imitation or modelling. In fact, in his discussion of imitation, Aronfreed,[14] like Bandura and Walters, insists on the need to assume that the imitator forms some kind of cognitive model or 'cognitive template' as he calls it, of the model's behaviour. Reinforcement is then provided by the imitator's perception of the degree of 'match' between his behaviour and the cognitive template. As far as the suppression of undesirable behaviour is concerned, Aronfreed,[12] following Mowrer, suggests that in internalized suppression of behaviour, two sequential processes are involved. First, anxiety becomes attached to behavioural or cognitive 'items' which are associated with the beginning of the transgression. Then, positive affective value becomes attached to items associated with reduction of the anxiety. Like Mowrer,[212] Bandura and Walters,[27] and Solomon et al,[255] Aronfreed stresses the timing of the aversive stimulation or punishment which creates the anxiety. Aronfreed and Reber (op. cit.), in an experiment with children of nine to ten years of age, showed that punishment at the beginning of a sequence of 'undesirable' behaviour was more effective than punishment after the sequence of behaviour had ended, in ensuring internalized suppression of the behaviour, i.e. in ensuring that the children did not indulge in the behaviour even when adult supervision was completely removed. Each child was presented with a selection of highly attractive and less attractive toys, and told to pick up the toy he wanted to tell about. He was told that some of the toys were 'only supposed to be for older boys', and he shouldn't choose these ones. On each trial, the child was allowed to pick up and describe one of the less attractive toys, but if he picked up one of the more attractive toys, he was 'told off'. Children 'punished' at the beginning were told off on reaching for the forbidden toy; children whose punishment was delayed were told off after picking up the forbidden toy. After a 'training session' in which they received the appropriate verbal punishment, the children were left alone with the toys. A child was judged 'resistant to temptation' if he continued to play with the unattractive toys. Aronfreed[14] points out a difficulty here. In real life, we are not likely very often to have the chance to stop a sequence of undesirable behaviour at the beginning of the sequence, though parents may sometimes punish behaviour which has been performed and is about to be repeated. However, most punishment will come after—perhaps some time after—the sequence of behaviour has been completed. How, then, can such punishment have any suppressive effect? Aronfreed attaches a great deal of importance to 'cognitive mediation'. As he says, 'cognitive structure facilitates internalized suppression by serving as an intrinsic mediator of anxiety which can intercede before the commission of a punished act, even though the original socialization process may generally transmit cognitive structure after the punished act has been committed'[15] (p. 276). Aronfreed regards 'cognitive structure' as any form of verbal 'definition of the situation' relevant to the probable effects of behaviour. By appropriate mediation by the socializing agent, anxiety may, in particular, become attached to the cognitive factor of the child's *intentions*. This, however, although it seems plausible, would be very difficult to demonstrate.

Aronfreed[15] reports an impressive series of experiments indicating that the provision of 'cognitive structure' in the form of 'labelling' does facilitate 'internalized suppression' when associated

with punishment. He feels that this justifies the view that cognitive structure acts by *mediating anxiety*. In general, more severe
punishment was more effective, but this was not independent of
the ease with which the situational cues relevant to punishment
or non-punishment could be discriminated, i.e. the ease with
which the child could recognize the signs that punishment was or
was not going to follow. Where discrimination was difficult, severe
punishment appeared to have a disruptive effect, and milder
punishment was more effective. Children were asked to select toys
to play with, and were punished when they played with certain
of the toys and not when they played with others. When the two
groups of toys could easily be distinguished (e.g. if the permitted
toys were red and the forbidden toys yellow), then more severe
punishment was more effective in suppressing choice of the
forbidden toys. But when the toys differed in a number of ways,
and the two groups had to be distinguished on the complex basis
of a number of cues, then milder punishment was more effective.
If, of course, the discrimination were sufficiently difficult, i.e.
entirely beyond the capacity of the children concerned, then the
children could not distinguish at all between the cues for
punished behaviour and the cues for unpunished behaviour. Discrimination is therefore crucial in making possible what Aronfreed[14] calls 'predictive control over the outcomes of (one's own)
behaviour'; and the verbal factor is crucial in enabling complex
discriminations to be made. 'It is therefore the verbal medium of
socialization that is the most pervasive determinant of the child's
ability to make active behavioural choices which are discriminative
before the occurrence of an overt act'[14] (p. 204).

So far we have been concerned with 'internalized suppression'
of behaviour. But not all undesirable behaviour is suppressed. We
all transgress sometimes, and there are different kinds of reactions
to transgression. These may be more or less 'internally' or 'externally' oriented, according to Aronfreed, and depend upon rather
different mechanisms for their acquisition. Aronfreed[11, 14] distinguishes four types of reaction to transgression, as follows. (1)
Self-criticism. (2) Reparation. (3) Confession. (4) Reactions
oriented toward external punishment. The first two of these involve
a degree of internalization in the sense that, once established they

take place independently of external authority. Confession involves much less internalization. Externally oriented reactions are largely oriented toward avoidance of consequences, although there may be an element of internalization, in so far as the motivating anxiety (or fear) may occur even when the transgression has not been witnessed by any relevant adult. According to Aronfreed, these different forms of reaction are acquired as a result of different kinds of experience in transgression.

(1) *Self-criticism.* In self-criticism, a child reproduces criticism from others which has resulted from the child's behaviour, i.e. he reproduces certain verbal aspects of punishment which he has received. Now, the committing of a transgression which has frequently been punished will be followed by anticipatory anxiety concerning the probable forthcoming punishment. The punishment, when it comes, will have the effect of *terminating* this anticipatory anxiety. Verbal criticism, as part of this punishment, will have acquired anxiety-reducing value because of its association with the termination of anticipatory anxiety. And since it is an *aspect* of the punishment complex which is particularly easy to reproduce, the child will tend to use self-criticism as an anxiety-reducing device. Because of the frequently short duration of punishment, criticism may also be associated with the termination of other aspects of the punishment, but for Aronfreed, the crucial factor is the reduction of anticipatory anxiety. Kohlberg[161] points out that if self-criticism is always an anxiety-reducing device, we should not expect it to be associated with resistance to temptation, whereas some studies (e.g. Mackinnon[190]) do find just this. However, it might be replied that if anticipatory anxiety can be attached by verbal mediation to *intentions* before committing the transgression, then if this anticipatory anxiety is on some occasions not sufficient to prevent the misdemeanour, self criticism *on these occasions* might reduce post-transgression anxiety, while in cases where transgression does not take place, anticipatory self-criticism might reduce the pre-transgression anxiety associated with the intention by reducing the strength of the intention.

In an ingenious experiment, Aronfreed[13] showed how children could learn verbal labels for their behaviour when these were used in a temporal association with the termination of a 'sign' indicating forbidden behaviour and the termination of punishment for the behaviour. A child had to guess how many out of four dolls (at least two) were looking in their direction, and to indicate by pulling the requisite number of switches on a machine. On some trials, a buzzer sounded, and when this happened, the child was deprived of some of a pile of sweets she had been given, and told that was because she had done it 'the blue way'. The 'other way', for which no sweets were removed, was called 'the red way'. The child was told that there were two ways of working the levers and these were called for convenience the 'red way' and the 'blue way'. After ten trials, the experimenter pretended not to be concerned with the buzzer, leaving it to the child to respond spontaneously, or if the child did not do so, asking, 'What happened that time?' The timing of the labelling as 'blue' was varied with different groups of children. (a) With one group, the child was told, 'You did it the *blue* way' *after* her sweets had been removed, and the buzzer was turned off and the switches re-set. In another group, the experimenter said, 'You did it the *blue* way,' and *then* took away the sweets, shut off the buzzer and re-set the switches. Aronfreed found that the children in the former group, i.e. those for whom 'labelling' occurred in association with the *end* of the punishment and the stopping of the 'signal' for the 'transgressing response, much more frequently attached the label 'blue' to their own behaviour when the buzzer sounded in the final 'test' trials. Aronfreed also found, in experimental attempts to *extinguish* the labelling, that it was rather strongly resistant to extinction.

These experiments, in themselves, do not actually involve the learning of real *critical* responses, but the implication is that a critical response is essentially a kind of label and that use of *critical* labels may be expected to follow the same kind of pattern as other labels which are associated with anxiety. The experiments represent, to use Aronfreed's term, a 'paradigm' or controlled demonstration of how the hypothesized underlying process can occur.

Aronfreed[13] and Aronfreed, Cutick and Fagen[17] emphasize that a clear cognitive structure facilitates self-criticism. Aronfreed, Cutick and Fagen provided cognitive structure by telling the subjects in the experiment that they had to be *careful and gentle,* and avoid being *careless and rough* in the task, which consisted in pushing a doll figure in a nurse's uniform off a board, while knocking down as few as possible of a number of 'soldier' figures which were in the way. After a number of trials, the experimenter remarked that the nurse doll had got broken, surreptitiously removing a hand. This provided the occasion for the occurrence of self-critical responses. More of those who had been provided with 'guiding' labels made self-critical responses.

Hill[137] had suggested that children learn to make self-critical comments because parents generally respond to such comments by forgiving their children and reinstating them to favour. Certainly, parents often do reward self-criticism in such a way, and this reinforcement is bound to contribute to the maintenance and consolidation of self-criticism. Grusec[124] showed that self-criticism might be reinforced by being associated with the termination of punishment. Aronfreed, however,[15] thinks that self-criticism is rarely *overtly* expressed, and so the reinforcement of self-criticism directly by parents cannot be the major factor in the acquiring of self-critical responses. But young children, in particular, may quite often express self-criticism overtly and in the hearing of adults who proceed to reassure them. If Hill's suggestion were correct, we should expect the children of highly 'nurturant' parents who reward their children for self-criticism to show more self-criticism than the children of less nurturant parents, since presumably the reward value of a return to grace should be greater. The experiment by Aronfreed, Cutick and Fagen[17] rather suggests that nurturance does not contribute much to the learning of self-criticism, although their manipulation of 'nurturance' may be questioned. Aronfreed, stressing the importance of aversive factors and the anxiety-reducing function of self-criticism, writes, 'The child will imitate the punitive behaviour of a model only to the extent that contingencies of aversive learning permit the behaviour to acquire some intrinsic representational value, and . . . nurturance can influence this kind of imitation only to the extent that it affects the aversive learning process'[15] (p. 290). He suggests that nurturance may have the effect of making the punishment salient, or of increasing the anticipatory anxiety experienced. In other words, the more loving the parents, the more important the fear of loss of their approval.

(2) *Reparation*. In reparation, the child takes some steps to deal with the adverse effects of his actions upon others. In other words, there is what Aronfreed calls 'a corrective orientation'. Aronfreed[12] reports that, whereas learning of self-criticism depended significantly upon cognitive structure and was not affected by the child's freedom to 'adjust' his own punishment in terms of the number of sweets he should lose, reparation (suggesting how the damaged doll might be repaired, behaviour which was rewarded by the experimenter's approval) depended upon the extent to which the child had control over the evaluation of his own behaviour and its punishment. Thus, the learning of reparative responses would appear to depend more upon assumption of responsibility for the consequences of one's own transgressions, and upon direct external reward for taking active steps to deal with one's transgression (for example, the child's depriving himself of sweets). Although the variations in cognitive structure which Aronfreed used in his experiment did not affect the tendency to reparation, it is obvious, as he remarks, that these children must have had *some* kind of cognitive structure. Aronfreed also points out that reparative responses may be learned in other ways as well. For example, if a child responds to signs of distress from another person, the cessation of these signs consequent upon the reparative action will have positively rewarding effects (although this would not explain how the reparative action came to be performed originally).

(3) *Confession*. Aronfreed suggests that confession is frequently instrumental in avoiding or reducing punishment, and that in this way it comes to have anxiety-reducing value. Confession also frequently has the function of terminating anxiety by bringing punishment, and children may find the continuing anxiety so unpleasant that they confess when there is little or no chance of their being found out otherwise. As distinct from self-criticism and (to a lesser extent) reparation, confession requires the intervention of another person to whom one can confess. In this sense, it is a more 'externally oriented' response to transgression than self-criticism or reparation.

(4) *Externally oriented reactions*. A variety of reactions is included

here. (i) A child who has been naughty may take steps to see that his mother finds him out, thus *seeking* punishment for his offence. This kind of reaction is very similar to confession with the same function. (ii) Again, a child may take evasive action to try to escape from the probable punishment; for example, he may hide or tell lies. (iii) He may interpret accidental misfortunes as punishment (like Piaget's immanent justice responses). Such reactions, though externally oriented compared particularly with self-criticism, nevertheless may be regarded as internalized to the extent that they occur in the absence of any potential punishing agent at the actual performance of the transgression. Aronfreed thinks that externally oriented reactions are more likely to occur when the child's experience has been one where he has tended to rely on external direction for the control of his behaviour, and when his experience has not provided him with the necessary cues to distinguish between behaviour which is likely to be punished and behaviour which is not. We would therefore expect to find externally oriented reactions where parental discipline has been inconsistent, and when little use has been made of verbal explanation in disciplining.

When he talks of the 'internalization' of control over behaviour and of 'internalized' reactions to having done wrong, Aronfreed means, as we have seen, that a particular pattern of behaviour will be maintained even when there are not likely to be any immediate consequences of the behaviour for the actor, and when other people, as mediators of possible consequences, are not present when the action is carried out. When one takes account of *cognitive* factors, one may speak of an orientation on the part of the actor toward his behaviour and its consequences. Some people's attention may be directed wholly toward possible external consequences; others may appear to judge, control and respond to their own behaviour with minimal regard for external consequences. In between, we have a whole range of 'orientations'. Self-criticism, reparation, confession and 'externally oriented reactions' represent decreasingly internal (and increasingly external) orientations. Though people may use all four types of reaction, it is implied that each person will develop a characteristic orientation, which will enable him to be placed at some point on an 'internal-external' continuum. One advantage of such a continuum is that it enables us to get away from the idea of guilt as the necessary basis for all internal control, and allows us to accommodate other reactions to transgression which may be but are not necessarily associated with the experience of guilt as indicated by self-criticism. It also enables us to avoid the pitfalls of the guilt-shame contrast, since a highly internal orientation may include elements of both guilt and shame, and shame may include both internal and external aspects.

There is evidence[14] (p. 317) that children whose parents tend to use *induction* techniques more freely show more highly internalized reactions to wrongdoing than children whose parents tend to use mainly *sensitization* techniques. On induction and sensitization techniques, Aronfreed writes, 'The induction category subsumes methods that should tend to induce in the child reactions to his own transgressions which could readily become independent of their original external stimulus sources. A mother who indicates her disappointment by rejecting or ignoring her child, or by showing that she is hurt or disappointed, is stimulating unpleasant feelings that are not closely tied to her physical proximity or its imminence. The arousal and termination of these feelings are less well defined by externally explicit punitive events conveyed through her immediate presence than would be the case if she were to punish the child with a direct attack. Likewise, if she reasons with the child or explains why his behaviour is acceptable, she is using a verbal and cognitive medium of exchange that can provide the child with his own resources for evaluating and modifying his behaviour. Finally, if she asks the child why he behaved as he did, insists that he correct the consequences of his acts or refrains from punishment when he takes the initiative in correcting himself, she is encouraging him to examine his actions and accept responsibility for them.'[11] The term 'sensitization' refers to direct physical punishment or scolding, which 'should give greater weight to the mother's punitive presence and be unlikely to induce reactions to transgressions that could easily become separated from their original external stimulus elicitation. They should instead merely sensitize the child to the anticipation of external demands and expectations defining appropriate responses' (*ibid.*). It should be noted that the distinction between induction techniques and sensitization techniques is by no means the same thing as a distinction in terms of severity of punishment. One cannot argue that induction techniques are less severe simply because they are primarily non-physical. 'Sensitization discipline,' says Aronfreed, 'tends to subject the child to punishment that is immediate and focussed in time. It makes the avoidance or the occurrence of punishment, rather than any act of the child the event that marks the resolution of a transgression. Under these conditions, the priority of avoiding or producing punishment would sharply curtail the probability that the child would acquire any self-corrective reactions to transgression'[14] (p. 322).

The main points in Aronfreed's version of reinforcement theory therefore seem to be the following. (a) Emphasis on aversive training, anxiety and the reduction of anxiety as the main mechanism by which internalization is enabled to take place. (b) The distinction between sensitization techniques and induction techniques of discipline, the latter including especially verbal explanation and reasoning. (c) The emphasis on cognitive structure and cognitive processes, especially verbal processes as the means by which anxiety is mediated backward or forward over time, and by which children may acquire the ability to react to their actual and possible behaviour in terms of general principles. (d) The elaboration of different possible reactions to having done wrong, with the implication that these may arise from different kinds of experience, and the further implication that one must look at various *patterns of behaviour* in their own right, rather than thinking in terms of a hypothetical entity like 'conscience'. (e) The development of the idea of internal and external orientations and an internal-external continuum as a means of ordering these different types of behavioural reaction. Of these, the idea of an internal-external continuum and (especially) the insistence upon the importance of 'inner' cognitive processes, including intentions, are the two which mainly distinguish Aronfreed from the more extreme varieties of behaviouristic learning theory. In a sense, Aronfreed may be said to occupy a position between the more extreme behaviouristic theorists and the cognitive developmental theorists like Piaget

E

and Kohlberg. He insists on the importance of cognitive factors, but does not accept the notion of developmental moral stages as put forward by Piaget, Kohlberg and their followers.

Cognitive dissonance theory

An interesting hypothesis concerning the internalization of moral values, particularly by means of aversive treatment or punishment, has emerged from the variety of cognitive theory sponsored largely by Leon Festinger and his followers and known as 'cognitive dissonance theory'.[83] We consider this approach here because, although it is not strictly a form of learning theory, it is similar in its regard for the experimental paradigm as the main source of empirical information relevant to the theoretical formulation, and because 'dissonance' seems to be regarded as a kind of drive which can be reduced and rendered more tolerable by appropriate response. According to Festinger, two cognitions or 'cognitive elements' concerning one's own behaviour, feelings, beliefs or attitudes are 'dissonant' with one another if they are not, or do not appear to be, mutually consistent. They need not be—indeed will seldom be—logically contradictory, but simply what would generally be accepted as being and would appear to the person concerned as being, more or less incompatible. For example, if I am aware that smoking causes cancer and am also aware that I am a heavy smoker, these two cognitions are said to be dissonant in the sense that awareness of the chances of getting cancer ought to be associated with *not* smoking. Now, the theory assumes that dissonance is unpleasant and that the person will be motivated to *reduce* the state of dissonance. This, of course, can be done in more ways than one. I might stop smoking. But if I am thoroughly committed to smoking, then I shall probably not give it up. In this case my cognition concerning the probability of getting cancer should tend to change. I may persuade myself that the evidence is not really all that convincing, and moreover, may tend to avoid reading any arguments which could be interpreted as supporting the danger of smoking, while I avidly fasten onto any arguments which could be interpreted as a defence of smoking. The theory has been applied mainly in studying the conditions under which attitudes may change. Many studies have used the 'forced compliance' technique, in which people are induced to *behave* in a way inconsistent with their known attitudes. If dissonance is aroused by this inconsistency, then the attitude should change in the direction of becoming more consistent with the behaviour. Now dissonance theory predicts that the *smaller* the inducement to engage in the behaviour, the *greater* the dissonance, and the greater the subsequent change of attitude. The *larger* the inducement, the *less* should be the dissonance and the *less* the change of attitude. In other words, with more reward, there is less need to *justify* one's behaviour in terms of one's own attitude, and therefore less need to change one's attitude. Festinger and Carlsmith[85] indeed, found that this was so, and numerous ingenious experiments have provided some support for the theory although some investigators have reported contrary findings. Essentially, it is a kind of 'equilibrium theory' or 'balance theory', which posits a constant strain toward consistency in the individual (though this may not operate under all conditions). It also has some similarity to the notion of 'rationalization', although it is of more general application. The theory and related experimental work in general have been subject to a good deal of criticism (see, for example, ref. 60) but it is not our present business to give a detailed critique of dissonance theory. An outline of the kernel of the theory has been provided simply so that we may better understand its application to our own sphere of interest.

The general hypotheses advanced by dissonance theorists concerning the internalization of values are that the less the temptation to 'wrongdoing' to which one gives way, the greater should be the tendency for the attitude toward the offence to become more lenient and conversely, the less the threatened punishment which is successful in inducing *resistance* to temptation, the more the attitude should change in the direction of 'outlawing' the behaviour. Mills[202] with student subjects, found that those who cheated in conditions of relatively *low* temptation or prospective reward became more lenient in their attitude toward cheating, while those who refrained from cheating in conditions of high temptation tended to take a more severe attitude. The other two conditions showed little change at all. This is precisely what dissonance theory predicted, although the results could also have been predicted as the probable outcomes of differently 'loaded' approach-avoidance conflicts—the more nearly equal the two opposing inducements (to transgress and not to transgress), the greater the uncertainty or anxiety produced by one decision or the other, and the greater the need to reduce this anxiety by convincing oneself that one had done the right thing. Aronson and Carlsmith, in a study reported in 1963[18] argued that compliance in the face of severe threats can more readily be justified without any change of values, whereas compliance in the face of mild threats is harder to justify according to pre-existing attitudes and should therefore lead to greater change in values. They had children of about four years of age play with toys and say which toys they liked best, putting them in order of preference. The children were then divided into three groups. (1) In the first group, there was no threat at all. The experimenter simply left, after telling the children that they could play with the toys, but removing their second preference. (2) In the second group, the children were left to play with the toys but were threatened with relatively severe consequences if they played with their second-preference toy. (3) In the third group, the children were left with the toys, but threatened with relatively mild consequences if they played with their second-preference toy. The children seem to have been exceptionally obedient as *none* of them transgressed by playing with the forbidden toy. Afterwards, preferences for the different toys were again collected. It was found, as predicted, that severe threat *increased* the preference for the forbidden toy, while mild threat *decreased* it. (These were average tendencies, with exceptions.) Decreased preference for the forbidden toy might be regarded as indicating greater internalization of the prohibition, as no *direct* supervision of the children was provided. If this is accepted, then the experiment might suggest (rather tentatively!) the general proposition that threats of punishment *just* sufficient to be effective are likely to produce the greatest degree of internalization. Festinger and Freedman,[86] however, argued that the results of the Aronson and Carlsmith experiment i.e. devaluing of the toy which was prohibited more under mild than under severe threat, though not incompatible with the hypothesis of greater internalization of the prohibition, is nevertheless not very convincing evidence that *internalization* has really taken place, since all we know is that under mild threat, children tended to say that they valued the object less. Freedman[89] thought it possible that the very mildness of the threat used by Aronson and Carlsmith may have made the children in this group feel that the experimenter could not attach much value to the toy, and thus have suggested to them that they were overvaluing it and should place it less highly on their lists. It is, of course, difficult to know in advance how 'severe' a 'severe' threat is, and how 'mild' a 'mild' threat is. If a punishment is *too* mild, presumably it will not be effective at all.

Freedman used a situation with toys including an attractive robot. As a severe threat he told the children, 'If you play with the robot, I will be very angry and will do something about it,' and as a mild threat, 'Do not play with the robot, it's wrong.' Instead of using valuation of the robot as a criterion, Freedman got another experimenter to allow the children to play with the toys 40 days later under a different pretext, and observed them. Twice as many of the children who had been in the severe threat group played with the attractive robot compared with those in the mild threat group. In Freedman's view, this is much better evidence for the dissonance hypothesis in relation to internalization. As a control, Freedman used a situation in which the experimenter did not leave the room after making his threat. Here, there was no difference between mildly and severely threatened groups, according to Freedman because no dissonance was created, since the experimenter was there to prevent playing with the forbidden toy. Unlike Aronson and Carlsmith, Freedman did not find the toy at all devalued, perhaps because it was *too* attractive.

According to Festinger and Freedman, the greatest amount of internalization of any desired moral value should occur 'if the person resists temptation under conditions of high motivation to succumb and low threat for yielding' (p. 234). But if the threat is not successful in deterring the person and he does give way to the temptation, a change in the relevant value should tend to occur 'in a direction opposite to that which, presumably, the culture is attempting to inculcate' (*ibid.*). Festinger and Freedman then go on to develop two interesting arguments. (1) As they remark, many modern parents frequently reason with their children, and provide them with external justifications, for example, for not cheating. The authors suggest that this may be self-defeating from the strict point of view of internalization of moral values, and that the more reasons a child has for not cheating, the less likely he may be to develop an internalized moral value against cheating. (2) They argue that in recurrent real life situations, children will sometimes give way to temptation on impulse and sometimes not. For example, a boy may sometimes suppress his aggression against his brother, and sometimes give way and express it. In so far as he inhibits it, he should tend to reduce dissonance by regarding it as 'bad'. In so far as he gives way, he should tend to reduce dissonance by justifying it. The total result, over all instances, should then be some kind of balance. Festinger and Freedman go on to argue further that very severe punishment may be likely to inhibit *behaviour* but not to lead to dissonance, and hence not to lead to internalization. At the other extreme, however, complete absence of punishment, which is associated with lack of inhibition, should also mean an absence of dissonance and hence also not promote internalization. There should, they argue, be an optimum level of punishment. If it is to produce the maximum degree of internalization, it should be just severe enough to stop aggression in most cases. If it is mild enough just to fail to inhibit the aggression (or other undesirable behaviour) in most cases, this should have the very opposite effect, producing the most positive attitude to aggression. Festinger[84] remarks that 'rats and men come to love the things for which they suffer'. Festinger and Freedman suggest that if the prospective punishment is effective in inhibiting aggression in about one half of the instances, then the likeliest outcome might be the development of discrimination between situations in which aggression is good and situations in which it is bad, with no overall effect on internalization of an anti-aggression value. However, whether such discrimination develops or not would seem to depend very largely on whether any properties of situations in which aggression is good could actually be distinguished, setting them apart from situations in which it is bad. Festinger and Freedman summarize their theory in the diagram below. (Taken from P. Worchel and D. Byrne (eds.), *Personality Change*, New York: Wiley, 1964.)

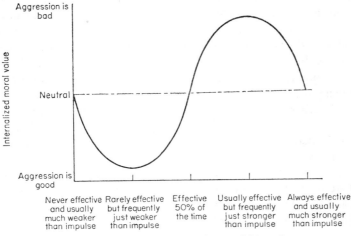

Strength and effectiveness of deterrent

This again is an attractively simple theory. It has, however, distinct limitations (1) The theory is (so far) wholly concerned with the internalization of prohibitions in the sense that if the prohibition has been internalized, the behaviour is not likely to occur even when direct supervision and the immediate prospect of punishment have been removed. One could, of course argue from dissonance theory that the less inducement is necessary to get a child to perform wanted behaviour (e.g. altruistic actions), the more likely the child is to internalize this *positive* value. But so far no directly relevant evidence seems to have been produced. (2) It seems to be implied that for any impulse, there is a level of threat which will be just sufficient to prevent the behaviour from taking place, but this is left to be a matter of judgment in any particular situation. It is not indicated how this judgment can be arrived at. (3) No account is taken of 'dissonance' which can arise from moral values which may be mutually incompatible, e.g. duty to one's parents and obligations to one's peers, or duty to refrain from stealing and obligation to feed one's family. (4) No allowance is made for 'seeing the point' of prohibitions or prescriptions. It is argued that 'reasons' given for suppressing undesirable behaviour such as aggression are likely to reduce the likelihood of the prohibition being internalized. Surely this depends on what *kind* of reasons are given. If these are selfish, 'utilitarian' reasons, e.g. that you shouldn't cheat because you are likely to get found out, or that it doesn't do you any good in the long run to cheat, then one might perhaps agree. One can argue that by giving a child such reasons one is doing nothing to induce the acceptance of a *moral* value against cheating, though one may be encouraging a habit of non-cheating. But if a child can be got to accept a moral reason, e.g. that cheating is unfair, or (at a more elevated level) that it involves betraying an implicit trust, then this *is* the acceptance of a moral value that cheating is bad. The difficulty partly arises from the assumption that moral values can *only* arise by being 'taken over' from outside as distinct from being 'accepted' as reasonable. Dissonance theory is, of course, no worse off in this respect than reinforcement theory.

It is difficult to formulate precise and specific deductions from psychoanalytic theory in such a way that the theory, or a part of it, might be said to be directly under test, although Calvin Hall did claim to have found 'a modest confirmation of Freud's theory of a distinction between the superego of men and women.'[125]* The role of psychoanalytic theory so far has rather been to suggest possible relationships between variables which may in some sense, however crudely, be 'measured'. In this way, psychoanalytic theory has stimulated much empirical work. Often, other points of view, especially those of various varieties of learning theory, have contributed to the investigators' formulations of their hypotheses, as was the case with Whiting and Child.[275] Other investigators have formulated their propositions entirely in terms of learning theory, although psychoanalytic theory has been an indirect influence in the background. Since psychoanalytic theory was so concerned with the early relations between parents and their children, it is natural that it should have had its greatest influence here.

In a relatively early study, Mackinnon[190] tried to examine the relationship between avoidance of wrongdoing, guilt and childhood experience. To obtain measures of wrongdoing, Mackinnon got his (student) subjects to take a paper and pencil test. Answers to the problems were provided, and the subjects were allowed to look at the answers to some of the problems, but told not to look at the answers to others. The subjects were watched through a one-way vision screen, and of 93 subjects, 43 were

* See p. 245

observed to violate the prohibition and 50 to do as they had been told. Thus, about one half of the subjects were labelled as transgressors and about one half as non-transgressors. A few weeks later, the subjects were asked if they had looked at any of the forbidden answers. About one half of the transgressors denied that they had cheated. Mackinnon then asked those who admitted cheating whether they had felt guilty or not, and asked those who had not cheated or who had not confessed, whether they would have felt guilty if they had cheated. Many more non-transgressors than transgressors said they would have felt guilty, and also that they often felt guilty in everyday life. The most obvious interpretation is, of course, that those with the strongest tendency to guilt avoid transgressing and thus avoid the discomforts of the expected feelings of guilt, as Brown[54] suggests, although Mackinnon's results are not incompatible with Freud's suggestion that every act of abstention increases the power of the superego. One should, however, put in a warning comment here to the effect that conceivably, those who *had* transgressed *knew* that they had not in fact felt very guilty, and the results may have been biassed in this way.

Mackinnon later got 28 of his subjects (all those he could lay his hands on) to check, on a list, those punishments which they had most frequently experienced as children. Although the numbers were by now small, 78 per cent of the transgressors checked physical punishments, against 48 per cent of the non-transgressors. This finding thus suggests an association between physical punishment and low resistance to temptation. However, one should again be cautious. In the first place, it is dangerous to draw general conclusions from such a small sample and with an index of transgression derived from a single relatively unimportant situation. In the second place, one cannot conclude that because some subjects *said* that they had received more physical punishments as children, this is necessarily true.

It is a long way from Mackinnon's 28 faithful subjects to Whiting and Child's[275] ambitious cross-cultural comparison of 40 different societies, and this may well be a tribute to the stimulating quality of psychoanalytic theory. Whiting and Child, influenced by both psychoanalytic theory and learning theory, argued that the widely practised and approved methods of child-rearing in any society should be associated with a tendency toward a particular kind of personality which, in turn, should express itself through particular kinds of cultural activity. Leaning upon Freudian theory, Whiting and Child argued that what they called the 'systems' of behaviour connected with oral training, anal training, sex, dependence and aggression should be related to adult institutions or beliefs in the society reflecting guilt associated with the corresponding system. In their terms, the 'oral system' includes all beliefs and practices associated with weaning, eating, drinking, sucking, vomiting and the like. The 'anal system' included everything relating to defecation, urination, cleanliness and orderliness. The sexual system includes normal and abnormal sexual behaviour, sexual exhibitionism and any beliefs or practices relating directly or indirectly to sex. The dependence system is concerned with the need for 'nurturance', including the desire for help, affection, support and attention. The aggression system includes fighting, swearing and other physical and verbal expressions of enmity and anger. Whiting and Child argued that indulgence during childhood of any or all of these systems would produce what they called a 'positive fixation', when a person would expect satisfactions to be associated with the system in question. A high level of frustration or harshness during childhood would tend to produce a 'negative' fixation, when a person would have a lot of anxiety or guilt connected with the system and expectations of harm or unpleasant experiences arising from it. These positive and negative fixations should then be associated with characteristic cultural beliefs and practices associated with the systems, reflecting positive expectations or guilt and anxiety. As the kind of cultural beliefs which could conveniently be used, Whiting and Child selected beliefs in the cause and treatment of illness. In respect of the positive fixations, we should expect to find people believing in treatment via the system in question. In the case of a positive oral fixation, for example, people should believe in treatment of illness by swallowing things. Treatment associated with dependence would involve such things as prayer (dependence on supernatural beings). In respect of negative fixations, we should find people believing that illness is *caused* by something connected with the system in question, this being taken as an indication of anxiety and guilt connected with the system. For example, in the case of a negative oral fixation, we should find people believing that illness is caused by something that has been swallowed. Whiting and Child, using the crudest of rating scales, recorded the presence or absence of beliefs concerning the cause and treatment of illness according to the criteria we have just indicated, for 40 different societies, on the basis of anthropologists' published reports. To assess the amount of early indulgence or frustration, Whiting and Child got judges to rate the published accounts of the 40 societies in respect of leniency or severity in each system. Care was taken to keep the two ratings independent, so as to avoid spurious relationships due to the influencing of ratings by the expectation of relationships. The two sets of results were then compared. As far as positive fixation was concerned, the results supported the hypothesis in four of the five systems (oral, anal, sex and aggression). However, the differences do not really carry much weight, since all were small and statistically insignificant. In respect of the negative fixations, the results were more convincing. For all five systems, the findings were in the predicted direction, and for three (oral, dependence and aggression) they were statistically significant. If we can make the assumption, reasonable on the basis of psychoanalytic theory, that belief in the causation of illness by factors associated with any system, e.g. sex, is likely to indicate the presence of guilt, then there is here some evidence to suggest that severe oral and anal training, and severe suppression of aggression, in particular, may tend to lead to guilt in respect of these systems. The fact that severe sex training seems to have less effect on beliefs about sexual activities and illness does not, of course, indicate that a severe upbringing in respect of sex may not produce a high level of guilt in relation to sex. It may simply be that in *this* case, belief in the cause of illness is not a good index of guilt. It is also possible that the causal relationship is the other way round, e.g. that if people believe that illness is caused orally, anxieties connected with oral activities may lead them to be more severe in their oral training. The significance of this study for moral development lies in its attempt to provide some evidence for the Freudian-derived hypothesis that severe training in inhibiting 'basic' needs or drives tends to produce guilt associated with these needs.

Whiting and Child go on to make a more direct attack on possible child-rearing factors associated with guilt. As a 'cultural index' of the prevalence of guilt, they use a measure of 'patient responsibility for illness', or 'the extent to which a person who gets sick blames himself for having gotten sick' (p. 227). They argue that 'guilt feelings . . . are just one form that anxiety about punishment may take, so that there would be no very important distinction between fear of external punishment and fear of guilt. The fear of guilt is merely one of a variety of specific types of behaviour that may be elicited by a broadly general fear of external punishment.' (*ibid*.). This time, the formulation is clearly in terms of learning theory. Whiting and Child use an index of general 'socialization anxiety' based on the average severity score for the five systems, and predict that 'patient responsibility' should be related to 'socialization anxiety'. Thirty five societies were rated on both variables, and the predicted relationship was in fact found. In fact, patient responsibility was related to severity of discipline in all five systems, especially the oral and aggression systems. All relationships were, however, rather small, and not as convincing as one would have liked.

In yet another part of their study, Whiting and Child had societies rated for the extent to which they appeared to use 'love-oriented techniques of discipline' (denial of love, threats of denial of reward and threats of ostracism) rather than 'physical techniques' (physical punishment, threats of physical punishment and ridicule), and compared these ratings with their ratings for patient responsibility. They argued that the threat of loss of love might work in two ways. (1) It might encourage the substitution of 'self-love or self-admiration' for the love of the parents, the child rewarding *himself* in the same way as his parents have rewarded him. (2) Imitation of parents' evaluative judgments might function to facilitate the obtaining of either parents' love or the substitute self-praise. Self-criticism would tend to prevent the repetition of behaviour which deprives the child of parental or self-approval. Physical punishment should stimulate some tendency to avoidance of the parents, which should interfere with the pursuit of parental affection and substitute self-approval. 'This analysis,' they write, 'suggests that the crucial thing about the techniques of punishment is whether they are likely to have the dual effect of keeping the child oriented toward the goal of parental affection and at the same time arousing uncertainty about the attainment of this goal' (p. 242). Once again, the predicted positive relationship between the two variables was found, but again it was quite small.

Rather higher relationships were found when estimates of 'age of onset' of training in the systems were related to ratings for patient responsibility. For weaning, modesty training, training in heterosexual inhibition and independence training, the *earlier* the beginning of training, the higher the patient responsibility rating. In the case of toilet training, the relationship was not established. Whiting and Child interpret their findings here to indicate that love-oriented techniques are more likely to be effective in developing guilt and a strong superego when training starts early, because the young child is more dependent on his parents' love. However, they did not find that degree of 'initial nurturance' was related to any signs of guilt.

The Whiting and Child studies can be criticized on various grounds. The measures used are not really adequate; the data was second-hand data derived from the reports of anthropologists (indeed, in the circumstances it could not have been otherwise); small correlations are apt to be misleading, as they can sometimes arise from incidental factors; and cultural beliefs and practices are not really a satisfactory index of individual variables like guilt and anxiety. The remarkable thing about their ambitious cross-cultural venture, however, when one thinks about the range of the data, how rough the measurements were and how many other criticisms may be made, is that it should have produced any results at all, let alone a set of findings which, on the whole, hang together reasonably well. It is also interesting that one part of their findings, in effect, confirmed the findings of Mackinnon, arrived at in such a different way.

Two of Whiting's followers, Hollenberg, studying individual differences *within* a Pueblo Indian group, and Faigin, in a rural white community in America (both reported by Child[62]), confirmed the relationship between guilt feelings and a relatively free use of love-oriented techniques of discipline. The child-rearing practices were assessed on the basis of interviews with the mothers, and guilt was measured by two projective tests. Similarly, Allinsmith and Greening[5] found that guilt associated with wishing someone was dead was higher among student subjects who were rated as having had mainly 'psychological' (love-oriented) discipline than among those who were rated as having had mainly 'corporal' discipline. Guilt was assessed on the basis of a story-completion technique, and the rating of the type of discipline favoured by the parents were made by the students themselves. In this case, it is not impossible that the subjects more inclined to give 'guilt' endings to the story were also more inclined to see or to remember their parents as having used more 'psychological' techniques, whether the parents actually did so or not.

Allinsmith[4] followed much the same approach, but with school-boys as subjects. He used three stories, one dealing with 'death wishes', one with theft and one with disobedience. From story completions, guilt was assessed by three criteria with the intention of including both conscious and unconscious guilt. The first was direct expression of self-blame or feelings of guilt. The second included indirect manifestations of guilt such as attempts at reparation. The third (and most dubious) included 'defensive distortions', in which, for example, the subject was judged to have hidden his guilt from himself by putting the blame on others, or by being punished by others without any direct expression of self-blame. Resistance to temptation was also assessed projectively by story completion. Three main child-rearing variables were used —age of weaning, severity of toilet training and use of psychological or physical discipline. Allinsmith reports that early weaning, severe toilet training and psychological discipline were all related to guilt scores based on the three criteria indicated, for the 'death wish' story. For the theft story, early weaning was associated with *low* guilt, and toilet training and type of discipline were not related to guilt at all. For the disobedience story, none of the relationships were significant. Thus the results are rather confusing. Allinsmith guesses that perhaps 'internalizations in different moral areas do not necessarily have the same developmental origins', and goes on, 'judging from our data, the person with a truly generalized conscience, either "punitive" or "psychopathic", is a statistical rarity' (p. 164). Allinsmith also concluded that resistance to temptation (by his projective measure) was related to *direct* acknowledgement of guilt, but not to the *total amount* of guilt by his measure. This seems quite in line with common sense (even if we accept that guilt may be unconscious). If a person is not *aware* of impending guilt, common sense suggests, we can scarcely expect guilt to motivate him to refrain from undesirable conduct or inhibit his impulses.

Allinsmith's study raises a number of important questions. The first is how far one is justified in using projective techniques like story-completion as a measure of psychological dispositions like 'guilt tendencies', without adequate, indeed without any, validation showing that they really do measure such tendencies. This is a criticism which applies whether guilt is regarded as a highly generalized disposition, or whether we regard 'total guilt' as consisting of the sum of a number of separate 'guilts' in different areas. It is assumed that a boy completing the story will identify with the hero, and that if he makes the hero express self-criticism, this indicates that he himself, in such a situation, would experience guilt. Perhaps he would, but we have no evidence to support this assumption. Even more striking, it is assumed that if the hero refers to punishment by others rather than expressing any self-criticism, or if an untoward accident befalls the hero, this can be interpreted as evidence of repressed or unconscious guilt. These assumptions, clearly deriving from Freudian theory, are in fact questionable and await proper empirical support. It also appears questionable to assume that guilt is necessarily indicated by any tendency to put right the wrong done. Allinsmith's ambiguous results might be due simply to the inadequacy and inappropriateness of the measures used. The fact that such measures have been used by others as well as by Allinsmith is a good indication of the difficulty of controlled investigations of this kind.

Sears, Maccoby and Levin, in their well-known book,[248] refer to three ways in which complex patterns of social and emotional behaviour may be acquired—trial and error, direct tuition and role practice. Role practice, by their definition, seems to corres-

pond in some measure to identification. It is, they say, 'the discovery and learning of new actions by observing what others do,
and then practising it by pretending to *be* the other person' (p.
369). This practice may be overt, in the form of observable
behaviour, but, more importantly, may be covert. Sears, Maccoby
and Levin suggest that children are more likely to practise the
parental roles if dependency is strong. Dependency, in the sense
in which it is used here, refers to the need to have the attention,
affection and approval of a caretaker (normally in the first
instance the mother), which have come to be rewarding because of
their association with the satisfying of physical requirements like
the need for food. That is, dependency in the sense of attachment is for these authors a secondary need derived from association with the satisfaction of primary needs. Shaffer and Emerson[250] and others, however, have indicated that dependency
may arise on the basis of perceptual familiarity and interaction
rather than by association with the satisfaction of primary
needs. It may very well be that both are relevant. In any case,
dependency has probably developed by the age of about six or
eight months. On the assumption that 'conscience' represents the
internalization or acceptance of parental requirements, we should
find that measures of 'dependency' are positively associated with
measures of 'conscience'. Sears, Maccoby and Levin[248] derived
such measures of conscience by interviewing the mothers of 379
five-year-old children, and asking them about the extent to which
the children confessed to wrongdoing and otherwise showed signs
of guilt after transgression. Ratings of the child-rearing methods
of the parents were obtained, also from interviews. These included
ratings for dependency of the children, parental warmth and
acceptance, and use of love-oriented techniques of discipline.
When the ratings for child-rearing variables were correlated with
the ratings for conscience, there did appear to be a *slight* tendency
for dependency to be positively associated with conscience, and
a clearer tendency for maternal warmth and acceptance, and
the use of love-oriented techniques of discipline, to be positively
associated. *Boys* (but not girls) who were rejected by their fathers
scored less highly on conscience ratings. It seems very reasonable
to suppose that love-oriented techniques, depending as they do on

the withholding of affection, can only be effective if some affection is given in the first place. Sears, Maccoby and Levin suggest—in line with common sense—that there must be a *balance* of discipline, with adequate but not too much control, as too much control might be expected to cause either an unnecessarily high level of guilt and anxiety, or resentment on the part of the children. The problem is, of course, to know what is a satisfactory balance, on more than just intuitive grounds, and how to achieve it. The problem is made no easier by the fact that children are individuals, and all children do not respond in the same way to the same kind of treatment. Sears, Maccoby and Levin also found that punishment for aggression did not seem to be very effective in reducing aggressive behaviour in general. Although such punishment might reduce aggressive behaviour within the home, it tended to be associated with a high rather than a low level of aggression outside.

A methodological objection to the work of Sears, Maccoby and Levin is that all their measures were derived from interviews with the mothers. It is quite likely that both reports of the children's behaviour and the reports of the reports of the parents' handling of their children may have been distorted unintentionally by the mothers reporting them. Indeed, it would be odd if they had not been so to at least some extent. Thus some caution is in order in relation to this study.

In a follow-up study of 160 of these children at the age of 12 years, Sears[247] used a number of self-report scales. He distinguished between aggression anxiety, pro-social aggression (energy and aggression in defence of socially accepted values) and anti-social aggression (disruptive). These were related to ratings from the interviews conducted when the children were aged five. Anti-social aggression was found to be related to high permissiveness for aggression, and to low punishment. This is of some interest when compared with the findings reported above, that (anti-social) aggression was associated with high punishment at age five. Pro-social aggression and aggression anxiety were also related to *high* rather than to *low* punishment. Sears interprets his findings in terms of the frustration-aggression hypothesis to mean that 'the successful inhibition of early forms of aggression in severely punished children would produce heightened amounts of aggression anxiety, pro-social and self-aggression at a later age' (p. 492). In view of various other reports of the association of early punishment with later anti-social aggression, however, it is difficult to know quite what to make of such a conclusion. Perhaps what adults label 'aggressive behaviour' may not be quite the same thing at different ages.

In a more recent study, Sears, Rau and Alpert[249] used a rather wider variety of methods to study the effects of 'identification'. They wanted to see first, how far different 'presumed products of identification' in young children were correlated, as identification theory seemed to suggest that they should be, and secondly, to see what child-rearing practices and parental attitudes seemed to be associated with the development of these 'identification-produced behaviours'. They used 40 nursery school children, 21 boys and 19 girls, as subjects. It was hypothesized that five kinds of behaviour—pro-social aggression, taking an adult role, sex-role behaviour, resistance to temptation and 'guilt'—would all be related, and that nurturance and warmth, love-oriented discipline, high expectations of mature behaviour from the child and the holding up of models for the child would be related to the measures of 'identification'. Seven measures of child behaviour and three measures of parental behaviour were collected. The child measures included the following. (1) Observations of behaviour in nursery school, defined to represent dependency, aggression and acting of adult role. (2) Standardized situations involving 'resistance to temptation' in 'guilt-provoking' situations, including an ingenious arrangement in which the child was told to watch a hamster in a cage, the hamster dropping through the bottom of the cage and 'getting lost' as soon as the child looked away. (3) Observer ratings. The four observers spent a great deal of time during the summer observing the children and rating them on a number of variables including aggression, attention-getting and amount of social interaction. (4) Permissive doll-play (free play with dolls and toys provided), which was scored in terms of the frequency of behaviour defined as indicating aggression, conscience, sex-typing and adult role-playing. (5) Story-completion doll-play. Here, the doll's house was used to present six incomplete stories in which a child doll of the same sex as the subject was made to do something naughty, and the subject was asked to tell 'what happens next'. These story endings were scored for indications of guilt, including confession. (6) Standardized mother-child interaction situations. In one situation, the child was given toys while his mother was given a job to keep her occupied, so as to stimulate attention-seeking on the part of the child, and afford an opportunity to observe the mother's response to it. In another situation, the child was allowed to get dirty playing and this provided the occasion for observing the mother's attitude to cleanliness and how far she interfered with the child. (7) Finally, interviews with the mothers elicited parental reports of the child's behaviour at home.

The parents measures were based on (a) interviews with both mother and father, (b) observations of the mother during the standardized mother-child situations and (c) questionnaires to assess the mother's attitudes. These covered a wide variety of child-rearing practices.

The results of this elaborate investigation are far from clear-cut. Eight different measures of dependency were obtained, including negative attention-seeking (getting attention by disruptive behaviour), reassurance-seeking and positive attention-seeking (seeking praise etc.). For boys, *none* of these measures were significantly related; for girls, there tended to be rather low positive correlations. If different measures of dependency are scarcely related to one another, then dependency as defined and measured in these ways cannot be treated as a single variable, and the hypothesis of a relationship between dependency and identification cannot be maintained in that form. Moreover, measures of the five variables hypothesized to be related were not highly correlated even *within* variables (i.e. different measures of the 'same' variable showed only slight agreement). For girls, pro-social aggression, sex-role behaviour and taking an adult role were modestly correlated but not related to either resistance to temptation or guilt. Resistance to temptation and guilt measures were found to be unrelated, as in other studies. Nurturance and high expectations were found highly related to dependency. Love-oriented discipline was if anything negatively related to dependency in girls and not related at all in boys.

Sears, Rau and Alpert consider that their results provide *some* evidence for a 'constellation of behaviour' in girls which *might* result from identification with the mother, and some evidence that parental expectations are relevant here. For boys, the findings do not seem to show even this level of consistency. One of the difficulties in this study concerns the nature of the measures used. In addition to criticisms which we have already indicated in relation to previous studies, there are further difficulties such as that the behaviours used to assess adult-role-taking in the nursery school setting were things like tidying up and helping younger children, which are *also* typically maternal behaviours, and a high score for adult role-taking by boys might tend to reflect a feminine rather than a masculine attitude. One is forced to the conclusion that the original hypotheses receive very little support, whether because the *measures* are unsatisfactory, because the reality is more complex than had been thought, or because the ideas are misguided. The most unsatisfactory thing about this kind of study is that one does not know *what* is wrong.

So far, on balance the evidence does suggest that the use of 'love-oriented' rather than 'physical' kinds of discipline is likely to increase the level of internalized moral control. However, since the use of such techniques may be associated with other factors which may possibly be relevant, such as wider use of explanation and reasoning by parents, and a higher level of intelligence and culture generally in the family, we cannot yet have too much confidence that it is the 'love-orientation' which matters.

As far as anti-social aggression is concerned, two studies support the earlier finding of Sears, Maccoby and Levin that a history of punishment tends to be associated with a high level of aggression. Sheldon and Eleanor Glueck[118] found a history of physical punishment to be relatively frequent in a sample of delinquents, while a history of parental use of 'reasoning' techniques appeared relatively more frequently in a sample of non-delinquents; and Bandura and Walters[26] found that delinquent boys had been more rejected by their parents and had received more punishment, especially from their fathers, while the parents of control boys made more use of reasoning. It is, however, conceivable that the delinquents had been more rejected and received more punishment *because* they were so badly behaved. This may seem on the whole unlikely, as the study by Bandura and Walters suggests, but we cannot be sure without more careful longitudinal studies or life-histories. It is extremely interesting that both Glueck and Glueck and Bandura and Walters stress the more frequent use made by control parents of *reasoning* with their children. Bandura and Walters, indeed, say, 'Of all the methods of correction that were investigated, only reasoning was associated with parental warmth and nurturance, and reasoning alone was associated with measures of the boys' guilt. In contrast, all other disciplinary measures—physical punishment, deprivation of privileges, ridicule, nagging and scolding, and withdrawal of love—were associated with parental rejection and punitiveness. ... While the parents of the control boys made greater use of reasoning as a method of control, the parents of the aggressive boys ... made more frequent use of all other disciplinary methods with the exception of withdrawal of love. The relationship of these latter methods with other aspects of the parents' behaviour and also with measures of the boys' behaviour, suggested that they were associated with the development of hostility and aggression.

'While it was assumed at the outset of this study that the use of threats of withdrawal of love would foster the development of control by guilt, it now seems likely that such threats, at least when used in disciplining an adolescent not only indicate parental rejection but may actually foster aggression'[26] (pp. 245–246). These comments by Bandura and Walters find some support from Sears, Rau and Alpert's finding that parental use of love-oriented techniques in early childhood was, if anything, negatively related to identification with parents. The importance of distinguishing between 'reasoning' and 'love-oriented' discipline has also been taken up and developed by other writers, especially Hoffman and Saltzstein.[142]

While Bandura and Walters found rejection and punishment by parents to characterize their sample of aggressive adolescent delinquents, they also found that the parents of these youths did not expect so much of them, nor give them so much responsibility. Very similar findings have been reported by McCord, McCord and Howard.[186] A study involving the observation of 174 non-delinquent boys and their (mainly working class) families over a period of five years indicated that aggressive boys were more likely to have had parents who (a) were rejecting and punishing, (b) did not make much use of direct control over their behaviour and (c) offered examples of deviant or odd behaviour (including other forms of deviance besides aggression). The non-aggressive boys were more likely to have had parents who (a) treated them affectionately, (b) applied consistent direct controls and (c) provided an example of socially approved conduct. In a later article, McCord, McCord and Howard[183] attempt a theoretical interpretation. They argue that rejection, punitiveness and threats should increase the strength of aggression as a drive, and that supervision, parental agreement, consistent discipline, high expectations and religious training should produce a 'controlled environment'. Distinguishing between anti-social aggression and socialized aggression (Sears, Rau and Alpert's 'pro-social' aggression), they then posit three 'types' of men, aggressive-antisocial men, aggressive-socialized men and non-aggressive men, and argue that high aggressive drive *plus* a deviant model *or* moderate aggressive drive *plus* a deviant model *plus* high controls should be antecedents of the aggressive-antisocial type; moderate drive *plus* low controls should lead to the aggressive-socialized type, while low drive *plus* high controls should lead to the non-aggressive type. It appears from this that they attach very great importance to the presence of a deviant parental model in the development of anti-social aggression, a factor which in their study seemed to be associated with anti-social aggression as indicated by convictions for larceny, assault and sex crimes. Although they found that their anti-social men showed a relatively high incidence of family discord, neglect and parental attacks, they write that 'the greatest direct influence on anti-social aggression seems to come from the nature of the parental model,' (p. 241)—i.e. from deviant or aggressive fathers.

So far, we have been concerned with correlational studies, which have either been entirely naturalistic, or in which experimental manipulations have been for the purpose of obtaining measures of relevant hypothesized variables, rather than to vary some independent variable in a controlled way in order to assess its possible significance. There are, however, also some laboratory studies which have used manipulation of a relevant independent variable. Thus, Bandura and Huston[23] got adults to use greater and lesser degrees of 'nurturance' toward children of four or five years of age, over two extended sessions, and found that nurturance greatly increased the degree to which the children then imitated the adult in an arranged situation; while Mischel and Grusec[205] found that even the *punishing* behaviour of a highly rewarding model was remembered better when the model was highly rewarding. In Ross's experiment,[238] 'dependent' children were more likely to imitate expressive behaviour by the model which was irrelevant to an experimental 'task', while 'independent' children were more likely to imitate the model's task-relevant actions. These studies, of course, are subject to the general criticism of short-period laboratory studies. They show that under certain conditions, in the laboratory, 'nurturance' as defined operationally for the purpose of the experiment *can* increase the influence of a model on a child. They do not show that in real-life situations, nurturance *does* have a corresponding long-term degree of importance. In so far as naturalistic and experimental studies are mutually confirmatory, the evidence is thereby strengthened. That is about all we can really say. Mussen and Parker's experiment[218] with five year olds may be regarded as falling between purely experimental studies of the Bandura and Huston type and more naturalistic studies. They used the children's mothers as models in a maze test, and found that the mothers who were classified as 'warm and rewarding' mothers were more frequently imitated by their children. These three studies support the idea that nurturance may be relevant to 'observational learning'. Aronfreed[12] and Aronfreed, Cutick and Fagen[17] failed to find nurturance to facilitate imitation. However, Bandura and Walters[27] think this may be because the 'nurturant' behaviour of Aronfreed's models was insufficiently prolonged and insufficiently great to make an adequate impact. The failure of Burton, Maccoby and Allinsmith[58] to find parental nurturance related to self-control (not cheating in a bean-bag game) may be due partly to the nature of the cheating situation used, and factors specifically connected with it (such as motivation to win). Their findings did, however, suggest that children whose parents were extremely high in nurturance, as well as children whose parents were extremely low, were more likely to cheat. Similarly, Bronfenbrenner[52] suggests that either too much or too little 'discipline' is likely to be associated with lower responsibility as assessed by teachers' ratings. Aronfreed[15] not unreasonably concludes that the relationship of 'nurturance' to moral development depends largely on the tendency for antisocial behaviour, low resistance to temptation and the like to be associated with extremely low nurturance, i.e. with parental rejection or excessive punitiveness. He believes that 'a certain minimum intensity of social attachment to a nurturant figure is required to produce effective internalization of the child's control over conduct. Beyond the requirement of this minimum threshold, however, internalization cannot be regarded as a generalized continuous function of parental nurturance' (p. 306). In other words, at one extreme we may have the rejected child, and at the other extreme the spoiled child. There is again the clear implication of a need for a balance; however, if Aronfreed's view is correct, there should be a wide range of nurturance within which variations should be of limited importance compared with the kind of discipline which the parents use, its consistency, and later, perhaps, other influences from outside the family. Bandura and Walters further suggest that 'the role of nurturance in the acquisition of self-punitive responses is not independent of the type of discipline employed by the agent of punishment. When the punishment takes the form of withholding or withdrawing reinforcers, and their reinstatement is made contingent on the child's performing some form of self-punitive response, the nurturant quality of the disciplinary agent assumes greater significance. Reports of a lack of relationship between parental warmth and nurturance and the self-control of children . . . may be expected as long as a possible interaction between parental nurturance and preferred type of disciplinary procedure continues to be overlooked'[27] (pp. 198–199). A similar view is expressed by Aronfreed when he comments that 'the nurturance of parents conditions their effectiveness as socializing agents only to the extent that it determines the acquired affective value of many more specific aspects of their behaviour, which are crucial to the power of their control over the child's behaviour'[15] (p. 308). For example, any action indicating withdrawal of affection might be expected to depend upon the general level of affection and the consequent expectations of the child.

Instead of distinguishing between physical and psychological or love-oriented techniques of discipline, Aronfreed,[14] as we have already seen, distinguishes between induction techniques and sensitization techniques. Induction techniques are techniques which may be expected to *induce* in a child an attitude to his transgressions which is likely to become independent of such external factors as punishment. Induction techniques include such measures as reasoning, asking the child for explanations and insisting upon corrective action. Sensitization techniques are techniques like physical or verbal punishment which may be expected to make a child sensitive to or alert to the probably external consequences of his behaviour for himself. Aronfreed includes three kinds of parental behaviour under the heading of 'induction techniques'—withdrawal of love, reasoning and insistence on correcting the consequences of actions. The last two of these are likely to depend largely on emphasizing the consequences of wrongdoing *for others,* or the need for maintaining general moral rules, and it would seem quite likely that when they are effective, they induce a rather different attitude from withdrawal of love. It would certainly seem reasonable to suppose that reasoning and emphasis on the consequences for others may help to promote a more 'moral' attitude than withdrawal of love, which might be expected, when effective, to produce an attitude compounded of anticipatory anxiety and guilt.

Aronfreed himself[11] used a story completion technique with sixth grade children, and classified their mothers, on the basis of interviews, into those predominantly using induction techniques and those predominantly using sensitization techniques. He found that children of 'induction-using' mothers more frequently gave story completions involving reparation, and children of 'sensitization-using' mothers more frequently gave responses involving unpleasant accidents to the transgressing hero of the story. Although 'self-critical' responses were also recorded, their incidence apparently was not related to type of maternal discipline.

It seems at least possible that the results reflect the specific effect of maternal discipline directed to reparation; and of course, the use of incomplete stories is open to the usual methodological objections to this technique.

Hoffman and Saltzstein, reported by Hoffman[141] used judgments about the violation of certain social norms, and found that boys with a more internal attitude had more permissive parents who used more love-oriented techniques, while girls with a more internal attitude often reported that their mothers threatened to have their fathers deal with them, and that their fathers more often used appeals to reason. Assessment of parental attitudes was based on the children's reports. In a later paper, Hoffman and Saltzstein[141] specifically distinguish between love-withdrawal and induction based on consideration for others. They propose three main types of discipline, 'power assertion' or authoritarian discipline based on fear associated with physical punishment and deprivation of material goods and privileges, 'love-withdrawal', and 'induction', in which a parent draws the child's attention to the harmful or unpleasant consequences of his wrongdoing for the parents or for others, thus stimulating the capacity for *empathy*. Among middle-class children, the use of induction in this sense by mothers was associated with a higher level of guilt and more internalized judgment in the children, and the use of power-assertion was associated with a relatively low level of moral functioning. Unfortunately, for 'lower-class' children, there was little relation between level of moral development and parental discipline. Hoffman and Saltzstein argue that power-assertion techniques tend to generate anger by frustrating the need of the growing child for autonomy, while too much love withdrawal or threat of love withdrawal may only produce a disrupting level of anxiety. Both power assertion and love withdrawal emphasize the consequences of wrongdoing *for the child himself,* while induction emphasizes the consequences *for others*. Induction *both* uses the capacity for empathy *and* induces awareness in the child that he is the *cause* of others' distress.

Various possibilities have been suggested as to *how* various kinds of 'psychological' discipline work. Whiting and Child[275] and Sears, Maccoby and Levin[248] suggest that love-oriented techniques keep emphasizing affection, and at the same time arouse uncertainty about attaining or retaining it. This seems to emphasize the importance of anticipatory anxiety. Allinsmith[4] thinks that a significant part is played by the fact that a parent who uses physical punishment is providing a model of aggression and implicitly condoning it, while a parent who uses more subtle techniques is providing a model of self-restraint in handling aggression. This 'modelling' view has also received support from Bandura and Walters.[27] Though the example of parents in this respect as in others no doubt counts for something, it seems unlikely that it could provide the whole explanation. Aronfreed, as we have seen, attributes significance to the fact that 'induction' techniques are less dependent upon the parent's actual presence, and that techniques involving reasoning are likely to increase the child's ability to analyse, judge and control his behaviour through cognitive mediation. With regard to the parents' presence or absence, anxiety over parental disapproval may be considerable and prolonged when the parent is not there, and the parent's return may provide the opportunity for action to restore or ensure the continuation of parental affection. Hill,[137] from an orthodox reinforcement theory point of view, thinks that the unpleasant experience associated with the withdrawal of affection is more likely to *end* when the child engages in corrective action (reparative action, confession, expression of remorse), while physical punishment is more likely to recur regardless of any action by the child, so that withdrawal of affection is more likely to be associated with corrective behaviour. Hoffman[140] points out that if 'feelings' are important, they may be of three kinds; (a) anxiety over loss of love, (b) shame over failure to reach an expected standard of conduct, (c) guilt over harmful consequences for parents (or others). He seems to suggest that the last of these is likely to be the most effective in promoting internalization when he emphasizes *induction* as involving both empathy and understanding by the child of how his behaviour affects others.

Hoffman[138, 139] puts the view that both love *and* punishment may have the effect of making a parent 'salient' for the child, and that the child may identify more strongly with a parent on the basis of a higher degree of such salience, i.e. the child will be the more ready to accept the admonitions and the values of a parent, the more important this parent appears as a source of either love or punishment. One can clearly argue that a child can be motivated both by a desire to receive affection and a desire to avoid punishment in whatever form. But the important point is that when the parent is more salient, the child should be more responsive to his or her reasoning and more ready to accept his appeals. Aronfreed[15] thinks that nurturance might increase the salience of punishment by increasing its significance as a sign of disapproval, or that it might increase the amount of attention given by the child to punishing and rewarding or approving and disapproving behaviour on the part of his parents, in both cases by increasing the affective value of various kinds of parental behaviour. The use of verbal methods of discipline might increase the importance of cognitive awareness of one's intentions as cues that some action is 'wrong'.

Kohlberg[166] takes the very simple and straightforward line that children are simply more likely to accept the admonitions of parents whom they *like*. This to some extent begs the question, since one may then ask what it is that makes children particularly like their parents. But clearly his view can readily be combined with the 'salience' view of Aronfreed and Hoffman. Liking can increase salience and can also add something of its own.

Kohlberg[164] has also suggested that children have a tendency toward mastering interesting events, and that modelling and identification follow upon *interest*. The child will tend to 'model' his parents because in many important ways they do interesting things. As Kohlberg points out, a two-year-old boy will frequently imitate his older brother rather than his mother because his brother is doing more interesting things. Perhaps 'interest' may also have the effect of making a parent more salient, then. There seems to be some similarity between the 'interest' view and the 'social power' notion of Mussen and Distler,[216] since the model may attract interest because of his *command over* interesting activities. Kohlberg, however, holds that modelling may take place regardless of the power or status of any model, as long as the model's actions are interesting or striking. There also seems to be some similarity between the 'interest' view and the 'status envy' notion of Whiting, since the model may attract interest because of his ability to do interesting things, or his access to interesting objects and materials.

We can thus see that there is a considerable range of opinion as to what factors in the 'family constellation' seem to be important for moral development and as to how such factors operate. A number of suggestions find a degree of empirical support, some more than others. There is, however, disappointingly little general agreement. The best-supported findings seem to be that some degree of familial affection and support favours moral development, and that the children of parents who *reason* with their children or use *induction* techniques are likely to function at a higher moral level.

A great deal of research deriving from Freudian theory and learning theory has been concerned with how we come to inhibit
impulses, to refrain from anti-social behaviour, to resist temptation—in other words with the negative aspects of moral control.
Much other research, deriving either directly or indirectly
from Piaget or other forms of 'developmental stages' theory,
has given attention to more positive aspects, but tended
(though not exclusively) to be preoccupied with cognitive and
judgmental aspects rather than behavioural aspects. Research into
the acquisition of positively valued *behavioural* dispositions—
which may indeed be relevant to resistance to temptation and self-
control—has been rather limited. There has been some study of
'concern for others' in animals (see Rosenhan[236]), indicating that
in at least some species there seems clearly to be a form of concern
for others and altruism within the species. As far as human beings
are concerned, Hoffman[141] speculated about a possible basis in
parental treatment, for the development of 'consideration for
others'. Using the familiar division into affective, conative and
cognitive, he hypothesized (1) that the positive emotional attitude
to others associated with 'consideration for others' (affective
aspect) results from parental acceptance of the child, which
provides a positive 'considerate' model; (2) that the ability to
control one's impulses (conative aspect) in consideration for others
results from the kind of parental discipline which directs the
child's attention to the consequences of his action for other people
and provides a model in the form of self-restraint; (3) that awareness of others and their needs (cognitive aspect) results from
parental discipline which directs attention to the needs of others.

He conducted a study with children of about three years of age to test these hypotheses. Relevant data concerning parental treatment was obtained from interviews and direct observation of mothers' behaviour toward their children. 'Scores' were found for acceptance, consequence-oriented discipline and other-oriented discipline. 'Consideration for others' by the children was estimated on the basis of observation of behaviour with other children. Unfortunately for these promising hypotheses, only very tentative support was found. This could, of course, be for various reasons; for example, either set or both sets of measures might have been unsatisfactory, or (as seems very likely), the children might have been too young.

Bronfenbrenner[52] attempted to establish parental discipline as a relevant factor in the development of a sense of 'responsibility'. The results which he reports are far from clear-cut. Adolescents who were rated by their teachers as 'low in responsibility' tended to describe their parents as frequently disapproving and complaining of them, as given to ridiculing them and comparing them unfavourably with others, and as spending relatively little time with them. In particular, lack of discipline by the father was associated with low responsibility in boys, while *strong* discipline by the father went with low responsibility in girls. However, those with *middle* scores for paternal discipline tended to have the highest ratings for responsibility. (Bronfenbrenner also found that the role of the mother was more important at the highest social level, i.e. parents who were college graduates.) Bronfenbrenner suggests that responsibility and leadership potential are fostered when the like-sex parent is salient in discipline. It is not quite clear why this should be so. He also suggests—tentatively—that 'the most dependent and least dependable adolescents describe family arrangements which are neither patriarchal nor matriarchal but equalitarian' (p. 267). That is, he suggests that the more 'democratic' family atmosphere, with decision-making shared between parents, tends to produce irresponsible rather than responsible adolescents. This would at first sight seem to cast doubt upon the idea of encouraging children to become responsible by sharing in decision-making and therefore sharing responsibility, of encouraging children to make decisions for themselves and to take at least some of the consequences. However, it may be that in Bronfenbrenner's 'equalitarian' families, (a) if responsibility is shared, then no one is really responsible for anything, (b) each parent avoids the 'responsibility' of giving a clear and unambiguous lead on many matters, particularly perhaps, moral matters, in which it is important that they should give a clear demonstration of their own responsibility in the sense of commitment to principles, e.g. consideration for others. To encourage children to make decisions and accept responsibility for them, a parent does not have to indicate that he does not care. To do so may be to signal his own refusal to accept the responsibilities of his parental role.

Doland and Adelberg[66] found that children of four and one half years of age could be got to share with others by social reinforcement. Verbal approval for sharing was given 'in advance' to elicit sharing. Nursery school children were more influenced by this kind of social approval than children who had not attended nursery school, no doubt, as the authors suggest, because they had had more experience of social reinforcement and were therefore more sensitive to it. In other words, they had learned to value adult approval more. This experiment is an interesting demonstration of what can be done with four-year-olds; but there is no indication whether the sharing continued after the social reinforcement was withdrawn. Perhaps it would be unreasonable to expect a 'short-period' experimental study to have any longer-lasting effects. But it could certainly be argued that, if social reinforcement (or for that matter other reinforcement) is given frequently for a range of sharing behaviours, a generalized 'sharing habit' could be established which could then be maintained by the intermittent social reinforcement that this kind of behaviour would be likely to meet with.

Berkowitz *et al.* held that 'a widespread ideal in our society . . . prescribes that the individual should help other people who are dependent on him and need his assistance. When someone . . . learns that a person needs his help, he presumably becomes aware of this moral standard and—assuming that he has adopted it—feels obliged to aid the dependent person even when no direct return benefits are anticipated'[34] (p. 47). Berkowitz calls this kind

F

of norm-oriented behaviour 'responsibility behaviour'. The reference to social norms and 'feelings of obligation' is welcome, but Berkowitz does not contribute anything directly to explaining how a person has come to 'adopt' the norm as 'obligatory'. The most interesting aspect of Berkowiz's work in this area is that which indicates social class and national differences in the conditions under which such a norm operates. According to Berkowitz and Friedman[85] in America adolescent boys from 'bureaucratic' middle class families tended to be relatively little influenced in helping another person by the amount of help they themselves had previously received. These boys were said to be relatively highly 'responsibility oriented', their helping being determined by their commitment to the 'helping norm'. Adolescents from entrepreneurial middle class families, on the other hand, were much influenced in the amount of help they gave by how much help they themselves had had. Their orientation was more in terms of reciprocity than in terms of a compelling norm, and they were therefore said to be less 'responsibility oriented.' English working class boys reacted much as the American entrepreneurial middle class boys had reacted, while the English bureaucratic middle class boys reacted much as their American counterparts. These findings seem to lend support to the view of the importance of 'perspective' associated with position in the class or occupational system taken by Kohlberg[165] and others.

Rosenhan and London,[237] like Bandura and Walters and other members of the 'social learning' school, emphasize the importance of 'imitation' and hence the importance of salient models. Rosenhan[236] reports an experiment in which 'charity' was shown to be encouraged in children by the behaviour of a 'charitable model'. A child and an adult model played a bowling game. Every time the adult 'won' he put two 'certificates' (actually redeemable at a toy or sweet shop) into a box labelled 'Orphans' Fund'. While the child played, the adult looked away from him to reduce the effect of the 'approval' or 'disapproval' which the child might expect to get from him. The child was then left alone to play, with the certificates there, and the Orphans' box. The child could, therefore, either keep all the certificates which he won, or contribute some or all to the fund. About one

half of the experimental group (who had seen the charitable
model) contributed to the Fund, while *none* of the control group
(who had not had the model) did so. Rosenhan refers to contributing in the absence of the adult as 'internalized' charity since the
child presumably had no grounds for supposing that any externally supplied reinforcement (such as approval) was likely to follow
his contributing (though we cannot be sure of this). Of 57 children
who contributed when 'unwatched', 51 had already contributed
in the presence of the adult model, and only six had not. According to Rosenhan, this indicates the importance not only of observing the model, but also of what he calls 'rehearsing'. When some
of the children were put under firm pressure to give ('enforced
rehearsal'), they actually gave *more* when not watched than
children who had watched the model contribute and contributed
in the model's presence but had not been under pressure to
contribute. This would seem to cast some doubt upon how far
the charity when unobserved could really be regarded as 'internalized'. A better though not perfect criterion of internalization was
used in an extension of the experiment. Later, 'left over' certificates were given to the children with envelopes for making
contributions if they liked. One half of the children got envelopes
marked 'Orphans' Fund' like the original collecting box, the other
half got envelopes marked with the name of another and well-
known charity. Contributions were all to be 'anonymous'. (The
certificate numbers had in fact been recorded so that it would be
known which children contributed.) This time, children in the
'enforced rehearsal' group gave less to the original fund, and also
less to the new charity, i.e. there was less generalization of giving
when the children had previously been under pressure to give.
However, Rosenhan holds that, in addition to the opportunity to
observe a model and to 'co-rehearse' voluntarily, a prerequisite
for the internalization of charitable behaviour is the capacity to
imagine oneself in the other's place; and since younger children
have less capacity for empathising with the needs of others as
distinct from feeling their own wants, they are less likely to be
able to internalize. It is clearly then, crucial to know at what
age to expect children to have sufficient capacity for empathy,

and what factors may contribute to the development of this capacity.

Rosenhan and London[237] suggest that 'vicarious arousal' or 'vicarious conditioning' may have a powerful influence. In vicarious arousal, there is no actual model whom the child can observe and copy. Instead he is told about (or may even see) someone in need or suffering, for example, a victim of oppression, and himself thinks of possible ways of relieving this suffering or preventing its recurrence. The question is, how does he come to empathise with the victim in such a way as to want to do something about it? Rosenhan and London suggest that the primary requirement is for the child to have had 'sufficient positive experience with others' (p. 271). It is commonly thought that experience of suffering oneself contributes to one's capacity for sympathizing with suffering in others, but Rosenhan and London, although they have no relevant evidence, are inclined to the opposite point of view—that experience of brutality, for example, tends to lead to its acceptance, both for oneself and for others. However, it may well be that experience of suffering and of having it relieved through the sympathetic action of others *is* relevant. This is suggested by Lenrow[176] who found that both verbal and active expressions of sympathy were more likely to occur in those who had formerly, in actuality or in role-playing situations, had distress relieved by others.

Rosenhan[236] in support of the importance of modelling and positive experience with others, refers to an extremely interesting study of civil rights workers in America. He found that dedicated (altruistic) civil rights workers nearly all identified strongly with an altruistic parent. Dividing the civil rights workers he studied into two classes, the fully committed and the partially committed, he found that the fully committed in interviews described their relationships with their parents as warm and satisfying and, reported at least one parent as dedicated to at least one cause. As Rosenhan and London[237] (p. 270) put it, at least one parent provided a consistent model of 'pro-social behaviour'. The partially committed, on the other hand, described their parents in either ambivalent or hostile terms, and showed signs of anxiety, hostility and guilt. Their reports also indicated that their parents were more confused and uncertain about their moral position, and tended to practise other than they preached. An inconsistent parental model might indeed be expected to create confusion and uncertainty. Personal uncertainties were also indicated by the fact that an appreciable number of the partially committed had had psychotherapy. Rosenhan suggests that for the partially committed, participation in civil rights activities may be largely a matter of reassuring themselves. For the fully committed, on the other hand, participation is the expression of a much more genuine concern for others based on their own relation with their parents and the atmosphere of altruistic concern for others in which they have grown up. People with such a genuine concern for the welfare of others would clearly be more genuinely moral and more truly committed to the principles involved. It would appear virtually certain that at least some degree of internalization of concern for others had taken place in the fully committed, and that their actions could not be explained wholly or even mainly in terms of possible social reinforcement.

In an analysis of altruism rather similar to but more detailed than that of Rosenhan and London, Aronfreed[14] posits two basic components in the acquiring of 'altruistic behaviour'. 'First, the child must acquire emphatic or vicarious affective sensitivity to the cues which serve as indicators of another person's experience of distress. Secondly, the child must acquire specific forms of overt behaviour which are instrumental to the reduction of the other person's distress' (p. 151). Aronfreed refers to two experiments by Vivian Paskal and himself designed to show how altruistic behaviour may be learned. The first study was intended to show how a child could come to attach positive affect to behaviour of an adult indicating the adult's pleasure at some event, and how a child could learn to *do* something to produce the signs of the adult's pleasure. This action, carried out to benefit another rather than oneself, is by definition altruistic. Aronfreed states that any action is altruisitic if 'the choice of the act, in preference to an alternative act, is at least partly determined by the actor's expectation of consquences which will benefit another person rather than himself' (pp. 138–139). However, this does not imply that the ensuing benefit to the other person has no affective value for the actor; on the contrary, Aronfreed mentions that it is precisely the positive affect induced by the consequences of one's action for another person, either directly observed or imagined, which reinforces and sustains the altruistic behaviour. The main problem is to see how such positive affect can become attached to consequences of one's own action for someone else.

Aronfreed and Paskal (reported by Aronfreed[14]), used an experimental situation in which a woman experimenter sat close to the child (subjects were six to eight years old girls) and showed the child how to work an apparatus with two levers, one of which produced sweets, the other of which switched on a red light. When the red light went on, the experimenter did one of three things. (a) She looked at the light, smiled and said 'in a pleased and excited tone of voice', 'There's the light.' These actions were called the experimenter's 'expressive cues'. Immediately after these, the experimenter gave the child a hug and smiled broadly, directly at her. This was called 'affection'. (b) The experimenter acted as in (a) but did not provide any 'affection'. (c) The experimenter acted as in (a) but did not provide any 'expressive cues'. In the test period which followed, the experimenter sat facing the child while the child operated the levers over a large number of trials. The one lever still delivered sweets, and the child was told that she could keep all the sweets she obtained. However, the light was disconnected, and the child told by the experimenter that whenever the child chose the 'light lever', the light would appear on the experimenter's side of the apparatus, but would not be seen by the child. Every time the child chose the 'light lever', the experimenter smiled and said, 'There's the light,' using the same expressive cues which she had used to indicate her pleasure during the initial session. Thus the child was in a situation in which she could, on each trial, either produce sweets for herself or the signs of pleasure in the experimenter. Children who experienced both the experimenter's expressive cues and signs of affection significantly more frequently chose the light lever in preference to the sweets lever, i.e. preferred to act in an 'altruistic' rather than in a 'selfish' way. (This experiment would seem to show that children *can* learn to be altruistic by having pleasurable affect conditioned to cues from another person expressing his or her satisfaction). The fact that the experimental condition which included *both* the expressive cues and affection was more successful than either the expressive cues or the affection alone seems to indicate that the children could not have been motivated entirely by anticipation of social approval for choosing the light lever. One can readily imagine a real-life situation corresponding to the experimental paradigm. For example, suppose that a mother buys a bag of sweets for her child, and then says, 'Let's share them with Mary', gives Mary a sweet and hugs her own child when Mary shows signs of satisfaction. If this *kind* of situation is relatively frequently repeated, it is easy to see how sharing with others could acquire positive affective value in the same way as in Aronfreed's experiment. Similarly, it is possible that cues from another person indicating termination of distress could come to have positive affective value. Whether this kind of conditioning is the *only* way or even the best way in which children become altruistic is, however, a different matter. Experiments of this kind can only suggest that 'natural' socialization *might* work in this way, but cannot conclusively show that it *does*.

Midlarsky and Bryan[201] in a very similar kind of investigation, report results indicating that similar effects follow when the expression of the experimenter's affection closely precedes rather than closely follows the expressive signs of pleasure. Midlarsky and Bryan argue that in this case, conditioning of positive affect to the signs of pleasure given by another person cannot be regarded as necessary conditions for the acquiring of altruistic behaviour, as Aronfreed's theory requires, on the ground that this would require 'backward conditioning', the unconditioned stimulus (hugs) preceding the conditioned stimulus (expressive cues); and there is a good deal of doubt as to whether backward conditioning of this kind can take place. Aronfreed, however, argues that 'backward conditioning might be especially viable when physical affection and expressive cues are blended together in close succession in the experience of a highly cognitive organism—particularly in view of the possibility that the positive affectivity which is aroused by a quick hug may reach its highest magnitude after the hug is terminated'[14] (p. 148). In other words, the child learns to *associate* the expressive cues with the demonstrations of affection which produce his own feelings of pleasure because the two occur in close contiguity—a way of putting it that really reminds us more of the 'association of ideas' than of conditioning in its strict sense. Perhaps too strict an application of the language of classical conditioning may be misleading. Midlarsky and Bryan argue that contiguity between expressive cues and demonstrations of affection is not a crucial factor, since altruistic behaviour in the test session was found even when the experimenter did not provide expressive cues when the child pressed the light lever. However, Aronfreed argues that the factor of contiguity was certainly relevant, since the 'altruistic effect' was greater when the experimenter did provide expressive cues during the test session, and that it is likely that, even when the experimenter did not provide expressive cues during the test, the children probably imagined them or, in Aronfreed's words, gave them 'cognitive representation'. While this may seem plausible, it might be objected that, in the absence of any more direct evidence of such 'cognitive representations', Aronfreed is introducing them 'ad hoc' in such a way as to explain away unanticipated or inconvenient results. It must be admitted, I think, that Aronfreed's argument sometimes gives the impression that he is trying to eat his cake and have it.

The second study by Aronfreed and Paskal is concerned with how children learn 'sympathetic behaviour'. Aronfreed defines a sympathetic act as one which is 'elicited through the actor's emphatic or vicarious affective response to the actual or anticipated distress of another person' (p. 150). As Aronfreed points out, apparently sympathetic behaviour may occur because it is instrumental in removing unpleasant stimulation (e.g. a child's crying), or because social reinforcement is expected, or because it is believed that it will create a reciprocal obligation. Such behaviour is in fact directly under the control of external positive or negative reinforcement, and should not properly be called 'sympathetic'. Aronfreed and Paskal's study, in many ways similar to their study of altruism, was designed to show how negative affect in children could be conditioned to the signs of distress in another person, and to see how far children could learn to

perform sympathetic actions as a consequence of observing the
action of a model who relieved their own distress. Again, children of seven to eight years of age were used as subjects with a
female adult experimenter. There were five separate experimental
arrangements or sequences. In the first sequence, the experimental
situation consisted of a classification task where objects had to be
classified into one of three categories as related to house, school or
dog, by working the appropriate one of three switches. The two
end switches were labelled 'house' and 'School' respectively while
the middle switch was labelled 'dog'. In fact, all the objects rightly
belonged either to the 'house' or to the 'school' category, so that
the middle switch would be very seldom used in the performance
of the task. On one half of the classification trials, *between* items,
the child heard an unpleasantly loud noise through a pair of ear-
phones. A few seconds before the noise in the child's headphones
started, the adult, also wearing headphones, began to show signs
of distress by clasping her hands to her head. During the second
phase of the first sequence, the experimenter did not wear ear-
phones and showed no signs of distress. She had a choice box of
her own, and told the child that she might be able to shut off the
nasty noise the child might still hear in the headphones. On one
half of the classification trials, the child heard the unpleasant noise
after a few seconds, the experimenter pushed the middle switch
saying she was doing so to stop the noise; that is, the experimenter
for the moment gave up the classification task in order to relieve
the child's distress. In the third phase of the first sequence, another
child was introduced who had in fact been trained by the experimenter to show signs of distress on certain trials. The first child
then took the role previously taken by the experimenter, and on
one half of the trials, the second child or 'stooge' subject clapped
her hands to her head. If the first child then moved the middle
switch, the stooge stopped showing distress; if she moved one of
the task-relevant switches, the stooge kept her hands to her head
for a further five seconds. This first sequence was designed, in
Aronfreed's words, 'first to condition empathic distress, then to
maximise the potential intrinsic reinforcement value of the child's
representation of the agent's sympathetic actions and finally to
provide external social stimuli which would emphatically motiv-

ate and reinforce the child's overt reproduction of the sympathetic behaviour' (p. 155). The second sequence was the same as the
first, except that the experimenter's signs of distress were not
contiguous with the unpleasant noise the child heard, but
occurred on the *other* trials of the series. The third sequence was
again the same as the first except that the noise was only of low
intensity. This was intended to reduce the value of the experimenter's sympathetic behaviour in reducing the child's distress.
The fourth sequence and fifth sequence were likewise like the first,
except that in the fourth, the stooge subject gave no signs of distress
and in the fifth, did not even wear headphones. This was to indicate how far the external, observable distress signs were necessary
for the sympathetic behaviour of the subject to occur. As predicted, children in the first sequence showed a markedly greater
degree of sympathetic behaviour, i.e. moving of the middle
switch to stop the noise for the stooge subject, than children in
any other sequence, thus indicating clearly the importance of
the conditioning of feelings of distress to the signs of distress in
others as a precondition for imitation of the experimenter's sympathetic behaviour. However, the fact that children in the fourth
sequence (in which the stooge subject wore headphones but gave
no signs of distress) also increased their use of the third switch
in the test stage compared with the first stage, indicates,
Aronfreed thinks, that they were influenced by cognitive representation of the *likely* consequences of their action in moving the
middle switch for the second child. In this experiment, some support was obtained for the idea of cognitive representation by
asking subjects about their experience, after the experiment was
over. A clear recognition that moving the middle switch would
have relieved the stooge's distress was associated with actually
moving the switch. Basically, then, it is changes of affectivity or
feeling which motivate sympathetic behaviour. Although
obviously sympathetic behaviour may be further reinforced by
external rewards, particularly social rewards such as approval,
Aronfreed is clearly of the opinion that the greater the extent to
which cognitive representation is involved, the more internalized
the 'sympathy' becomes, in the sense that it is less dependent upon
directly observable cues to distress, more on the actor's recon-

struction of the other's situation. Once again, the caution about the experimental paradigm is in order. To show that it *may* happen like that is not to show that it *must* happen like that. Nevertheless, the two experiments of Aronfreed and Paskal are ingenious, highly provocative and quite impressive demonstrations of the role of the experimentally created 'model' situation.

So far, we have devoted most of our attention to approaches in terms of psychoanalytic theory and learning theory. In this chapter, we shall be concerned with a different kind of approach in terms of (a) attempts to establish useful *types* of moral character and (b) attempts to establish a useful sequence of *stages* of moral development.

(a) *Types of moral character*. Types may be of two kinds, empirically derived and theoretically derived. Empirically derived types represent the result of classyifying data in a way which seems to fit or to be required by the data. There is a sense, of course, in which no classification is entirely empirically derived, since the way in which we view—and even select—data inevitably depends on the notions, perhaps implicit, with which we approach our data. But the classification has not been predetermined by theoretical considerations. Havighurst and Taba[132] say that their personality types are empirically, not theoretically derived, since they emerged from a study of the data which they had accumulated. The first function of such a classification is to introduce order into data in the sense that when data can be meaningfully classified, similarities between different events such as items of behaviour become clear and some general statements become possible. A second function is to suggest relationships to other variables, such as social class, and to suggest possible causal or facilitating factors. The value of the classification or typology depends partly on the extent to which it fits data other than that from which it was derived, partly on the degree to which it enables relationships with other variables to be established and hypotheses as to further relationships and possible explanations to be suggested.

Theoretically derived types are types which are 'implied' by theory. For example, the four types of McCord and Clemes[182] were derived from their two basic dimensions, rather than from an examination of data. In this case, the types enable the data to be ordered in a way compatible with the theory. But the most important function again is to suggest relationships and possible explanations. Here, however, the discovery of such relationships as, on theoretical grounds, might have been expected, not only demonstrates the usefulness of the types but also provides justification for the theoretical conceptions from which the types were derived. For example, McCord and Clemes were able to show that the incidence of their four types varied in different kinds of social groups as they expected, thus justifying the use of their types and the ideas behind them.

Havighurst and Taba[132] are concerned with defining 'character types' among 16 year olds and trying to find background factors of experience differentiating the various types. They define four character types, plus an extra category labelled 'unadjusted'. The four types are the defiant, the submissive, the adaptive and the self-directive.

(1) The defiant person 'is openly hostile to society' (p. 158). He does badly at school, does not conform to social conventions and may be delinquent. Typically, he has a chip on his shoulder which prevents him from being able to make any realistic adjustment to family, peers, school or occupation. 'In general, the defiant person is one who has had early and continued experiences of neglect and frustration. . . . He is unable to cooperate with other people in the pursuit of any social end' (pp. 163–164).

(2) The submissive person 'is one who will not initiate action' (p. 146). He relies mainly on authority, and may have a reputation as a responsible person based on conscientious performance of what he is required or expected to do. He tends to have strong moral standards and a well-developed sense of duty and obligation, and so may sometimes show an unexpected moral stubbornness. But he has formed his standards as a result of *accepting* standards imposed by authority, and is little capable of thinking

or acting independently. He tends to come from 'a home dominated by authoritarian parents . . . in which there is a lack of emotional backing and warm attachments to offset the influence of harsh and sometimes puzzling parental requirements' (p. 157).
(3) The adaptive person 'is sociable, friendly, vivacious and outgoing in manner' (p. 134). He adapts easily to most social situations and almost unconsciously tends to follow customary standards of 'good' behaviour. He is a social conformer, but less obsessively so, less authority dominated and with less commitment to standards than the submissive person. He 'must have had an affectionate, permissive family environment. Discipline must have been easy, and the child must have been given a complete feeling of security and affection in the early years. The moral views of the parents are broad and tolerant so that they do not set restrictions on their child's social participation' (p. 144).
(4) The self-directive person 'is conscientious, orderly, and persistent. He sets high standards for himself and is seldom satisfied with his performance. He is ambitious, strong-willed, and self-sufficient, yet characterized by self-criticism and self-doubt' (p. 124). He has a strong and active conscience, and tends to suffer from anxiety and feelings of guilt which are, however, generally managed successfully. 'This person has probably had less than the usual amount of emotional warmth in his relations with his parents and with other adults. They have taught him that he can attain security only through performance. He learns not to expect to be appreciated for himself but for what he can accomplish' (p. 132).

The additional category is for the 'unadjusted person'. He is 'discontented, insecure, frustrated' (p. 165). Usually he is in difficulties with his family and at school. But he is unsuccessful in his adjustment rather than hostile to society like the defiant person. The unadjusted is not a character type like the other four. He is rather a 'potential self-directive, adaptive or submissive person who is barred by adverse circumstances from achieving a reasonably good adjustment in one of these roles.' He can often find a solution to his problems if the adverse circumstances in his environment can be removed. Most of their unadjusted persons came from the upper-lower social class, and Havighurst and Taba think the lack of adjustment is due to the fact that their peer-group was largely 'geared to middle-class values and expectations' (p. 175).

Although they are not intended as specifically 'moral' types, these types can clearly be applied *as* 'moral' types. The adaptive person is essentially externally oriented and pragmatic, taking situations as they come, but because of his social intelligence, generally following the socially accepted line. The submissive person has internalized over-efficiently the standards which parents and other representatives of society have imposed upon him and is thus unable to question them on his own account. The self-directive person has both a strong conscience and a strong sense of personal responsibility for his own decisions.

McCord and McCord[185] have proposed a rather elaborate typological scheme. They start by distinguishing *five* levels of conscience, the unconscious-inhibitory level (repression), the conscious inhibitory level (conscious conflict), the retrospective inhibitory level (guilt), the ideal prescriptive level (where 'oughts' are nominally accepted) and the active prescriptive level (where prescriptions actually guide behaviour). They then propose four 'orientations of moral anxiety'. (1) Hedonistic orientation, corresponding to fear of external consequences, (2) authority-oriented orientation, corresponding to fear of losing approval of authority and of losing status, (3) other-directed orientation, corresponding to fear of loss of love, with consistent following of the dictates of a primary group, (4) integrity orientation, corresponding to fear of loss of identity or integrity, with strongly internalized standards. These four 'orientations' correspond almost exactly to Kennedy-Frazer's prudential, authoritarian, social and personal orientations (see p. 182). However, McCord and McCord use them more as *dimensions* than as orientations, and on the basis of their own investigations, using story completion techniques, they develop a much more elaborate classification of types of conscience. The main types are as follows. (1) *Authoritarians*. These are people who are concerned with popularity and fame. Their values centre on authority, approval and achievement. They tend to have idealized images of kind, loving parents. Interestingly, Adorno *et al.*[2] reported very similar parent images for their 'authoritarian personality'. (2) *Integral-authoritarians.* These have more thoroughly internalized their moral anxieties, though they still place a high value on approval. They tend to regard their mothers as kind, but not their fathers. (3) *Other-directed conformists.* These are also concerned with winning approval from others, but are less inhibited and less oriented to authority than the authoritarians. They show less internalized anxiety than the integral-authoritarians. (4) *Integral-conformists.* These are the most inhibited of all. They were the only subjects to report that moral conflicts often involved conflict *between* ethical principles. In general, they did not consider the views of others. They tended to dislike their fathers. (5) *Hedonist-conformers.* They are relatively uninhibited. They fear consequences and loss of status, but do not experience moral conflict. (6) *Integral deviants.* These have a high regard for individual freedom, and have strongly internalized anxiety. (7) *Hedonist-deviants.* These have a hedonistic individual orientation. The other *five possible types* of conscience which McCord and McCord indicate are as follows. (8) *Psychopathic hedonists.* These are people who pursue the immediate satisfaction of their impulses in an amoral way. It is suggested that such persons result from early emotional deprivation or brain defect. (9) *Other-directed deviants.* These depend upon the support of a 'deviant group'. Where parents do not personify such a deviant group, they may have suffered from parental inconsistency and early parental rejection. They may, in fact, have a very high need for affection and approval. (10) *Authoritarian-other-directed.* These tend to vary between dependence on authority and need for group approval. (11) *Compulsive deviants.* These, although they have internalized standards, seem *driven* to deviant behaviour in one particular area (e.g. sex, theft). (12) *Supra-moralists.* Such people orient their life around their moral beliefs. These beliefs are 'actively prescriptive', requiring them to carry out the implications of their beliefs in behaviour.

It will immediately be evident that the 'authority orientation' of McCord and McCord corresponds fairly well to the 'submissive person' category of Havighurst and Taba, the other-directed orientation to the 'adaptive person', and the integrity orientation to the 'self-directed person'. One difficulty with the analysis of McCord and McCord is the relatively large number of 'types of conscience' proposed. A much more compact scheme is provided by McCord and Clemes.[182] They start with two bipolar, dichotomous and logically derived dimensions. (1) The deontological-technological dimension represents the distinction between Kantian views of the moral worth of an action deriving 'not from the purpose which is to be attained by it, but from the maxim by which it is determined' (*qu.* p. 18) (deontological view), and the views of philosophers like G. E. Moore that the moral worth of an action depends upon its probable consequences. (2) The extrinsic-intrinsic dimension represents the distinction between those who believe that standards of morality are *extrinsic to* or independent of man's desires, and those who believe that one should judge in relation to the desires and preferences of men, i.e. that standards must be *intrinsic to* these desires. These two dimensions give rise to four theoretical moral orientations, thus:

	Deontological emphasis	*Teleological emphasis*
Extrinsic standards	Normativist	Integratist
Intrinsic standards	Phenomenalist	Hedonist

(1) *The normativist* should show the following characteristics. (a) His standards are extrinsic—he rejects desires as a basis of value; he tends to be resistant to group pressure. (b) He attends to *procedure* rather than results and is thus inclined to ritualism. (c) He has a desire for order, associated with an emphasis on law, self-control and authority supported by a belief that man is naturally 'evil' or dangerous. He is sensitive to status differences.

(2) *The integratist* should be as follows. (a) Like the normativist, his standards are extrinsic, he rejects desires as a basis of value, and is resistant to group pressure. (b) He is more concerned with results than procedure. (c) He values independence, privacy and autonomy highly, and thus values intelligence and the ability to make discriminations relevant to achieving goals he regards as important. He is not concerned with authority or status. He does *not* believe that man is naturally evil or dangerous.

(3) *The phenomenalist* appears as follows. (a) He believes that the desires of men are appropriate guides for behaviour and tends to believe that most people are similar. (b) Like the normativist, he stresses procedure and inclines to ritualism. (c) He is concerned with conformity and agreement with others, rejecting the possibility of fundamental and unresolvable conflicts. He is concerned with how he appears to other people.

(4) *The hedonist* appears as follows. (a) His first 'good' is pleasure. (b) Like the phenomenalist, he believes that most people are similar. (c) He believes that every man can act as his own judge. (d) He has confidence that man's desires are an appropriate guide to choice. (e) He rejects ritualism and external controls. (f) He adjusts readily to environmental requirements and change. It can at once be seen that the 'normativist' corresponds to the 'authority orientation', the 'phenomenalist' to the 'other-directed' orientation, the 'integratist' to the 'integrity orientation' and the hedonist, of course, to the 'hedonistic orientation'. The difference lies in the fact that, in the more recent formulation, there is a 'rationalistic' basis for the four basic orientations, which are derived by combining the two basic dimensions. It is also clear that various 'combinations' of the four orientations would be logically possible. As we have previously mentioned, McCord and Clemes found that different groups of subjects did tend to differ in expected ways. For example, Mormon subjects were high in 'Normativist' orientation, members of the Peace Corps lower in 'Normativist' and higher in 'Integratist' orientation.

Stephenson[259] distinguishes between (1) 'other-directed anxiety', referring to 'the individual's susceptibility to external moral sanctions, reflected in the tendency to anticipate and avoid disapproval'; (2) 'intropunitive guilt', referring to 'the self-inflicted remorse and unhappiness which may follow wrong-doing'; and (3) 'conscience motive', referring to the positive aspect of conscience. On the basis of scores derived from scales designed to assess these three dimensions, Stephenson proposes eight types of conscience, defined in terms of the three dimensions. His is thus a theoretically derived system of types.

Type of Conscience	Conscience motive	Intropuni- tive guilt	Other-directed anxiety
Susceptible	High	High	High
Prescriptive-intropunitive	High	High	Low
Prescriptive	High	Low	Low
Prescriptive other-directed	High	Low	High
Intropunitive other-directed	Low	High	High
Intropunitive	Low	High	Low
Other-directed	Low	Low	High
Psychopathic	Low	Low	Low

In a sample of 15 year olds, the most frequent 'conscience types' were the susceptible and the 'psychopathic', which was actually the most frequent of all, with 24 of the 100 children falling in this category. The label 'psychopathic' may be a little misleading. Stephenson mentions 'the cheerful, nonchalant self-interest' of many of the responses of children of this type. 'Amoral' or 'non-moral' might be a better term, especially since Stephenson warns us against confusing the 'psychopathic conscience' with the 'psychopathic personality'. The person with the 'psychopathic conscience' appears to be governed almost entirely by purely hedonistic considerations. However, the conscience of the 'psycho-path' is not *merely* hedonistic; the psychopath is impulsive, frequently aggressive and does not readily profit from experience. One may, after all, be governed predominantly or purely by hedonistic considerations, and still be a respected and useful citizen, although one does not act for reasons of moral principle.

Wright[279] refers to four 'dimensions' of conscience, which he labels and defines as follows. (1) Resistance to temptation, or the inhibition of behaviour defined as 'wrong'. (2) Post-transgressional behaviour, or the reaction to having done 'wrong', such as feelings of guilt, restitution, confession or apology. (3) The impulse to pursue virtue, or to perform 'good' actions. (4) The capacity to distinguish between right and wrong, or moral judgment. Wright suggests that 'the four strands of moral behaviour can combine to form frequent character types' (p. 752), and indicates four types, depending upon the relative influence of adult authority and the peer group. (a) The non-moral man largely follows hedonistic considerations. He has been little influenced by either parents or peers. (b) The autonomous man tries to decide 'rationally'. In his case, there has been a balance between authority and peers. (c) The conscientious man tends to conform to the dictates of 'conscience' but not without a struggle. He has had a close attachment to an exacting authority. (d) The conformist man does 'what he ought' unreflectively because that's what everybody does. He has been influenced largely by peers. These categories or types are quite similar to Stephenson's, and also to those of Havighurst and Taba, and McCord and McCord. The agreement is highly comforting. It should be noted that these are all systems of classification, and that there is no necessary implication of any developmental sequence, although in general, one would expect the 'autonomous' character or its equivalent, for example, to occur relatively late. About all the systems, however, there is some implication that the types can be arranged in order of their 'morality', the autonomous conscience being the most *moral*. This provides a bridge to the idea of stages of development of conscience.

*(b) Stages of development.** Stages must also enable data to be ordered in a number of categories, but these categories must now be related to each other in a temporal sequence. In the case of moral development, this implies (1) that children in general become more moral as they mature, up to early adulthood, and (2) that development proceeds in a fixed sequence of stages, each stage being distinguished by special defining features; although it may be possible for a stage to be 'skipped' or for there to be some alternative sequences of stages. An interesting question with stages is whether the stage concept is regarded as implying some kind of discontinuity of development. There are really two possibilities. (1) Stages may represent simply a convenient way of dividing up a continuous process of development, rather as one may divide people according to age into decades, for convenience. (2) We may regard the transition from one stage to the next as involving

---

* For a sophisticated and comprehensive analysis of the idea of stages of development in general, see Tran-Thong[264]

a *qualitative* difference in attitude or orientation. This is the way in which most stage theorists have used the term. However, this does not necessarily require us to think in terms of sudden changes. We may regard a child at a given point or stage of development as gradually progressing toward the point at which he seems to show unmistakably that he *can* think or behave in the way which defines the next stage, and we may regard this capacity to think or behave in terms of the higher stage as grounds for regarding the child as having attained this stage, although the child may continue to respond in ways characteristic of earlier stages. We may alternatively require the child to respond more frequently in a way characteristic of a given stage than in ways characteristic of any other stages before we regard him as 'belonging' at that stage. Again, we may regard the concept of stages as referring to units of response or units of behaviour rather than to children. Children might then be described or located in terms of a profile representing their use of each stage. The underlying notion of development with age, however, implies that responses or behaviour defined as characteristic of an earlier stage should be found predominantly among younger children, and responses or behaviour characteristic of a later stage should be found predominantly among older children. None of these alternatives requires us to assume any basic discontinuity; rather, the idea of stages of development assumes emergent qualitative differences between stages.

Now, suppose we find a series of stages which seems to fit our findings at different ages very well. How are we to interpret this? Does it indicate natural stages of growth or does it reflect largely the kinds of changing demands which are being made of children? Does a change from an authoritarian to a social orientation, for example, simply reflect the fact that as a child is required by the nature of the society in which he lives to have progressively increasing interaction with his peers, he becomes more sensitive to the kinds of rewards which they, rather than authority figures, may provide? If stages reflect a natural process of growth, we should expect to find the same (or nearly the same) stages in different societies, though some will not have advanced as far as others, and the specific content of the stages may differ. If stages reflect largely cultural expectations, we should not be surprised to find that the same developmental scheme does not fit different societies, that stages may be missing, or may be different in nature. A stage-developmental point of view will tend to emphasize the natural process of development (though environmental factors cannot be ignored), and to regard different social arrangements etc. rather as factors likely to facilitate or impede development through natural stages. A behaviouristic or reinforcement point of view will tend to emphasize the history of the rewards and punishments to which children are subjected during growth as the main basis for explaining the particular patterns of development with age which can be found in different societies.

In his famous *Social Psychology*,[187] William McDougall distinguishes four levels or stages of conduct, each stage being a necessary precursor of the following stage. (1) In the first stage, instinct controls behaviour, subject only to 'the influence of the pains that are incidentally experienced in the course of instinctive activities' (p. 156). (2) In the second stage, 'the operation of the instinctive impulses is modified by the influence of the rewards and punishments administered more or less systematically by the social environment' (*ibid.*). (3) In the third stage, 'conduct is controlled in the main by the anticipation of social praise and blame' (*ibid.*). (4) In the fourth and last stage, 'conduct is regulated by an ideal of conduct that enables a man to act in the way that seems to him right regardless of the praise or blame of his immediate social environment' (*ibid.*). These stages are thus defined in terms of the type of sanction judged to predominate in the orientation at each stage. It will readily be seen that these four stages are in fact defined in terms very similar to these in which McCord and McCord define their hedonistic, authority, other-directed and integrity orientations. McDougall's four stages were described by Kennedy-Frazer[156] as the prudential, the authoritarian, the social and the personal respectively, and directly and indirectly, this formulation has had considerable influence. McKnight[189] found that, in fact, there was a shift in the dominant orientation from the prudential to the personal with increasing age.

Swainson[262] found four sequential stages corresponding quite well to those suggested by McDougall and Kennedy-Frazer. Her first stage, up to the age of five years, is characterized by prudential and authoritarian attitudes. In the second stage, from five to eight years, she thinks that the main attitude is one of deference to authority, with 'introjection' of authority being completed. Her third stage, from eight to twelve years, is marked by a growing ambivalence of attitude to authority owing to the increasing influence of peer groups. Her final stage of adolescence, from 12 to 19 years of age, shows the development of moral conflicts, and the emergence of an altruistic attitude of concern for the well-being of others, or attitude of 'love'.

Kay[154] (ch. 5) suggests four stages, again defined in terms of the 'dominant' sanction. (1) At the first stage, the child is controlled simply by the necessity of complying with externally imposed restraints. (2) At the next stage, control is through 'introjected irrational values' (p. 127), which seems to mean the unquestioning acceptance as binding of restrictions and demands imposed by authority. (3) The third stage is the stage of control by group opinion. 'At this point,' says Kay, 'an empathic morality emerges where moral conduct displays altruism and concern for people, without necessarily being based on reciprocity' (p. 128). (4) There is then a stage when control is through an ego-ideal or ideal self-image (though Kay seems to include this in his third stage). (5) Finally, 'reasonable, personal moral principles control the individual's behaviour' (ibid.). In a short appendix to the same chapter, Kay thinks, on the basis of his own research, that the five stages can conveniently be reduced to four. (1) The prudential (nursery and infant school children). (2) The authoritarian (junior school). (3) The social (secondary school). Kay finds that this kind of sanction 'operates in a subtle way. With girls it is an ideal self-concept; with boys a reciprocal mode of moral thinking' (p. 142). (4) The personal, which 'slowly emerges but does not dominate at any stage.' He also suggests that if the stages are further compressed into three, these will correspond to Kohlberg's three levels—the amoral, the pre-moral and the moral.

Bull,[56] like McDougall, distinguishes four stages, again, like Kay's stages, defined in terms of the dominant sanction. (1) The stage of anomy or pre-morality where there are no rules or standards, and pleasure and pain are the only factors exercising any control over impulses. Bull refers to this stage as characteristically 'animal'. (2) The stage of *heteronomy* or external morality, in which rules are imposed by others, especially by parents, teachers, police and religious precept. Reward and punishment are still the dominant sanctions, but they have become associated with *rules*. At the beginning of the stage of heteronomy, punishment is mainly physical, this being replaced later by deprivation, and then by verbal approval or disapproval. Negative sanctions (punishment in its various forms) are particularly important here. This stage may be regarded as a stage of externally imposed discipline, necessary for the later development of self-discipline. (3) The stage of *socionomy* or external-internal morality, in which the main sanctions are the essentially *social* sanctions of public praise or blame. Responsiveness to these sanctions is based on the child's submission, first to the authority of his parents, and later to the authority of public opinion. Bull suggests that other relevant motives here are fear, derived from the child's earlier fear of punishment, sympathy and fear of isolation, and forms of 'altruistic' motivation, including 'reciprocal affection' and the desire to experience pleasure by giving pleasure to others. In summary, the two main features of the stage of socionomy are (a) an increasing realization of the responsibilities which one owes to other people, and (b) an increasing sensitivity to the opinions of other people. Conformity to the moral code of the society or group is still primarily egoistic, although tinged with genuine altruism. (4) The stage of *autonomy* or internal morality, in which morality is guided by the individual's *own* standards. Bull makes the valuable contribution of distinguishing three aspects of autonomy, (a) freedom from restrictive emotional ties to one's family, (b) freedom to criticize conventions and the values of others, and (c) freedom to apply one's own standards or principles in action. 'Freedom' here, of course implies freedom from the subjective point of view of the person concerned. He feels *himself* to be free to act according to his beliefs. It does not mean that he is necessarily going to be free from penalty exacted by society for doing so. In a sense, the use of the term 'freedom' here may be misleading, for if the individual truly is committed to his principles, then he is, in a very real way, *not* free to act *at variance* with them, though he may feel free from the need to consult others as to how he should act.

Although Bull names only four stages, he found it necessary, in his own research, to introduce *intermediate* levels in the assessment of children's moral judgment. For example, a 'pure anomy' response (rather rare even with seven-year-old children) was scored as 1, and a 'pure heteronomy' response was scored as 2, while a 'mixed' response, involving aspects of *both* anomy and heteronomy, was scored at $1\frac{1}{2}$. Thus, if the four stages of anomy, heteronomy, socionomy and autonomy are indicated by scores of 1, 2, 3, and 4, we would in effect have *seven* score categories. This raises an interesting kind of question. If these seven categories are adequate, then this might suggest that seven stages could perhaps be defined. For example, stage $1\frac{1}{2}$ might be defined in terms of an orientation to rewards and punishment given by adults for actions that they approve of or disapprove of. Stage 2 would remain the stage of 'rules imposed by others'. Stage $2\frac{1}{2}$ might be defined by *acceptance* of authority, stage 3 (socionomy) in terms of deference to group norms and public opinion, stage $3\frac{1}{2}$ by reciprocity and mutual obligation and stage 4 in terms of individual standards. This would not, however, meet the case of a response where, in fact, *two* answers are given, for example, in a question about saving life 'He might get a reward. . . . He'd like to be saved himself.' But it would also be misleading to score this as intermediate between the values of the two answers given, since it clearly indicates that the respondent *can and does* think at the higher level. To an appreciable extent, the number of categories, levels or stages used is a matter of empirical convenience. But if we also feel that a certain 'system' of stages has logical or *a priori* justification, then we are prepared to go to greater lengths to 'fit' data to the schema. And if, like Piaget, we regard each stage as representing a *qualitatively* different mode of organization, then there may be genuine 'intermediate' stages when a new mode of organization is in process of emerging. But in this case, the mere presence of responses characteristic of more than one stage is not really grounds for assuming that a process of reorganization is taking place. This can properly be decided only on the basis of a thorough examination of the child's way of thinking. At this point, it is always a good thing to remember that when we are *investigating* the child's thinking and behaviour, the pattern of results which we get out will depend to a very considerable extent upon the kind of material which we use for our investigation.

As far as his stage of 'autonomy' is concerned, Bull allows that 'autonomy may vary greatly in its quality'[55] (p. 35). It may, at one extreme, involve a 'harsh and rigid superego' with a large irrational component, while at the other extreme, it may be highly rational and genuinely altruistic. This raises the question of whether a person dominated by a rigid superego is really more moral than one dominated by a 'socionomous' orientation. The difficulty arises from the definition of 'autonomous' as 'no longer dependent upon fear of authority or fear of public opinion', i.e. as relatively independent of immediate external sanctions. But just as we should hesitate before regarding a compulsive neurotic as 'free' in his actions, we must, I think, hesitate before regarding a person driven by an excessively harsh superego as 'autonomous'. There seems to be something not quite right about a developmental scheme which includes both in the same stage or level. This point is well taken by Stephenson[255] in his distinction between 'intropunitive guilt' and 'conscience motive'.

A further problem is, as Bull indicates, that if we regard the most advanced kind of autonomy as characterized by plasticity or fluidity, rather than rigidity, we may be liable to confuse *moral uncertainty and confusion* with the highest level of moral functioning. Fluidity must mean a capacity for applying, adapting and modifying principles in the light of events and reason. It *cannot* mean simply non-commitment.

Stephenson,[259] although not primarily concerned in his book with developmental stages, does propose a rather loosely defined developmental scheme related to his typology, to which we have already referred. He suggests very tentatively the following stages. (1) The earliest stage is characterized by 'object anxiety', an impersonal kind of anxiety in relation to the objects in the environment. (2) The next stage comes when the child is able to differentiate self from other people, and feels anxiety in relation to the behaviour of people toward him. This is the basis of other-directed anxiety. (3) The child then learns to respond in terms of other people's expectations, and learns to react in terms of avoiding failure to meet these expectations. (4) Next, he begins to realize that he can 'please' and 'hurt' other people, and may feel sorrow or guilt. (5) Then, he becomes aware of his own position and status, and of 'wanting' to be something, e.g. good or kind. He 'may come to see the relation between the collection of tabooed acts about which he feels guilt, and the moral precepts he accepts. He may also come to demand that what is forbidden by authority tallies with the moral precepts he is being taught' (p. 120). (6) Later still, the child 'acquires the ability to consider alternative reasons and explanations and weigh up their merits. . . . In his thinking about people he will become able to consider the reasons behind their actions, and to appreciate that, like himself, they have needs, deficiencies and peculiarities' (ibid.). The 'conscience motive' may develop at this stage. (7) Finally, the child 'realizes that other people besides himself have aspirations, good and bad', and 'a new guilt factor may then emerge—a disquiet about loss of integrity, about failing and hurting oneself' (p. 121).

It is important to note Stephenson's explicit statement that 'with the attainment of successive levels of maturity, different conscience factors will not automatically emerge. Whether they do or not will depend upon the conditions affecting the child's relationships with others' (p. 121). It is not clear, however, whether Stephenson thinks it necessary to progress through *all* the earlier stages before reaching any given stage.

Bobroff's[39] stages of 'socialized thinking' correspond fairly closely to Bull's stages. His first stage, about the age of six years for normal and eight for retarded children, he describes as the stage of impulse, at which no distinction is made between rules and habits, games behaviour is self-oriented and situations are appraised entirely in subjective or egocentric terms. His second stage, from about eight years for normal children and ten years for retarded children, is characterized by the acceptance of the 'prescriptions of authority' as desirable, and there are some tentative attempts to evaluate situations in a more adult manner. However, there is little understanding of the roles, functions or feelings of authority figures, and of the reasons for the rules and expectations they provide. In Bobroff's third stage, from about ten years for normal children and twelve years for retarded children, the child shows that he is beginning to understand adult roles, shows some signs of being able to take a model's point of view as a basis of judgment and to seek values by reference to groups. The child often attempts to modify his feelings according to the requirements of others. However, sanctions are still mainly external, although there are some signs that internal control is developing. In the fourth stage, from about 12 years for normal children and 14 years for retarded children, the child has a better understanding of *reasons* for rules in terms of interrelations between groups of people, he has developed some hierarchy of values which facilitates internal control, he can better grasp adult opinions and attitudes, and can adapt his own desires to the requirements of group functioning without feeling that his individuality is thereby frustrated. As Bobroff suggests, the problem of moral education is the problem of balancing the need for self-expression against the need to conform and of balancing the need to foster originality against the need to ensure good adjustment.

All the schemes of stages of moral development which we have considered so far imply that development is linear, through a series of levels or stages. In general, it is assumed that progression through each stage is necessary to reach the next stage, although Stephenson, for example, does not make it clear whether he thinks it possible for any stage to be 'skipped'. Peck and Havighurst,[224] however, use a scheme which is *not* linear, but allows for two alternative paths of development. Basing their approach broadly on psychoanalytic principles, they propose five 'character types', each of which is 'conceived as the representative of a successive stage in the psychosocial development of the individual' (p. 3). The five character types can therefore be regarded as equivalent to stages, and are defined in 'motivational' terms. (1) The *Amoral* type is characteristic of infancy. Such a person, like an infant, is wholly self-centred, follows the immediate satisfaction of impulses, and sees other people only as a means to such satisfaction. 'In a real way,' say Peck and Havighurst, 'this is a picture of an infant, in its first year. Adults who show such a pattern are spoken of clinically as fixated at an infantile level. To the best of our knowledge, they act so because they have never learned to accept prohibitions or sanctions from others' (p. 5). (2) The *Expedient* type is characteristic of early childhood. Such a person is, like the amoral person, wholly self-centred, but is better able to take account of others, as possible means of facilitating, or as possible obstacles to, reaching satisfaction. 'External sanctions are always necessary ... to guide and control their behaviour, and keep it moral. In the absence of such controls, they immediately relapse into doing what they please, even if this involves shoving other children around, taking what they want, or otherwise gratifying their self-centred desires' (p. 6). At this point, Peck and Havighurst introduce the 'bifurcation' of their scheme. The third and fourth types are *both* regarded as characteristic of middle and late childhood. (3) The *Conforming* type accepts social restrictions and requirements as such, regarding conformity as good for its own sake. 'A conformist may frequently ignore chances for personal advantage, if they require departure from the prescribed rules of conduct. ... He defines 'right' as acting by the rules ... he has no abstract principles of honesty, responsibility, loyalty etc.' (p. 7). (4) The *Irrational-conscientious* type conforms 'to a code he has internalized and believes in. ... If he fails to live up to his own idea of what is moral, we call his anxiety "guilt" '. This is the outlook of the rigid moralist, 'characteristic of children who have accepted and internalized the parental rules, but who have not attained awareness that the rules are man-made and intended to serve a human, functional purpose' (*ibid.*). Perhaps the most interesting thing about Peck and Havighurst's scheme is that they regard this type of moral attitude as 'an alternative form of childlike morality, occurring at the same developmental level as the Conforming type, and thus parallel with it as far as concerns any measure of the maturity of character development' (p. 8). Thus, there would be two possible routes to the moral maturity of the 'Rational-altruistic' stage or orientation, one through the 'Conformist' stage, the other through the 'Irrational-conscientious' stage. The idea of a 'branching' rather than a linear pattern of development is an interesting one well worth exploring, although to date it has received little attention. (5) The *Rational-*

altruistic type is found mainly during adolescence and adulthood. 'Such a person not only has a stable set of moral principles by which he judges and directs his own action; he objectively assesses the results of an act in a given situation, and approves it on the grounds of whether or not it serves others as well as himself' (*ibid.*). In fact, the picture which Peck and Havighurst draw of the 'ideal type' of the 'Rational-altruistic' person is pretty well their idea of the perfect person. They say that their picture 'represents an ideal goal . . . to be sought, perhaps to be approached by adulthood, but probably never to be perfectly achieved and unfalteringly maintained by the best of mortals' (p. 9). All their types are, in fact, 'ideal types' in the sense that each type as they describe it is to be regarded as a 'perfect example', not as referring to actually existing persons.

Although the Peck and Havighurst classification may be regarded as a sequence of stages, since they regard each type as reflecting a particular stage of development, they themselves use their types rather as dimensions or 'components' of character. But they regard a person who functions predominantly at the level of any stage prior to his present developmental stage as being fixated at that stage of development. And it is interesting that in their own research they found it necessary to use eight rather than five 'type groups'—five groups corresponding to a clear predominance of any one type, plus three additional groups; (i) a 'CEA' group in which there is more or less equal predominance of amoral, expedient and conforming orientations, coming between the moral and expedient groups, (ii) an 'IAE' group in which there is more or less equal predominance of Irrational-conscientious, amoral and expedient orientations, coming between the expedient and conforming groups, (iii) a 'near-R' group in which there is an appreciable but not predominant incidence of rational-altruistic ratings. This eight-point scale they then called a scale of *maturity of character*. Scores on this scale were obtained, in their research, from ratings based on a considerable range of data, including interviews and various kinds of tests. It should, however, be noted that although they use eight 'type groups' for their scale of maturity of character, they do not suggest that the three 'mixed groups' correspond to any *stages* of development. Peck and

Havighurst's scheme, in fact, points up rather well the difference between a sequence of stages and a dimensional or component analysis. Their scheme is nevertheless based, as we have said, on concepts related to stages of development. The main use which Peck and Havighurst make of their type groups is to relate maturity of character to other variables—personality variables, family variables and social variables like social class, school background, and so on. In particular, they found that maturity of character ratings were positively related, especially to measures of ego strength, superego strength, and friendliness, and negatively related to a measure of the predominance of feelings of guilt and hostility. Although moral variables are practically certainly related to some qualities of personality, it is difficult to know how far *measures* of both kinds of variables are independent, and therefore how one should interpret such observed relationships. It seems very likely, for example, that the kind of things on which one based judgments of moral character and on which one based judgments of ego strength would both include the same kind of things. In an important sense, many qualities of personality may include aspects which are also aspects of moral character.

There seems therefore to be a fair amount of agreement among the 'stage' theorists we have mentioned as to the nature of the general process of moral development through different stages. At the most general level, we have agreement that development proceeds from an early amoral stage to a mature stage of moral autonomy, through an intermediate stage or intermediate stages where the dominant influence is that of other people, whether authority figures or peers. Different authors differ somewhat as to the number of stages regarded as necessary. For example, Kay[154] suggests that perhaps only three stages are really necessary—the amoral, the premoral and the moral—while Stephenson proposes seven stages; the most popular number of stages is four. In addition, there are differences in the content or definition of the stages of development by different writers. These, however, are relatively minor differences, and the amount of agreement is quite impressive.

Piaget is well-known for his advocacy of 'stages' in child development, and his classic work, *The Moral Judgment of the Child*,[227] represents his application of 'stage' thinking to the development of moral judgment. Piaget's main argument, like that of other 'stage' theorists, is that the development of moral thinking involves a progression through a sequence of stages; each of Piaget's stages is characterized by thinking of a particular 'quality'. For Piaget, the most important aspect of this development lies in advance from an earlier stage where social relations are characterized by, and are seen to be characterized by, heteronomy or constraint, an attitude of one-sided respect on the part of the child for his elders, and acceptance of rules as sacred, to a later stage where social relations are characterized by co-operation and an attitude of mutual respect, and acceptance of rules as binding by mutual agreement rather than by any intrinsic compelling or constraining quality of rules as immutably given by authority. The moral attitudes associated with these two types of social relations Piaget refers to as 'heteronomous' and 'autonomous' morality respectively.

Piaget works out his approach in three 'areas'. (1) 'The rules of the game'—how rules in games come to be accepted, and how children regard these rules. (2) 'Moral realism', or the 'tendency ... to regard duty and the value attaching to it as self-subsistent and independent of the mind, as imposing itself regardless of the circumstances in which the individual may find himself' (p. 106). (3) The idea of justice, and the development from 'retributive justice' to 'distributive justice', defined by 'equality' or 'equity'.

(*1*) *The rules of the game*. Piaget documents his analysis here by reference to the game of marbles as played by Swiss children, and claims, on the basis of his observations and questioning of children, that there is 'a certain correspondence (not simple but yet quite definable) between children's judgments about rules and their practice of these same rules'. (p. 111). He distinguishes, however, between the application of rules and the *consciousness* of rules.

(a) *Application of rules*. Here, Piaget indicates four stages of development.

(i) Up to about three years of age. This he calls the stage of 'motor behaviour', when the child develops habits or 'individual rules' only. (ii) Roughly between the ages of three and seven years of age, when the child begins to take an interest in the rule-regulated behaviour of older children and want to play with them but shows no proper appreciation of the nature and function of the rules. Piaget describes this stage as 'egocentric'. He says, 'Egocentrism in so far as it means confusion of the ego and the external world, and egocentrism in so far as it means lack of co-operation, constitute one and the same phenomenon. So long as the child does not dissociate his ego from the suggestions coming from the physical and from the social world, he cannot cooperate, for in order to cooperate one must be conscious of one's ego and situate it in relation to thought in general. And in order to become conscious of one's ego, it is necessary to liberate oneself from the thought and will of others. The coercion exercised by the adult or the older child is therefore inseparable from the unconscious egocentrism of the very young child' (p. 87). By coercion, of course, Piaget does not mean simply physical coercion, but refers to the fact that the older person's authority imposes itself of necessity upon the 'egocentric' child. By the end of the egocentric stage, i.e. by about six years of age, the child's attitude to rules is that they are something sacred and immutable which come from without. (iii) Roughly between the ages of seven and ten years, when the child develops a genuine social sense and acceptance of common rules through appreciation of the need for cooperation. (iv) From about ten years of age, children show that they have mastered the rules of the game, 'and even take pleasure in juridicial discussions whether of principle or merely of proce-
G

dure, which may at times arise out of the points in dispute' (p. 33). The difference between the third and fourth stages Piaget refers to as only one of degree. In the fourth stage there is interest in the rules for their own sake.

(b) *Consciousness of rules.* Here, Piaget distinguishes *three* stages.

(i) Up to the age of about five years, the child may either have purely motor rules, or apprehend rules 'unconsciously' as factors in his environment but not as being constraining upon him.

(ii) From about five years until about ten years of age, children develop a kind of respect for the 'given' and sacred character of rules, which are endowed with the same kind of respect and authority as parents, other adults and older children. The fact that the child's definition of a rule, and the way he applies it, may be changing and arbitrary, is not incompatible with his attitude to a rule at any time as indisputably given, but is due to the young child's lack of organized memory and his inability to 'differentiate between the impulses of his personal fancy and the rules imposed on him from above' (p. 49). Adult constraint, in Piaget's view, 'is always the ally of childish egocentrism. . . . With regard to moral rules, the child submits more or less completely in intention to the rules laid down for him, but these, remaining as it were external to the subject's conscience, do not really transform his conduct. That is why the child looks upon rules as sacred though he does not really put them into practice' (p. 53). Towards the age of about seven or eight, we have a degree of genuine cooperation developing which, however, is not sufficient to displace wholly the attitude of mystical respect to authority. By the end of this period the child typically has learned, by cooperation, 'the existence of possible variations in the use of rules, and he knows, therefore, that the actual rules are recent and have been made by children. But on the other hand, he believes in the absolute and intrinsic truth of rules' (p. 55). The respect for the rules of the game at this stage is 'inherited from the constraint that has not yet been eliminated by cooperation' (p. 56). It takes some time for cooperation in action to bring about the proper corresponding attitude, since thought always lags behind action.

(iii) During the third stage, from the age of about ten years, the rules of the game cease to be regarded as sacred, externally imposed laws, and come to be viewed as the result of free interaction and reciprocity between equals, deserving to be respected because they are the product of mutual agreement. At this point, says Piaget, 'we can actually put our finger upon the conjunction of cooperation and autonomy, which follows upon the conjunction of egocentrism and constraint' (p. 61).

Thus, in his discussion of the rules of the game, we see Piaget's conception of the nature of rules emerging. There are three kinds of rules, (a) the *motor* rule, (b) the *coercive* rule and (c) the *rational* rule. (a) The motor rule is relatively asocial and arises out of habit. It results from the perception of regularity and repetition, but includes no element of the obligation or necessity of the real rule. (b) The coercive rule is associated with unilateral respect and constraint and also with egocentrism in the sense of the child's inability to discriminate between his own self and his social environment. (c) The rational rule is associated with mutual respect and reciprocity, and with autonomy in the sense of the child's awareness of the boundaries between himself and others, and his understanding of others and an ability to make himself understood by them. The distinction between constraint and cooperation is indeed the corner stone of Piaget's whole theory of moral development. It will be clear that, in Freudian terms, Piaget lays much more stress on ego factors than on superego factors.

Although Piaget does give ages for his developmental stages, he does not stick strictly to these ages himself, stressing the sequence of development rather than age as the important thing. Indeed, he is careful to remind us that the ages are likely to be influenced by cultural factors. In a footnote, he says, 'We take this opportunity of reminding the reader of what has not been sufficiently emphasized in our earlier books, viz. that most of our research has been carried out on children from the poorer parts of Geneva. In different surroundings the age averages would certainly have been different' (p. 37n.). Elsewhere in his writings, for example in *The Child's Conception of the World*,[226] Piaget also indicates that he does not regard development as being too closely tied to chronological age, but believes that it is the sequence of development which should be more or less invariant, even although development may be fluctuating, with both leaps ahead and regressions.

(2) *Moral Realism.* According to Piaget, moral realism is characteristic of childhood up to the age of about nine years. He refers to three aspects of moral realism. (a) What is good is what is in obedience to adult rules or adult instructions. (b) The letter rather than the spirit of the rule must be followed. (c) Objective responsibility—responsibility for actions is viewed not in accordance with the motive which has prompted them but in terms of their exact conformity with established rules' (p. 107). Actions will be evaluated more in terms of the consequences of the actions as defined by adults as good or bad than in terms of the intentions of the actor. In fact, in his discussion of moral realism, Piaget is largely concerned with the question of consequences versus intentions.

It is important, in order to understand Piaget, to realize that for him, moral realism is closely related to moral constraint, and moral constraint to intellectual constraint. Piaget felt that the same *basic* principles applied to both intellectual and moral development, although the various stages of each did not coincide. He writes, 'Moral constraint is closely akin to intellectual constraint, and the strictly literal character which the child tends to ascribe to rules received from without bears . . . a close resemblance to the attitudes he adopts with regard to language and the intellectual realities imposed upon him by the adult. We can make use of this analogy to fix our nomenclature and shall speak of *moral realism* to designate on the plane of judgments of value what corresponds to 'nominal realism' and even verbal or conceptual realism on the plane of theoretical reasoning. Not only this, but just as realism in general (in the same sense in which we have used the word in our previous books, see *The Child's View of the World,* first part) results both from a confusion between subjective and objective (hence from egocentrism) and from the intellectual constraint of the adult, so also does moral realism result from the intersection of these two kinds of causes' (pp. 105–106).

In his studies of moral realism, Piaget is concerned with how children *evaluate* actions and the basis for these evaluations. The method which Piaget uses is that of telling children short stories concerning transgressions and asking them to say in which of two stories the transgression was worse, this method being supplemented by questions. Piaget is fully aware of the difficulties that such a method presents—for example, the possibilities that children answer as they think they are expected to answer, that their answers to hypothetical test questions do not correspond to their judgments of the same situations in real life, that judgments do not correspond to actions; but he thinks that the study of the judgments which children make in hypothetical situations should be of great interest in at least suggesting the nature of their moral thinking. In discussing the more general question of the relationship of verbalizations to action, Piaget writes, 'Is man merely a maker of phrases that have no relation to his real actions, or is the need to formulate part of his very being?' (p. 109). And he feels that in his study of the game of marbles, he did find 'a certain correspondence between judgments and the practice of rules'. The stories which he uses are concerned with 'objective responsibility', and deal with clumsiness, stealing and lying. In the case of clumsiness, the stories to be compared are about children who do a relatively large amount of damage by accident or with the best intentions, and children who do a relatively small amount of damage while doing things they know they should not be doing, or on purpose. In the case of stealing, the comparisons are between stealing motivated by selfish greed and stealing motivated by good intentions. For these two sets of stories, Piaget reports that evaluation by consequences and evaluation by motives exist side by side up to the age of ten, and children are not always consistent in their preference for one or the other type of judgment. 'But', he says, 'broadly speaking, it cannot be denied that the notion of objective responsibility diminishes as the child grows older' (p. 120). No clear case of judgment by objective responsibility occurred after the age of ten. The material was not suitable for children under the age of six, and so the age range is from about six to ten years. Some of even the youngest children, Piaget found, did in fact judge in terms of intentions. He thinks that the 'objective responsibility' attitude is occasioned by adult constraint, in the sense that at least some adults *apply* their sanctions in such a way as to indicate or suggest objective responsibility, e.g. a mother who has 15 cups broken is likely to be angrier than one who has only one broken, other things being equal, and perhaps even independently of the offending child's intentions. The adult rules, whether imposed by admonition, by punishment or by signs of displeasure, are for the child 'categorical obligations'. Piaget is careful to point out here, however, that 'those parents who try to give their children a moral education based on intention, achieve very early results, as is shown by current observation and the few examples of subjective responsibility we were able to note at six or seven' (p. 130). The importance of emphasizing inten‑ tions is also stressed by Aronfreed[14] who refers to the role of avoidance responses which became conditioned to intentions as 'symbolic' cues.

In the matter of lying, Piaget asks children to evaluate the act of lying in several pairs of stories; in each pair, one story contains a 'smaller' lie told deliberately to deceive, and a 'larger' lie told without any bad intentions. For the younger children, there was a strong tendency for the bigger lie to be judged worse, another example of thinking in terms of objective responsibility. Piaget also refers to younger children who 'look upon lying as naughty because it is punished, and if it were not punished, no guilt would attach to it', which he regards as objective responsibility 'in its purest form' (p. 165). Again, judgment in terms of intentions became more frequent about the age of nine. The older child‑ ren, of ten to twelve, generally viewed lying as bad on the grounds that truthfulness is necessary for fruitful cooperation and mutual agreement and trust. There seem to be three stages in attitude to lying. In the first, it is regarded as wrong because it is punished; in the second, it is regarded as wrong in itself, while in the third it is regarded as wrong because it undermines trust.

Piaget feels that, although his inquiries into responsibility did not indicate 'any stages properly so called', yet they suggested 'processes whose final terms were quite distinct from one another' (p. 171), and that these processes essentially reflect principles of unilateral respect and mutual respect, thus leading to conclu‑

sions confirming those from the study of the game of marbles. Thus, Piaget suggests that moral realism is due partly to the intrinsic nature of the child's mental development and partly to the way in which children are treated by adults. Moral realism is closely associated with unilateral respect or heteronomy, but for Piaget realism is not a phenomenon distinctive of the moral sphere, as we have already seen. On the contrary, it is associated with intellectual realism as shown, for example, in the child's tendency to draw things, not as he sees them, but as he *knows* they really are. It is an important aspect of Piaget's thinking that 'physical regularity is not dissociated from moral obligation and social rule' (p. 186) and that for the child, both physical and moral rules are part of a general world order.

(*3*) *The idea of justice.* Piaget here starts with a consideration of punishment. There are, he says, two ways of looking at punishment; one may regard punishment retributively, as the proper expiatory consequence of wrongdoing; or one can regard punishment as essentially not a matter of expiation, but a matter of seeing that the transgressor puts right any wrong he does, or himself carries the consequences of his wrongdoing. Again Piaget uses the technique of story-telling. In these stories, a child does something wrong, and the subject is asked to say how the child in the story should be punished. Then three alternative forms of punishment are suggested, and the child has to say which is the most severe. He is then questioned to find whether he judges the punishment in terms of its severity or according to some other standard. The punishments suggested are either 'expiatory punishments' or 'punishments by reciprocity' (p. 203). For a sample of about 100 children, Piaget found that there was a definite increase in the proportion of punishments by reciprocity between the ages of six to seven years and eight to ten years. Approximately one third of the responses of the youngest group were reciprocity punishments, as against four fifths for the oldest group. As Piaget himself admits, the numerical values should not be taken too seriously, but the results point to a marked shift from expiation to reciprocity with increasing age. As Piaget also admits, however, when children are themselves required to suggest an appropriate punishment, they generally select an expiatory one, and often a very severe one. Children choosing expiatory punishments tended to think that the *fairest* punishment would be the most severe. Piaget's view of reciprocity may also be criticized on the grounds of its inclusiveness, since it covers a whole *range* of punishments from the primitive one of doing to the offender exactly as he has done to others ('an eye for an eye') to simply ensuring that the offender realizes that he has infringed the rules of mutual obligation, or 'broken the bonds of solidarity' (p 207).

The next question considered by Piaget is the question of 'collective' or 'communicable' responsibility. Once again, he used the story-telling technique. Situations were described involving transgression by children, in which the adult concerned (a) punished the whole group without bothering to find out who was the guilty child, (b) wanted to find the guilty child but could not, since he did not own up and the group would not give him away, and (c) wanted to find the guilty child but could not because nobody knew who he was. The children were then asked whether it was fair or not for the whole group to be punished. In situation (a), all Piaget's children, both younger and older, thought it unfair for the group to be punished without any concern for who had actually committed the offence. Thus, here, no tendency to collective responsibility was found. In situation (b), both approval and disapproval were found among both younger and older children, but on the whole, younger children were more inclined to think that all the group should be punished because they all knew who the offender was, and shared his guilt by not denouncing him, as duty to the adult required, while older children were more inclined to think that group punishment was fair because, by deciding to shield the offender the members of the group had recognized their group membership and solidarity. In situation (c), the younger children thought that everyone should be punished because there must be punishment after transgression, even if the innocent suffered as well as the guilty. All children over the age of eight or nine years thought collective punishment in situation (c) more unjust in situation (c) than in situation (b).

Piaget concludes that, where group punishment is regarded as fair, this is 'not because the group is responsible as a whole for the faults of one of its members, but simply because the guilty one is unknown and that there must be a punishment at all costs. The fundamental fact in these cases is not the feeling of solidarity of the group, but of the necessity of punishment' (p. 242). We may wonder whether Piaget was indeed right on this point, and whether he did not underestimate the real feeling of group solidarity.

Piaget then turns to what he calls 'immanent justice'. By 'immanent justice' he means the belief in 'automatic punishments which emanate from things themselves' (p. 250), a belief which he believes to be characteristically held by young children. Again with the story technique, he finds belief in immanent justice to decline from the age of six, when he found about four fifths of the children taking this view, to age 12, when only one third believed in immanent justice. Once again, Piaget thinks the belief in immanent justice to be associated with the idea of a general world order. The belief 'originates in a transference to things of feelings acquired under the influence of adult constraint' (p. 260), and tends to disappear partly as the child's intellect develops, but partly in consequence of his realization of the imperfections of adults and their justice, which takes him in the direction of a more cooperative attitude. Thus once more, we find Piaget emphasizing the dichotomy between 'adult constraint' on the one hand and 'cooperation' on the other.

Piaget also compares 'retributive justice' with 'distributive justice'. 'Retributive justice' refers to the belief that each should be rewarded strictly according to his deserts, i.e. according to how 'good' or 'naughty' he may have been, 'distributive justice' to the idea that equality of treatment should often be the norm, e.g. in the distribution of cake. Piaget found that 'for the little ones, the necessity of punishment is so strong that the question of equality does not even arise. For the older children, distributive justice outweighs retribution' (p. 265). Similarly, when authority and equality are pitted against one another, younger children tend to feel that the authority of their parents is absolute, and that whatever they say must be right, whereas older children feel that equality should prevail over authority. Children 'in between', as it were, may accept the parents' right to obedience without acceptance of the justice of their impositions. The oldest and most 'advanced' children apply what Piaget calls 'equity', which goes beyond equality to take account of the particular situation in which each individual finds himself. For example, 'the special relations of affection existing between parent and child should be taken into account' (p. 282).

Thus, from his study of justice, Piaget distinguishes three broad stages in the development of the sense of justice. (i) Up to the age of seven or eight, what is just is what is enjoined by adult authority. (ii) Between eight and eleven, equality becomes the governing principle of justice. (iii) After about eleven, equalitarianism is replaced by equity, taking account of individual circumstances, e.g. respect due to age or previous service rendered. Thus, Piaget is led to his view of the importance for the development of the sense of justice, of social relations and cooperation between peers, although the example of adults, and genuine reciprocal relationships between adults and children may also be important contributing factors, especially with older children. It is interesting to see that Piaget, like Freud, admitted that a great many adults never attained to the more highly developed forms of morality—all, according to Piaget, 'who have not succeeded in setting autonomy of conscience above social prejudice and the written law' (p. 319).

The developmental stages which Piaget finds in his three 'areas' thus do not correspond, and there is no *single,* simple scheme of developmental stages. There is, however, as we have already indicated, the major *underlying* developmental progression from a 'heteronomous' to an 'autonomous' attitude or orientation.

Piaget's theory, then, lays stress on the importance of interaction with peers, and, unlike Freudian theory, does not regard relations with parents as crucial except in the negative sense, that parents, by their authoritarian treatment of their children, may discourage the emergence of true morality through cooperation. The theory also emphasizes (though in fairness one must say, by no means exclusively) the spontaneous development of the child and his active role in relation to his social environment, unlike learning theory, which lays major emphasis on the experiences which make their impact upon him. And it is primarily, indeed almost exclusively, a cognitive and 'rationalist' theory, differing in this way from psychoanalytic theory, which stresses emotional factors, and learning theory, which stresses both emotional and behavioural aspects. We shall presently review research which has been stimulated by Piaget's theory, and see how far such research has tended to support the theory. First, however, we shall look at a number of general criticisms of the theory which have been made by various writers, most recently by Bull[55] and earlier by Bloom.[37]

(1) Piaget unwarrantably ignores the non-cognitive, orectic element in moral development. This point is well taken. However, it is only fair to say that Piaget *ignores* rather than discounts emotional factors, probably because of his primary interest in cognitive processes. (2) Piaget ignores the processes of modelling or imitation, and of 'identification' with parents, and the 'intro- jection' of parental values, and thus underestimates the import- ance of *internalization* of adult values in favour of the *discovery* of values in interaction with peers. This criticism also seems justifi- able, although it may be said that Piaget's emphasis on interaction with peers represents a useful corrective against the possibility of an *overemphasis* on the role of parents, especially of early parental influence. (3) Piaget overemphasizes the extent to which parental authority acts in a negative way, restricting or imped- ing development, and underestimates the positive contribution of parental and other authority. Bull mentions that many of his subjects referred to their parents as having 'drummed into them' principles or values which they later accepted as their own. Piaget might claim that such principles were accepted by the children as their own in spite of, rather than because of, their parents. For Bull, however, as for many other writers, discipline imposed from without is a necessary preparation for self-discipline or autonomy. This seems a very reasonable view. The merit of Piaget's position, as Bull readily concedes, is to emphasize that continuing authoritarianism is not the best way to encourage the self-reliant, moral decision-making which constitutes the core of

genuine moral autonomy. However, we need not go to the opposite extreme. Piaget himself allows that parents may *contribute* to development, but only in so far as they emphasize 'equality' and 'cooperation'; and Piaget seems to stress interaction with peers because the parent-child relationship *cannot* be one of *genuine* equality, since this relationship is inevitably characterized by unilateral respect. Only grudgingly and in passing does Piaget grant any role to parental authority. 'Thus adult authority' he writes, 'although perhaps it constitutes a necessary moment in the moral evolution of the child, is not sufficient to create a sense of justice' (p. 319). (4) Piaget, in devoting so much attention to contrasting the heteronomous, constraint-dominated attitude of the younger child with the cooperative attitude of the older child, ignores the stage of 'anomy' *preceding* the heteronomous stage. A similar criticism is made by Kohlberg.[162] It is true that practically all Piaget's attention is devoted to children between the ages of six and 12 years, although he does indicate his awareness of earlier development in his discussion of the 'rules of the game', when he refers to the earlier two stages as (a) that at which the child develops habits or 'individual' rules only, and (b) that at which he is aware of other children as potential playmates, but has no sense of the proper social nature of rules. (5) Piaget, by not extending his studies beyond the age of about twelve years, failed to come to grips with the development of *true* autonomy, which only properly emerges during adolescence. In Bull's view, Piaget assumed that the cooperation or reciprocity would tend, from the child's very nature, to lead on through 'equity' to a stage of genuine autonomy characterized by love and humanity rather than by mere reciprocity, but in fact produces little or no evidence for this assumption. Bull finds 'reciprocity' in the sense of giving back what one receives, to persist up to the age of 17. However, Piaget does not require that everyone should necessarily develop in the direction of equity and true autonomy. Durkin[70] has also suggested, on the basis of her own results, that if Piaget had continued his researches with older subjects, he would have found 'strict reciprocity' declining again. This, however, would not seem to be truly at variance with Piaget's position when, for instance, he asserts that strict returning of blow for blow represents an unstable equilibrium. The real grounds for criticism seem to be that Piaget simply *assumes* that development *must tend* to occur toward the 'stable equilibrium' of humanity and forgiveness. What Piaget does not tell us, as Bull indicates, is how this takes place. (6) Piaget is given to ignoring or reinterpreting unwarrantedly data which do not fit his theory. For example, writing of the three reasons which Piaget found given by children for not cheating—that it is against authority, that it is against the principles of equality, and that 'it is useless' or 'one learns nothing'—Bull refers to Piaget's 'astonishing rejection of this third type of response as being no more than the reproduction of adult sermons'.[55] (p. 139). Certainly, this seems to be an arbitrary and cavalier procedure, though one might also doubt Bull's suggestion that such responses may in fact represent the beginnings of genuine autonomy. It is hard to see in what sense a judgment of 'one always gets caught' can be regarded as even an incipient autonomous moral judgment. May it not simply reflect an appreciation of the fact that, in general, cheating does not *pay?*—in other words, reflects the purely pragmatic ethic that honesty is the best *policy?* (7) Piaget does not give sufficient attention to individual differences or to sex, social class or cultural differences. This is a perfectly justifiable criticism, and once again, it can be said that Piaget ignored rather than discounted such differences. In fact, as we have seen, he does specifically allow that his results would have been affected if his studies had been carried out under different conditions. However, the crucial point is not whether there might have been differences between different groups or individuals in the rate or extent of development, but whether, under different conditions, Piaget would have found results which enabled him to maintain the main structure of his theory. (8) Piaget virtually ignores the whole question of moral conflicts, their possible effects and different possible modes of resolving them. This point was specifically made by Bloom[37] in 1959, and seems a legitimate point. As we shall see, Kohlberg makes more allowance for moral conflict and its effects. (9) Piaget's notion of 'reciprocity' is too wide. He includes, for example, under the heading of 'reciprocity punishments', returning a blow given, *and* censure intended to indicate transgression of group standards, *and* making good the damage one has done. In fact, Piaget seems to include as 'reciprocity punishments' simply *all* kinds of punishment which are not 'expiatory'. This criticism again seems a sound one. Acceptance of such different forms of punishment may reflect very different kinds of underlying psychological processes, and important differences may be obscured by including everything under the general heading of 'reciprocity'.

A considerable volume of research has been generated by Piaget's thinking on moral development, and most of his ideas have been put to some kind of test—some to more, or more adequate, tests than others.

(*1*) *Moral realism—intentionality.* Piaget's claim that the basis of judgment shifts with increasing age from a consideration of consequences (moral realism) to a consideration of intentions has received a great deal of support. Lerner[177] and Macrae[191] in America, and more recently Loughran[179] in England all found 'intentionality' to increase with age. Macrae, however, found that the 'intention-consequences' factor was unrelated to a 'retributive-reciprocity of punishment' factor and to a 'perspective' factor, and that none of these three factors was related to parental authority as assessed by specially constructed measures, thus casting doubt on whether 'development' in terms of Piaget's measures is a more or less unitary process, and suggesting that one may, in fact, have relatively independent dimensions of moral judgment which are all age-related.

Boehm and Nass[43] confirmed approximately Piaget's finding that regard for intentions acquired predominance about the age of nine, but their American children seem to have been rather more advanced than Piaget's, since *most* of the American children of nine years of age gave 'intentional' responses, compared with only 50 per cent of the Swiss children. Their results also showed considerable variations between stories, thus drawing attention to the specific as distinct from the general factors involved in judgments in different situations. Boehm,[40] with children of from six to nine years of age, noted that academically gifted children made the change to intentionality earlier than less gifted or less fortunate children. She also found the gifted children to be more independent of adults, but unfortunately did not find maturity of moral judgment related to independence of adults. In a further article, Boehm[4] found that American children in Catholic schools were more 'intentionality minded' at an earlier age than children in state schools. Whether this greater maturity would have been reflected in spontaneous judgments of 'real' situations is another matter, and it also seems doubtful whether such a difference would have continued to appear as the children grew up. A further interesting point made by Boehm in this article is that *within* the Catholic schools, the advantage of the academically gifted children did not appear. One can think of various possible explanations, but without further information this would be no more than speculation. However, Boehm's work does at least draw attention to the importance of experience—something which Piaget never in fact denied, though he was not primarily interested in the effects of differential experience.

Medinnus[197] was concerned with objective responsibility and intentionality as shown in children's attitudes to lying. Using stories taken from Piaget, Medinnus had four judges classify children's responses according to criteria relevant to Piaget's three stages of development in attitude to lying (cf. p. 198). He did find some evidence for an age progression, but found only a relatively small number of responses (10 out of 55) at the first stage among his youngest subjects (six years of age) and only a relatively small number of responses (15 out of 36) at the third stage among his oldest subjects (12 years of age). After a closer examination of the children's answers, Medinnus classified them into 'a number of fairly specific meaningful themes' (six in all), as follows. (a) You get punished. (b) It is naughty; it isn't right; God, Jesus or parents don't like it. (c) You get into trouble. (d) You hurt others. (e) You don't get any place; It just leads to more lies. (f) You always get found out anyway. He then grouped themes (a) and (b) together because they appeared to be based on the idea that lying is wrong because it is forbidden and results in punishment, and the last four themes, (c) to (f) together because they all had some notion of consequences which might follow from lying. When responses were classified in this way a clear age trend was found indicating an increasing concern with consequences and a decreasing tendency to view lying as wrong only because it is contrary to prohibitions imposed by adults. It is interesting that the answers given by Zarncke's[282] German children to the question, 'Why mustn't we tell lies?' seem to follow very much the same pattern as those of Medinnus. Zarncke remarks that moral values were seldom referred to by her subjects, who ranged in age from five to fourteen years, and that many of the children seemed to have no idea at all of moral principles. However, even at the age of nine, she did find such answers as 'When once you've told a lie, nobody believes you again'. She seems to think, probably rightly, that this represents a concern for consequences likely to be a nuisance to oneself rather than an appreciation of the requirements for the maintenance of an order of mutual trust.

Caruso[59] used picture material to present pairs of situations to children of six years of age, so as to minimize the importance of purely verbal understanding of stories. He found that an appreciable number of his six-year-olds were already able to employ the criterion of intentionality. With older children of from eight to 15, he presented a range of stories about children's transgressions in which the children had to say, for each story, whether the child in the story was naughty or not. He found a steady increase in the use of intentionality as a basis for judging 'not naughty', with increasing age, though there were differences between stories. The younger children, of eight years of age, seldom failed to judge the fictitious child naughty. When, however, the children were asked to say which was the *more* naughty of two transgressions differing in the nature of the underlying motive (e.g. 'James wanted to give something to a poor man and he stole a slice of bread and butter. Louis stole a slice of bread and butter because he was very greedy. Which was the naughtier?'), three quarters of even the youngest children used intention as a criterion and, although there was an increase from 76 per cent to 87 per cent between age eight and age nine, there was no further age increase. This indicates that by the age of eight, most children were at least capable of *understanding* the significance of intentions. But here, the children were being asked to make a simple discrimination in respect of intention. They were not being asked in such a way as to allow for *spontaneous* use of intentionality, nor was the judgment a complex one requiring the comparison of different possible criteria. Caruso also gave 'double-barrelled' tests ('tests à double dimension'), in which the transgression was greater when the intention was worthy, or where there were bad intentions but no actual transgression (e.g. 'To please his mother, who was ill, John said he got five good marks whereas in fact, he had had one bad mark. Peter said he got a good mark when in fact he hadn't, and he said it to boast. Which was the naughtier?') These were similar to the items used by Piaget. The results again showed a steady increase from age eight to age 15, from roughly one half to something above 80 per cent. In this case, as Caruso points out, the child is being asked to *compare* 'a deplorable result obtained *without* any evil intention with a *less serious* result obtained with evil intentions,' (p. 155) and he remarks that 'the results show the difficulty that the youngest subjects have in making a clear choice' (*ibid.*). This distinction between the simpler and the more complex kinds of situation has been further investigated by Crowley[64] and by Turner,[268] as we shall see.

In recent years, Kugelmass and Breznitz have published an interesting series of articles. In a study[169] of Israeli children of 11 to 17 years of age, they found a very similar increase of intentionality with age among city children brought up in their families and in Kibbutz children brought up in communal settlements. If anything, the city children tended to score rather higher for intentionality, thus failing to confirm the hypothesis that children more dependent on peer-group relations should show greater intentionality. The authors refer to support from Kohlberg's observation[163] that there appears to be no association between intentionality and peer-group participation. They think it possible that intentionality has a stronger cognitive basis than other areas of moral judgment, and is therefore more likely to be strongly age-linked and less likely to be affected by relational factors which do not directly involve cognitive components. Breznitz and Kugelmass[49] somewhat refine Piaget's rather crude schema by suggesting four stages in the development of intentionality. (1) Preverbalized usage. At this early stage, a child may indeed use intentionality as a criterion, but he is unable to *say clearly* on what basis he is judging. His use of intentions as a criterion seems to be limited to situations which closely resemble his own experiences. (2) Verbalization of principle. At this stage a child *can* specify the criterion he is using and though he does not yet apply it systematically, it is now potentially applicable to all situations. (3) Recall of principle. The child can now recall and phrase the principle of intentionality spontaneously, thus greatly increasing the chances of its being applied over a wide range of instances. (4) Refined application of principle. By this stage, the child is able to use the principle in a complex and highly differentiated way. Obviously, not all children progress through all four stages.

In a third article, Kugelmass and Breznitz[170] suggest that intentionality increases slowly between the years of 11 and 14, fairly rapidly from 14 to 17, and then less steeply again. Obviously cognitive and intellectual factors must be important here, and Kugelmass and Breznitz suggest that the cognitive ability to abstract principles is crucial. They have also drawn up a *scale* of verbal items for the measurement of intentionality. They presented their children with variations of a transgression, constructed so as to differ in intentionality and results (including carelessness, insanity, deliberate planning on the intentions side, and killing, wounding or hurting another person on the consequences side). The children were asked to judge the extent to which they thought the actor in each situation should be blamed, on a four-point scale. Items were then subjected to a Guttman scale analysis, and it was found possible to form a genuine scale which was the basis of future measurement. While this more sophisticated method has considerable advantages, it is true that it introduces an even more restricted and artificial experimental situation than Piaget used. If this has any effect, then it would mean that even greater care should be taken in extending conclusions beyond the experimental situation.

Bandura and McDonald,[24] who also find intentionality or 'subjective responsibility' to be linked to age, question Piaget's basic interpretation. Since they found that subjective orientation increased *gradually* with age, and that children at all ages showed both types of response, they concluded that Piaget's ideas of sequential stages was invalidated. However, Piaget does not suggest that the transition from one stage to the other is abrupt and discontinuous—on the contrary, he states that development is gradual, but that nevertheless, *qualitative differences* between earlier and later stages can be seen. Nor does he suggest that when the later stage is reached, the behaviour characteristic of this stage entirely replaces that of the earlier stage. What is essential in his view is that there must be a point at which the *later* forms are not found. If some responses of a more 'mature' kind are found at *all* ages studied, one might suggest that children young enough not to show any such responses have simply not been included. Bandura and McDonald, however, finding that children's moral judgments can readily be influenced by the example of adult models who express judgments contrary to the children's own 'dominant orientation', suggest that children *acquire* their judgment response tendencies simply by imitating models. Once again, Piaget would certainly not wish to deny the influence of adult example, particularly with younger children, though he would emphasize interaction with other children. But he would stress the developing capacity of the child to assimilate and actively accommodate to environmental events in an understanding way, rather than the nature of these events themselves, or the relatively non-constructive act of *imitating*. As far as the experimental modification of judgment is concerned, we do not know from Bundura and McDonald how genuinely and enduringly the subjects' judgment tendencies may have been affected. The changes observed by them may possibly represent little more than superficial conforming without genuine acceptance, in situations involving rather specific responses.

Crowley[64] has also experimented in influencing the judgment of young children by 'training' them in the 'labelling' of items in terms of intentions. He found that training in labelling was quite effective, and that its effectiveness was not increased by a discussion of the principles and reasons involved. Crowley himself is inclined to view his results as indicating modification at the level of specific response tendencies, without implying that there *are* no deeper-reaching processes of development. He found that children rarely verbalized spontaneously the underlying principle, and that children trained in 'intention labelling' of non-moral stories did not show much transference of the concept of intentionality to moral stories. Crowley thinks that the good 'learning' of the children in his experiment suggests that frequently, children may fail to use intentionality as a criterion, not because they are *unable* to grasp the significance of intentions, but because they fail to *focus on it* when a striking competing cue in the form of extent of damage is present. Crowley's observations fit quite well with the view of Breznitz and Kugelmass.[49] For them, it is the ability to recall and formulate principles spontaneously which leads to their general application. If this is not developed, then judgments are likely to represent specific and easily influenced response tendencies.

Crowley's point that stories like those which Piaget used to study intentionality may make development or change difficult to interpret because the child is in fact being faced with variations in *both* intentions and consequences together, a point also raised by Caruso,[59] is further developed by Turner,[268] as reported by Lunzer and Morris.[180] Turner argues that in Piaget's story of the two children, the first of whom broke many cups but with good intentions while the second broke only one cup but did so deliberately, we have, in the first case (child A), good intentions *plus* catastrophic results, and in the case of the second child (child B), bad intentions plus bad but much less disastrous results. To arrive at an *overall* judgment that child B is the more blameworthy, the results of child A must be more than balanced by his good intentions, while the less serious result of child B is more than balanced by his evil intentions, and these two positions must be compared. Turner goes on to predict an *intermediate* stage in development. The youngest children would not be able to take both intentions and consequences into account at the same time, and weigh them one against the other; and so child A and child B would both be judged by the obvious consequences, and child A would therefore be adjudged the worse. At the intermediate stage, children would say that child A was really good, while child B was really bad, but would be unable to *retain* this judgment, and their comparative judgment would therefore be the contradictory one that child A, who had been judged to be 'really good' was worse than child B, who had been judged to be 'really bad' when the two children had been judged separately. This contradictory state of affairs would be resolved only at the third stage, when the judgments of child A as 'really good' and child B as 'really bad' could be retained and used as the basis of the comparison of child A with child B. In his research, Turner did in fact find that 'first stage' judgments of both children as bad but of child A as worse than child B declined steadily with age, while 'intermediate stage' judgments of child A as 'really good' but 'worse than' child B increased from five to eight years and then decreased, and 'last stage' judgments of child B as worse than child A because of his intentions, steadily increased. Turner's emphasis on the importance of 'retaining' judgments and using these as a basis of comparison may perhaps remind the reader of Breznitz and Kugelmass'[49] third stage, recall of principle, and their reference[170] to the cognitive ability to abstract principles. Lunzer and Morris suggest that the older child becomes 'capable of dissociating the purpose with which an action was conceived from the action itself, while the judgment of the younger child remains global,' just as, in relation to the causes of natural phenomena,[144] young children cannot properly separate their actions from the results of their actions. 'To put the matter another way', say Lunzer and Morris, 'in order to give due weight to motivation in moral judgment the child must be in a position to represent his own behaviour and that imputed to others sufficiently clearly to pick out the moments of decision .... both the initial judgments implying a rigid morality of constraint and the final judgments which represent a logically consistent morality are attempts on the part of the child to assimilate and identify himself with the moral attitudes which he finds around him. The difference between primitive morality and more mature forms should be attributed primarily to a difference in cognitive capacity' (pp. 343-344).

The young child, according to Lunzer and Morris, assimilates the attitudes of his parents as far as he can understand them, and thus may be able to *anticipate* their behaviour. But he cannot carry his thought back and isolate 'moments of decision', and so cannot refer to 'motives' as the basis of judgment. Actions which express love or obedience, because of their effects come to be approved of, other actions, such as aggression, destruction or disobedience, come to be disapproved of; but the basis of such approving or disapproving attitudes lies in consequences. Lunzer and Morris suggest that there are five 'steps' in the development from this point to a mature adult moral attitude. (1) Children learn to distinguish between things done accidentally and things done on purpose, because the reaction to the situation is different when it is done intentionally, because the child is in a different 'state'. (2) This is followed by distinguishing between the intentional and accidental actions of others (i.e. attributing or not attributing intention). (3) This attention to motives is reinforced because it has functional value in so far as it enables the child to predict reactions to his behaviour. (4) The child, with increasing maturity and experience, is able to classify actions as 'good' and 'bad', and to locate them along a good-bad dimension, and to isolate the moments of decision relevant to actions. (5) The final stage 'is essentially a matter of reconstructing a coherent system, based on the abstraction of general principles, being ways of relating actions rather than the actions themselves and their relations' (pp. 345–346). The relevance of intelligence or cognitive ability, particularly to the last step, is obvious. A highly developed mind is necessary for the elaboration of an internally consistent, well-differentiated system of moral principles. This analysis by Lunzer and Morris is one of the most enlightening to emerge from what we may call the Piaget tradition, particularly as it enables important ideas from reinforcement theory and imitation learning theory to be incorporated.

Bull[55] finds little support for Piaget's idea that children move away from a 'moral realism' attitude to lying as wrong because it is against adult prohibition, to a more proper appreciation of the significance of lying because they discover in the course of interaction with their peers that it is necessary to tell the truth if relationships based on mutual respect are to be maintained. Bull found, in fact, that his 'lying test' produced very few responses showing 'mutality'. Bull agrees with Piaget in finding that his nine year old children thought it worse to lie to an adult than to lie to another child, but did not find that many of these younger children thought that a lie told to other children was justified. The expectation that children should think it bad to lie to adults but not to children seems to stem from the view that lying to adults is bad because of the child's 'unilateral respect' for the adult rather than for the adult's *rules*. But if the child's attitude is to the *rules* laid down by the adult, then surely a great deal would depend on whether the adults indicated that lying to adults *was* particularly bad. If the adult rule emphasizes that *all* lying is bad, then one should hardly expect even young children to think that lying to adults is bad but lying to other children quite permissible.

In his 10 to 13 year old children, Bull found many *fewer* children than Piaget who thought it equally bad to lie to children, and also 10 per cent of his children who thought that it was worse to lie to an adult on the grounds that to do so was to betray an adult's trust. Bull concluded, on the basis of his own findings, that 'lying as a breach of trust, falls within the sphere of close personal relationships' (p. 94), including relationships with both adults and peers, and takes the view that disapproving of lying is a function, not of mutuality with peers, but of *conscience* as a system of internalized values. He proposes the reasonable view that lies are first regarded as wrong because lying is proscribed by parents; that lying to other children *then* becomes regarded as wrong by extension or generalization; and that lies by adults to children may be regarded as especially wrong because this sets a bad example to children. We should in the main agree with this, except that we think it likely that lying to other children comes to be regarded as wrong not so much by extension, but because parents, other adults and older children convey directly that lying to other children, just like lying to parents, *is* wrong, as we have indicated above. Most of Bull's subjects referred to parental influence as the main factor in their conviction that lying is wrong, and he thinks that identification with parents and introjection of parental values are the most influential factors. Bull found that as children increased in age, they gave more responses including such phrases as 'It all depends. . . .' This might appear to be in line with Piaget's idea of an increasing regard for 'equity' or the special circumstances of any case, and certainly seems to reflect increasing flexibility. Bull's interpretation, however, is different from Piaget's. He feels that this kind of relativity comes about as a result of the 'increasing subordination of moral principle to persons, though not its abandonment' (p. 211). He thinks, in fact, that we find the application (and refinement) of a *principle* of truth-telling to situations involving peer relationships, but *not*, as Piaget would have it, the *discovery* of the principle in these situations. There would seem to be a lot to be said for this view.

(2) *Reciprocity*. Piaget's idea about the change from an 'expiatory' to a 'reciprocity' view of punishment has also been the subject of a fair amount of examination. Two very early studies by Barnes and by Schallenberger, both in 1894 (reported by Johnson[149]), report results very much in keeping with Piaget's view, formulated so much later. Barnes found with American children of from seven to 16 years of age that the younger children in particular, tended to regard punishments as just because they were administered by adults, and to think that suffering punishment could atone for offences, these beliefs declining with age. A further study by Barnes in 1902 (*see* 149) found English children to favour 'restitutional' rather than 'punitive' punishment to a greater extent than the American children. Schallenberger, with children of from six to 16 years of age, found that restitution was suggested by children at all ages, but increasingly frequently with increasing age.

Harrower,[127] in an early replication of Piaget's study found the same development in the direction of reciprocity in children from five to ten years of age in a London County Council school, but found that for children in a private school, the younger children showed few signs of the more authoritarian point of view. Harrower thought that these children learned the more 'mature' attitude directly from their parents rather than that their development was simply expedited by their parents' influence, i.e. that children's attitudes reflect their parents' expectations rather than their own processes of organization of their experience.

Harrower and Bull are on common ground in stressing parental influence.

Whereas Piaget had studied children up to but not beyond the age of about 12 years, Morris[210] was primarily concerned with the development of value judgments during adolescence. His pupils showed a distinct tendency to greater autonomy and greater reciprocity and equity with increasing age, but there were large individual differences. Johnson[148] found the use of reciprocity to increase with both chronological age and intelligence quotient. Goldman,[119] primarily interested in the development of religious ideas, asked his children questions about 'divine justice', for example, 'Was it fair that all men in the Egyptian army should be drowned?' and found that elements of 'authority' and 'constraint' were very common in the responses of children of all ages, but that there was a progression from a retributive or expiatory view, commonest in children of nine years of age or under, through an intermediate stage at about ten years, to a 'distributive' view in children of about 12 and over. Goldman, observing that his children seemed to make the transition to a more fair and impartial view rather later than Piaget's, suggests that this might be a function of one or all of three possible factors —sampling and cultural differences, differences in the content of the items used and the possibility that religious material is more 'difficult' in the sense that it requires thinking to be transferred to a remote and unfamiliar situation.

So far, the results of research on reciprocity and distributive justice in general support Piaget. In one series of researches, however, the results are less confirmatory. Durkin[68, 69, 70, 72] was concerned less with the more general aspects of reciprocity and equity than with a rather specific assertion of Piaget's that 'children maintain with a conviction that grows with their years that it is strictly fair to give back the blows one has received'[227] (p. 301). In her first article,[68] Durkin used a story about physical aggression by one child against another, and was concerned to see how her subjects thought the other child should have reacted —e.g. told the teacher, hit him back. She found that children of approximately 11 years of age more frequently believed that it was right to 'give back what you get' than children of about eight, but that older children (of 13 to 14) more frequently felt that it was right to refer the matter to authority. Moreover, the more intelligent children were more likely to refer to authority. In the matter of property rights (e.g. if someone refuses to lend you something of his, should you later refuse to lend him yours if he wants it?) and character rights (e.g. if child A is caught cheating and child B calls him names, what should child A do if B is later caught cheating?) Durkin[69] found reciprocity in the sense of 'doing as you were done to' to be negatively related to age, and unrelated to intelligence at three age levels (eight, 11 and 13). However, in a further study[70] involving physical aggression, with children of approximately eight to 17 years of age, Durkin did find *equity*, defined as 'overt concern for particular circumstances' to increase with increasing age, though 'reciprocity' was not favoured by the children of about 13, and less so by those of 17. In yet another study, Durkin[72] compared reciprocity responses for stories involving physical aggression, taking the property of another, and defaming another's character. The percentage of reciprocity responses varied from five per cent to 40 per cent, and apparently similar responses were sometimes given for quite different reasons.

Bull[55] found the approval of 'expiatory' punishment to decrease much less with increasing age than Piaget had indicated, and found the approval of 'reciprocity' punishment to increase rather less with age from eight to 11 years. Bull is in *general* agreement with Piaget here, but (rightly) thinks that things are much more complex than suggested by Piaget. Bull finds, for example, that the youngest children tended to favour punishment by censure (for Piaget, a form of reciprocity punishment) for its relative leniency, while older children tended to favour it for its appropriateness and effectiveness. Again, Bull, like Durkin, found reciprocity to increase to a peak and then to decline again, the peak being about the age of nine, while a concern for motives continued to increase with age.

Of her failure to find reciprocity increasing strictly with age, Durkin observes that 'older children, at least on the basis of the reasons they give for their responses, are more experientially aware of what happens when the adults' admonition, "Don't fight" is ignored; and therefore they are willing, at least at this verbal level, to seek justice in the authority person. If Piaget had questioned subjects older than 12 years, he too might have found similar reactions'[70] (p. 256). It may well also be that the oldest children appreciate that the business of 'returning a blow' is not the end of it, but that this may mean starting a fight (in which one may be worsted), or even creating a feud. As children get older, there tends to be more pressure *against* fighting and *against* physical retaliation. Further, while the youngest children may oppose retaliation because it is 'naughty' to hit someone, and prefer the exercise of arbitrary adult control, the oldest children may prefer to refer the matter to an adult arbiter because they trust him to see that the matter is dealt with *justly*. In fact, it is pretty certain that if an adult in this position does not deal with incidents in a way which is regarded as just, then the children will soon *cease* to have recourse to him.

Again, we must distinguish between what children do to one another as individuals and what is administered as punishment. For example, even if children believe in returning a blow they get, they will not necessarily believe that if the offender is to be punished, he should receive a similar blow, or even any physical punishment at all. Children might well decide as a group that 'sending to Coventry' for a period or exclusion from the group (which Piaget also regards as a form of reciprocity punishment in his wider and more important sense of 'reciprocity') would be more appropriate, or he might be required to make some form of restitution. After all, the doctrine of 'an eye for an eye and a tooth for a tooth' is not a particularly moral one, and in so far as children growing older may be expected on the whole to grow more moral, we should scarcely expect them to go on being committed to such a doctrine, still less to become more committed to it. It would indeed, be very odd if this were the case. And in fact, Piaget himself writes, 'In our view, it is precisely this concern with reciprocity which leads one beyond the rather short-sighted justice of those children who give back the mathematical equivalent of the blows they have received. Like all spiritual realities which are the result, not of external constraint but of autonomous development, reciprocity has two aspects: reciprocity as a fact, and reciprocity as an ideal, as something which ought to be. The child begins by simply practising reciprocity, in itself not so easy a thing as one might think. Then, once he has grown accustomed to this form of equilibrium in his actions, his behaviour is altered from within, its form reacting, as it were, upon its content. What is regarded as just is no longer merely reciprocal action, but primarily *behaviour that admits of indefinitely sustained reciprocity*. The motto"Do as you would be done by" thus comes to replace the conception of crude equality. The child sets forgiveness above revenge, not out of weakness, but because "there is no end" to revenge . . . reciprocity implies a purification of the deeper trend of conduct, guiding it by gradual stages to universality itself. Without leaving the sphere of reciprocity, generosity— the characteristic of our third stage—allies itself to justice pure and simple, and between the more refined form of justice, such as equity and love properly so called, there is no longer any real conflict'[227] (p. 323). Where one may differ from this is in thinking that Piaget overestimates the extent to which behaviour is 'altered from within' and underestimates the part played by precept and example.

(3) *Immanent justice.* Using picture material and questions, Caruso[59] found that the number of immanent justice responses decreased markedly between the ages of approximately six and eight years. With older children, Caruso used (i) a multiple-choice cause-and-effect test, in which children were free to select or not to select an explanation for a misfortune, which indicated that the child had previously been naughty and that was why the misfortune had occurred; (ii) a multiple-choice test of what consequences might be expected to result from wrongdoing; and (iii) two stories from Piaget, of misfortunes which followed in time an act of disobedience, for which children had to say whether the misfortune would have occurred if the child had not disobeyed. In all three tests, the number of immanent justice responses decreased steadily with age from eight to 15 years.

Johnson[148] also found a decline in belief in immanent justice with increasing age, and a tendency for IQ and belief in immanent justice to be negatively related. Abel[1] in a study of subnormal children who had been institutionalized for more than six years, in an atmosphere believed to be one of high moral realism, showed a higher frequency of belief in immanent justice than other subnormal children of the same mental age. This receives support from Johnson's finding that 'parental constraint' was also related to immanent justice. MacRae[191] with children of from five to 14 years of age, found an overall tendency for belief in immanent justice to decrease with increasing age, but there was a curious reversal in his findings. *Fewer* five and six year olds gave immanent justice responses than nine and ten year olds. Perhaps this might be due to some specific factor connected with the particular sample of subjects used, or with the particular material. If not, it is difficult to see what could lie behind such a reversal at this age. Medinnus[196] also failed to find unqualified support for the decline of immanent justice from six to 12 years of age. He used the following two stories. STORY I. There was once a little boy who didn't mind his mother. He took the scissors one day when he had been told not to. While he was trying to cut some paper, he cut his finger. Why did he cut his finger? If his mother had said it was all right if he used the scissors, would he have cut himself just the same? STORY II. Once there were two children who were walking by a house in the country. There were some apple trees out in the yard in front of the house. No one was around so they went into the yard and stole some apples. Suddenly a man came out of the house and ran after them. He caught one of the boys but the other one got away. This one crossed a river on a rotten bridge and he fell into the water. Why do you think the boy fell into the water? If he had not stolen the apples but had crossed the river on that rotten bridge, would he have fallen into the water anyway? Why?

Answers were scored as immanent justice responses if the scorer felt 'that the subject conceived of the accidents described in each of the two stories as forms of punishment administered by the objects themselves, or by God, or by the "moral force" in the Universe through these objects' (p. 258). They were scored as not involving a belief in immanent justice if they 'invoked a rational explanation'. Instead of finding a clear decrease in belief in immanent justice with increasing age, Medinnus found no statistically significant age trend. In Story I, the number of immanent justice responses did decrease, though insignificantly, with age, but in Story II, they actually increased (again insignificantly) with age. In both stories, there was a large number of non-immanent justice responses, even at the age of six years. In Story II, the number of immanent justice responses was less at every age than in Story I. As Medinnus points out, there is a crucial difference between the two stories. 'In Story I no rational explanation is provided to account for the boy's misfortune. . . In Story II, on the other hand, mention is made of the fact that the bridge . . . was rotten' (p 259). Medinnus suggests that the less information relevant to a 'rational' explanation is given, the more likely the child is to resort to 'magic' or immanent justice. 'The present findings,' he says, 'indicate that a child's expressed belief in immanent justice is dependent upon a number of such factors as the meaningfulness of the situation to him, the presence or absence of rational alternative explanations, the range of his experiences, the concreteness of the young child's thought, and so forth' (p. 260).

Magowan[192] examined Medinnus' suggestion that children should give more immanent justice responses to stories about unfamiliar situations than to those about familiar situations, and this was clearly confirmed for children between nine and 12 years of age. He also found that an open-ended test encouraged children to give more immanent justice responses, while in a multiple-choice test, they were more likely to select the more 'rational' alternatives. Children, both boys and girls, gave more immanent justice responses when the main character of the story was a male. This may be, as Magowan suggests, because they believed that boys ought to be more severely punished than girls. An interesting feature of this research is that the author controlled for the factor of 'projective fluency', which may well confound the results when projective or semi-projective devices are used, and indeed, has also to be guarded against when interview techniques such as Kohlberg's[162] are used.

The possibility that the 'immanent justice' effect might be largely due to cultural factors, or at least might be strongly influenced by cultural factors, has stimulated various cross-cultural studies. Dennis[65] found considerable belief in immanent justice among Hopi Indians, which decreased markedly with increasing age from 12 to 18 years. The relatively high frequency of immanent justice responses among these Hopi subjects strongly suggests the importance of cultural factors in the persistence or non-persistence of the belief with increasing age. Dennis does, however, think that an early belief in immanent justice is a universal feature of children's mentality in any culture. Havighurst and Neugarten,[131] however, report an *increase* rather than a decrease in belief in immanent justice in a study of American Indian children. This appeared to support Piaget's view that in *primitive* societies, the moral constraint exercised increases rather than decreases as one grows older. However, Havighurst and Neugarten believe that instead of thinking in terms of Piaget's oversimplified concept of 'primitive societies' differing from modern societies in moral constraint, we must look to the particular structure and beliefs of each different society. This eminently sensible position is also taken by Jahoda,[147] who further considers that the incidence of beliefs in immanent justice 'cannot be quantitatively assessed, in any culture, without further conceptual clarification' (p. 248). Jahoda is very critical of the finding of Havighurst and Neugarten that immanent justice in American Indian societies increases with age, and advances a very reasonable argument for the view that their findings may be an artefact of their method of investigation. Jahoda reports an investigation which he himself carried out in Ghana. He classified the responses to his material into five categories as follows. (1) Pure immanence, in which 'the injury is viewed as the direct consequence of the misdeed, without the intervention of any external agency or any naturalistic explanation being offered'. (2) Act of God. (3) Inconsistent—partly immanent, partly naturalistic. (4) Magical causation—the consequence of being cursed. (5) Naturalistic. (a) Causal guilt—'the sequence crime-injury is conceived as a causal one, but mediated by a natural process' (e.g. the boy was nervous as a result of his transgression and he couldn't handle the knife properly). (b) Pure accident. Categories 5a and 5b are included as sub-classes of the same category, because both involve 'rational' or 'naturalistic' explanations compared with the other four. Jahoda found a marked decrease between his younger group of Ghana subjects (age six to 11 years) and his older group (age 12 to 18 years) in 'pure immanence', and the appearance of naturalistic responses among the older subjects. However, if 'acts of God' are included under the heading of 'immanence', then many more of the younger children show immanent justice responses, and even more of the older children, so that the decrease is then much less. As Jahoda points out, Piaget himself was not very clear as to whether 'acts of God' should be regarded as indicating a belief in immanent justice; Jahoda felt that they probably should be. The clear implication here is that, in the absence of an unambiguous definition of 'immanent justice', what is included under this heading must be somewhat arbitrary, and will also almost inevitably vary from culture to culture, making quantitative comparisons difficult.

Najarian-Svajian[219] provides another useful cross-cultural comparison in a study of Lebanese children and adults. He found an incidence of immanent justice responses below the age of eight years, comparable with that reported by Piaget, but found no marked decline beginning about the age of nine. For children at school, there was a marked decline in the belief from the age of about 15 years, and in college students, naturalistic thinking was highly developed and belief in immanent justice rare. It was, however, still as high among illiterate Lebanese adults as among elementary school children. Najarian-Svajian emphasizes the importance of cultural factors in the incidence and decline of belief in immanent justice and in moral thinking in general. Such findings, however, are not necessarily at variance with Piaget's view, since Piaget does not deny that cultural factors may facilitate, postpone or even prevent development. Indeed, in view of the very widely reported frequency of immanent justice responses in young children, and the fairly general reports of decline with increasing age, we may conclude that Piaget's views have found a very fair amount of support.

(4) *'Decentration' and moral judgment.* A most interesting investigation was carried out by Stuart[261] into the relation of 'decentration' to moral judgment as assessed by story items relevant to
H

immanent justice, expiatory punishment and objective responsibility. By 'centration', Piaget means a tendency to concentrate on some striking aspect of an object or a question, to the neglect of other more relevant features. 'Decentration' refers to the ability to 'see beyond' such striking features, and to take into account other relevant features. For example, if a child 'centres on' the *length* of two pieces of clay to the exclusion of thickness, he will not be able to see that there may be the same amount of clay in each piece. Stuart used the ability to see graphic representations of figures seen from different points (perceptual decentration) as his measure of decentration, and had as his subjects a sample of children of from seven to nine years of age, and from 11 to 13. He found, as predicted, that decentration was related to moral judgment, but also to age and intelligence; and he suggested that minimum age and intelligence are necessary for decentration, that older and more intelligent children learn to differentiate more readily, and that training in decentration might *possibly* help children to earlier cognitive maturity and thereby, perhaps, to earlier maturity of moral thinking as well. This suggestion does not seem to have been put to test so far, but it is clearly an interesting and testable proposition.

Lawrence Kohlberg[162] bases his work partly on the work of Piaget, but has greatly elaborated it in a number of ways. In his scheme of developmental stages, he proposes three *levels* of development, the premoral level, the level of conventional role conformity and the level of self-accepted moral principles. Each of these three levels is divided into two stages, so that we have the following scheme of six developmental stages (see Kohlberg[162, 165] and Kohlberg and Kramer[167]).

Level I Premoral. At this level, the child is responsive to cultural rules and evaluative labels but views them in terms of pleasant or unpleasant consequences of action, or in terms of the physical power of those who impose the rules.

Stage 1 Obedience and punishment orientation. Egocentric deference to superior power or prestige, or a trouble-avoiding set. Objective responsibility.

Stage 2 Naively egoistic orientation. Right action is that instrumentally satisfying to the self's need and occasionally other's. Awareness of relativism of value to each actor's needs and perspective. Naive egalitarianism and orientation to exchange and reciprocity.

Level II Conventional Role Conformity. At this level the child is oriented towards actively maintaining the expectations of his family, peers etc. as a value in its own right, and with justifying these expectations as such.

Stage 3 Good-boy orientation. Orientation to approval and to pleasing and helping others. Conformity to stereotypical images of majority or natural role behaviour and judgment of intentions.

Stage 4 Authority and social-order-maintaining orientation. Orientation to 'doing one's duty' and to showing respect for authority and maintaining the given social order for its own sake. Regard for earned expectations of others.

Level III Self-accepted Moral Principles. The child is concerned with defining moral values and principles apart from the supporting authority.

Stage 5 Contractual legalistic orientation. Recognition of an arbitrary element or starting point in rules or expectations for the sake of agreement. Duty defined in terms of contract, general avoidance of violation of the will or rights of others, and majority will and welfare.

Stage 6 Conscience or principle orientation. Orientation not only to actually ordained social rules but to principles of choice involving appeal to logical universality and consistency. Orientation to conscience as a directing agent and to mutual respect and trust.

It is not hard to see how and how far Kohlberg's scheme represents a modification and elaboration of Piaget's. For example, Piaget's starting point is respect for rules and the authority of those who impose them. Kohlberg's stage (1) orientation reflects the desire to avoid punishment rather than unilateral respect. This is, according to Kohlberg, because children cannot yet distinguish hedonism from respect for authority. Punishment is simply something one avoids if one can. 'Only as children reach a level of cognitive development at which the meaning of moral concepts can be differentiated from punishment can they attain either a definite hedonism or a degree of disinterested respect for authority'[159] (p. 22). Kohlberg claims that children of four years of age whom he himself studied with a simplified version of his material did in fact respond more in terms of reward and punishment than in terms of adult imposed rules and respect for them. Stage 2 judgments are more oriented to relativism based on an appreciation of one's own needs, thus involving some degree of reciprocity. Stage 3 judgments involve more reference to helping others, thus showing a further degree of reciprocity, and to intentions. Stage 4 judgments are more concerned with respect due to authority. Stage 5 involves reference to the mutual obligations involved in laws and rights, while stage 6 involves reference to something like an idea of justice which may form the basis for making decisions between conflicting alternatives, and seems to be quite close to Piaget's notion of 'equity'.

Kohlberg's method, like Piaget's, involves interviewing children and asking them questions, but his procedure is more elaborate and searching. The children are taken individually and told a number of standardized stories, each involving a moral dilemma, different ways of resolving which may be justified on different grounds. For example, a man who steals to feed a starving child might be regarded as 'wrong' because he has broken the law, but right on humanitarian grounds. The children are questioned about each story and asked to say, in answer to each question, what is right, and to explain why. Further questioning and probing are used to make sure that a child's answer and what he means by it are perfectly clear. Responses are evaluated according to the nature of the grounds given rather than according to the alternative chosen. It is not, therefore, a case of giving 'the right answer'. An example will help to make this clear. Kohlberg himself cites the following case. Suppose we have a story in which the problem is whether a boy should tell his father a confidence about his brother's misdeed, or should refrain from betraying a confidence. One of Kohlberg's ten year old children, Danny, replied, 'In one way, it would be right to tell on his brother or his father might spank him. In another way, it would be right to keep quiet or his brother might beat him up'[162] (p. 13). This is a stage 1 response, made by reference to which line of action is likely to produce the more severe punishment.

Twenty-five 'aspects' or 'dimensions' of moral thought are covered, including the value of human life, motives as a basis for judging conduct, the concept of rights, and attitude to punishment. Each aspect is viewed as having six levels corresponding to the six stages of development. For example, the six levels or stages to which answers relevant to motivation can be assigned are defined as follows. (1) Punishment by another. (2) Manipulation of goods or rewards by another. (3) Disapproval by others. (4) Censure by legitimate authorities, followed by feelings of guilt. (5) Community respect. (6) Self-condemnation[162] (p. 14). The levels or stages for the concept of rights are defined as follows. (1) No real conception of a right beyond obeying authority. (2) Rights defined in terms of factual ownership (right to do as one likes with what one owns). (3) Similar to (2) but qualified by the belief that one must not do evil. (4) Recognition of a right as a claim, generally earned, on others. (5) Idea of unearned, universal human rights. (6) Similar to (5) but including the idea of respect for the lives and personalities of other people.

Scoring of the material is quite difficult to carry out until one has had some experience, but Kohlberg provides useful examples, and the agreement of independent judges, once they have had training experience, is quite high. The method does preserve the flexibility of Piaget's technique, while enabling quantification to be carried out more satisfactorily. A child may be assessed in terms of a 'global' score for moral maturity, or by means of a 'profile' indicating the proportion of his responses which fall at each stage. The stages are regarded as forming a linear age-related sequence, in order of increasing morality, the ability to function at any stage being regarded as resulting from a reorganization of experience which is only possible because of preceding organization at the previous stages, and representing the child's continuing efforts to make sense of his social and moral experience as a whole. The following examples from Kohlberg[165] (pp. 4–5) illustrate the kind of responses characteristic of each stage. The aspect here involved is 'the worth of human life'.

Stage 1 The value of human life is confused with the value of physical objects and is based on the social status or physical attributes of its possessor. Tommy, age ten: (Why should the chemist give the medicine to the dying woman when her husband couldn't pay for it?) 'If someone important is in a plane and is allergic to heights and the stewardess won't give him medicine because she's only got enough for one and she's got a sick one, a friend, in back, they'd probably put the stewardess in a lady's jail because she didn't help the important one.' (Is it better to save the life of one important person or a lot of unimportant people?) 'All the people that aren't important because one man just has one house, maybe a lot of furniture, but a whole bunch of people have an awful lot of money and it doesn't look it.'

Stage 2 The value of human life is seen as instrumental to the satisfaction of the needs of its possessor or of other persons. Tommy, age thirteen: (Should the doctor mercifully kill a fatally ill woman requesting death because of her pain?) 'Maybe it would be good to put her out of her pain, she'd be better off that way. But the husband wouldn't want it, it's not like an animal. If a pet dies you can get along without it—it isn't something you really need. Well, you can get a new wife, but it's not really the same.'

Stage 3 The value of a human life is based on the empathy and affection of family members and other toward its possessor. Andy, age sixteen: (Should the doctor mercifully kill a fatally ill woman requesting death because of her pain?) 'No, he shouldn't. The husband loves her and wants to see her. He wouldn't want her to die sooner, he loves her too much.'

Stage 4 Life is conceived as sacred in terms of its place in a categorical moral or religious order of rights and duties. John, age sixteen: (Should the doctor kill the woman?) 'The doctor wouldn't have the right to take a life, no human has the right. He can't create life, he shouldn't destroy it.'

Stage 5 Life is valued both in terms of its relation to community welfare and in terms of life being a universal human right.

Stage 6 Belief in the sacredness of human life as representing a universal human value of respect for the individual. Steve, age sixteen: (Should the husband steal the expensive medicine to save his wife?) 'By the law of society he was wrong but by the law of nature or of God the chemist was wrong and the husband was justified. Human life is above financial gain. Regardless of who was dying, if it was a total stranger, man has a duty to save him from dying' (Slightly modified from Kohlberg[165]).

Although Kohlberg treats his six stages of moral judgment or orientation as sequential and age-related, we must not think that the later, more mature stages wholly replace the early stages. Many people, for instance, though making stage 4 judgments, may still from time to time make stage 2 or even stage 1 judgments. However, Kohlberg's position is that the central tendency of judgment moves up with increasing age (although of course not everyone will pass through the whole sequence), and one expects, in the main, to find a limited range of stages used. The next step at any time is in the direction of the next stage up. If we look at the age pattern which Kohlberg reports from America, we find that at the age of ten years, the types of judgment used are, in descending order of frequency of use, 1–2–3–4–5–6; i.e. stage 1 responses are most frequent, followed by stage 2 responses and so on. Stage 5 and stage 6 responses are equally infrequent. By the age of 13 years, the frequency of stage 1 and stage 2 responses has declined very considerably, while the frequency of stage 6 responses has increased a little. Thus, at age 13, we have the following sequence of frequency of use of the stages : –4–3 – – – 5–2–1–6, with stage 4 responses most frequent and stage 3 not very far behind. Then, appreciably less frequently used come stages 5, 2 and 1, all about the same, with stage 6 still least used. By the age of 16, stage 4 and stage 5 responses have increased further, while stage 6 responses remain at a low level of frequency. It seems very likely that with increasing age beyond 16, there will be some tendency for a relative increase in the frequency of stage 5 and stage 6 responses.[162] Kohlberg and Kramer,[167] in fact, report a (barely significant) increase in stage 6 thinking between the ages of 16 and 25, though stage 6 responses remain rare. They also say that there is no new stage or mode of moral thinking which is to be found in adulthood and not found in adolescence. Kohlberg and Kramer support the view that adult development seems to consist in the dropping out of less mature, lower stages of thinking. In particular, thinking typical of stages 1, 2 and 3 tends to drop out while stage 4 thinking increases. From the age of 14 to the age of 25, the range of stages used becomes less, indicating greater consistency. Kohlberg and Kramer think of this adult process of 'moral stabilization' as a form of socialization rather than of moral development. This is because it involves 'settling down' to level II thinking, i.e. in terms of conventional role conformity. It is a kind of adjustment rather than development. These authors comment that 'the breed of conventional morality which stabilizes in adulthood depends upon one's adult

social sex role'[167] (p. 108). Women, they observe, seem to stabil-
ize more at stage 3, men at stage 4. 'Stage 3 personal concordance
morality is a functional morality for housewives and mothers;
it is not for business men and professionals. Adult moral stabilization, then, appears to be more a matter of increased congruence
between belief and social role than of novel integration of experience' (*ibid.*).

Kohlberg and Kramer do, in fact, report a study by Kramer in
which it was found that between late high school and second or
third year at college, 20 per cent of middle class subjects actually
'retrogressed'. (This was true only of college students). Retrogression was defined as a drop greater than any found in a two-month
test-retest sample. Retrogression was mostly from stages 4 and 5
to stage 2 (hedonistic relativism) and was often accompanied by
'high-flown jargon'. *All* these subjects had returned to stages 4 and
5 by the age of 25, with rather more of stage 5 than at high school.
The correlation of moral maturity scores between the ages of 16
and 25 was +.89, from high school to college only +.41 and
from college to age 25 and +.41. Kohlberg and Kramer regard
the retrogression as 'functional' rather than 'structural', and occasioned by *protest* against authoritarian-based morality and
against a world of 'immoral people' who don't themselves live
by the precepts they teach. They think this interpretation supported by the fact that the 'backsliders did return to their previous
level, that they did continue to use *some* stage 4 or stage 5 thinking, and that when asked what the world in general would regard
as 'moral responses' they tended to give stage 4 responses.

If Kohlberg's technique really does assess moral development
through a sequence of age-related stages, then we should expect
to find a fair degree of internal consistency and some degree of
consistency over time. Kohlberg reports[166] (1) that on average,
50 per cent of expressed judgments fit a single stage, although
judgments cover numerous different aspects; (2) that correlations
between stories had a median value +.51; and (3) that correlations between scores at ages 13 and 16, 13 and 24 and 16 and 24
ranged from +.78 to +.92. Turiel has also argued[267] that if the
developmental stage view is correct, then children should be
particularly responsive to attempts to influence them in the direc-

tion of the stage above that at which they most typically respond. Turiel used a role-playing situation in which children of age 12 to 13½ years were exposed to moral reasoning at their own stage and at other stages. Forty-four subjects whose own reasoning was typically at stage 2, stage 3 or stage 4 were used. These stages were chosen so that moral reasoning could be provided at one stage below and at one and two stages above the typical level for each subject. The typical level for each subject was established for each subject on the basis of six of Kohlberg's nine stories. The remaining three stories were used for the purpose of 'supplying' the subjects with moral reasoning at levels other than their own. After each story was read, the subject was asked to play the part of the main character in the story and to ask advice concerning the issue posed from two friends, played by the experimenter. The experimenter supplied 'advice' at the appropriate moral level, first supporting one alternative solution to the dilemma posed and then supporting the other alternative. Subjects were later tested again with the original six stories. The results did in fact show a tendency for the children to be most influenced by arguments one stage above their own, and in particular to be more influenced by arguments one stage above their own than by arguments one stage below. As Turiel points out, the children in this experiment did not learn *solutions* to the problems, but learned to *apply* a more mature form of argument to problems other than those used by the experimenter in the 'treatment' session. He suggests that what happened was that the experimenter's reasoning stimulated cognitive conflict which the children could grasp, and that the more mature reasoning provided a means of dealing with this conflict. Turiel argues that his results support the view that each stage represents a reorganization of thinking at the previous stage, but in view of the limited statistical significance of his results, this argument is perhaps not too convincing.

Rest, Turiel and Kohlberg[234] used Kohlberg's material with two groups of children of approximately 11 and 14 years of age. The children were well above the average in intelligence. First, the stories were read to the children and then they were presented with three alternative 'pieces of advice' about how the dilemmas should be resolved, at one stage below and two stages above their own stage, which was established beforehand. The children at the different stages were approximately of the same mean chronological age and intelligence. They were asked which piece of advice was best and which worst, and why. Their understanding of the arguments was also assessed on the basis of their ability to summarize the advice given. The results indicated (a) that the children *preferred* advice which was either one or two stages above their own to advice below their own stage; (b) that the children found thinking two stages above their own stage more difficult to understand than thinking one stage above, and thinking above their own stage in general more difficult to understand than thinking below it. The authors think that in general, children will prefer reasoning at as high a stage above their own as they can understand. Kohlberg also reports[166] (p. 403) an unpublished study by Blatt, who elucidated in class arguments of stage 3 children as against stage 2 children on hypothetical moral conflicts, then stage 3 against stage 4, and finally presented stage 5 arguments himself. Blatt found that this raised 45 per cent of the children by one stage as compared with eight per cent in a control group. Blatt's discussion classes were held once a week for three months, and so were spread over a longer period of time than Turiel's, and this may be why they had more effect. It may also be that they stimulated a greater sense of conflict. It is part of Kohlberg's general position that a child does not simply absorb certain values from some other people, and other values from different people, but arrives at his own values by a holistic process of coping more or less effectively with the demands and expectations of all the groups to whose pressures he is subject, and that conflicts in values may stimulate moral growth as a means of coping with these conflicts.

If the structural, developmental point of view is correct, then we should expect that, once 'restructuring' in terms of a higher stage has taken place, it would be rather difficult to reverse this restructuring. Kohlberg and Kramer, as we have indicated, suggest that the 'retrogression' between high school and later college years which they found is a temporary, functional phenomenon rather than a basic, enduring and structural one. Kohlberg argues that experiments which show reversibility, such as that of Bandura and

McDonald[28] may be misleading. Bandura and McDonald claimed to have shown that a tendency to judge in terms of 'intentionality' could be reversed by social learning, and that its emergence was therefore also likely to be due to a similar process of learning from adults. However, Kohlberg claims that the reversal found by Bandura and McDonald was more likely to be a temporary phenomenon, representing an adjustment to the specific nature of the experimental influence situation. After all, if a child is rewarded or encouraged for saying that black is white, he is likely to go on saying that it is as long as it looks like the 'right' answer. But this does not mean that he is now really unable to discriminate black from white. Kohlberg reports[166] (p. 409) an unpublished study by Cowen *et al*, which repeated Bandura and McDonald's experiment, but found 'downward' learning to be less stable over time than 'upward' learning. Similarly, Le Furgy and Woloshin,[175] with rather different material based on Piaget and intended to assess moral realism versus moral relativism over a number of situations, also found that children who were influenced away from their own relativistic position in the direction of greater realism mostly reverted to their previous position within about three months, while children who were influenced in a relativistic direction tended quite strongly to retain the effects of this influence. This does seem to provide some support for the structural argument as against the 'pure learning' view.

Kohlberg's developmental point of view is an attractive one in that it attempts to provide the child with an active, creative role in relation to his social environment. However, it can be criticized in two ways, one specific to Kohlberg's scheme, the other general to any similar developmental approach based on the idea of sequential stages. In the first type of criticism, the appropriateness of the particular sequence of stages which Kohlberg proposes may be questioned. It may be found, for instance, that not all data seems to fit as well into Kohlberg's scheme as the data which he and his colleagues have reported. Other writers, for example Bull or Kay, prefer other developmental schemes. In particular, it may be suggested that Kohlberg's scheme is not likely to fit data from different cultures. To some extent, however, this is a matter which can be settled empirically. We simply want to find the most appropriate scheme, the one which best fits the empirical data, and which at the same time can be agreed to entail a series of *moral* stages. It would not be suggested that Kohlberg's or any other developmental scheme should be impervious to change and modification if change should be called for. The second kind of possible criticism is a general one which can be brought against any similar kind of developmental scheme. Three such criticisms may be made. (1) Such a scheme of sequential stages does not indicate how, by what mechanisms, the change from one stage to the next is actually brought about. At present, this criticism does seem to have a good deal of justification. (2) It may seem questionable how far cross-cultural studies are likely to support the universality of stages based on one particular society. However, Kohlberg does provide *some* cross-cultural support for his stages, and thus for the idea of a developmental approach. He reports[165] that studies carried out in Taiwan, in a Malaysian tribal village and in a Turkish village indicate 'a similar sequence of development in all cultures, although they suggest that the last two stages of moral thought do not develop clearly in preliterate or tribal communities' (p. 11). Similarly, Kohlberg reports that, in American society, 'middle class' children advance more rapidly through his stages than working class children. We ourselves confirmed this tendency, although it was relatively small when verbal intelligence was controlled. No doubt this middle-class advantage (if it can be regarded as such) in general is due partly to differences in intelligence, partly to the more verbal and liter-ate way in which middle class parents tend to treat their children, and partly to differences in social 'perspective' or outlook, due to different positions in the socio-economic system, and corres-pondingly different attitudes to decision-making and responsibil-ity-taking. Kohlberg claims that in the case of aspects of Piaget's scheme which have been shown to be so subject to cultural influence as to cast doubt on the idea of cross-culturally valid stages, the aspects concerned have not really been genuinely *moral* aspects. For example, he says, there is nothing essentially moral about being influenced by one's peers rather than referring to adult standards. Moreover, no one defending the developmental point of view would maintain that *everything* can be explained in terms of stages of development, or that the specific nature of experience is not important. (3) As Aronfreed maintains,[14] it is very probable that increasing cognitive capacity (for discrimination and abstraction) enables more abstract principles to be adopted. Since self-direction is a common Western value, this increasing cognitive capacity manifests itself in an increasing tendency to accept principles allowing and encouraging (up to a point) autonomy or internally oriented decisions, while in other societies, increasing cognitive capacity might mean the development of different kinds of principles. Certainly a great deal more cross-cultural evidence is needed.

Some Relevant Parameters: Intelligence, Sex, Religion, Social Class

Intelligence

Chassell[61] deals exhaustively with the relationship between intelligence and morality and shows how frequently these were found to be associated, up to 1935. Hartshorne and May[130] found resistance to temptation (e.g. to cheat, to steal) to be firmly related to intelligence, and other studies have confirmed this. In an investigation which we ourselves carried out, we found cheating to be significantly and inversely related to intelligence, the more intelligent cheating less, as other findings had led us to expect. Cheating was assessed by an academic test situation which was so constructed and scored as to equate for *opportunity* to cheat. This was necessary since otherwise, children who are better at doing a test have less opportunity to cheat in it. The factorial study by Nesbitt[220] supports the association of honesty with intelligence. Measures of intelligence had a substantial loading on his first factor, which he labelled 'honesty'. It is an interesting fact that, while a number of studies, including our own, have found cheating to be related to intelligence, it also appears that cheating is *not* related to chronological age over a wide age range. If the intelligent child tends to avoid cheating because he is more suspicious of the situation in which cheating seems to be so easy, it is difficult to see why older children do not cheat less. It would appear that at any age, the less intelligent children feel more *need* to cheat in order to 'do well' than the more intelligent children, but that the amount of cheating felt to be necessary remains more or less constant across a wide age range, although the *tasks* which elicit cheating of course grow more difficult with increasing age. Moreover, it is quite possible that, although the average amount of cheating seems to remain constant with increasing age, the view which children take of the situation may change, and thus as they grow older, they may be cheating for different characteristic reasons or motives.

Kohlberg indicates[163] that the correlations reported between intelligence and ratings and measures of 'character' generally fall within the limits of $r = +.20$ and $r = +.50$. He observes that the correlation is generally higher in studies using ratings of moral character than in studies using experimental measures or indices of behaviour such as incidence of delinquency. Terman and Odin, for example[263] found intelligence quite highly related to moral reputation. Some caution is, however, called for. Brogden[50] found his measures of moral character in the main unrelated to intelligence, while Havighurst and Taba[131] found the relationship between school achievement and character reputation to be significant, but not that between intelligence and reputation. The relationship between intelligence and reputation, however, though not statistically significant, was positive, and the population was a selected one in respect of intelligence, having an average Binet intelligence quotient of appreciably above 100. It is therefore quite likely that the relationship was attentuated by this selection, and appears less than it would have been in an unselected population. This may also be true of the rather low correlation of $+.29$ which Havighurst and Taba report between intelligence and 'moral beliefs' (beliefs about friendliness, moral courage, honesty, loyalty and responsibility, and about what course of action it is 'right' to follow in various circumstances).

A number of studies have related Piaget's concepts of moral development to intelligence, most finding a significant relationship. Abel[1] found mental age inversely related to the tendency to interpret events in terms of 'immanent justice'. However, Najarian-Svajian[219] with Lebanese children and adults, concluded that the incidence of 'immanent justice' below the age of eight years in his population was comparable with Piaget's finding, but that there was no marked drop after the age of nine years in his Lebanese subjects, and that increasing mental age at this point does not in itself necessarily imply a reduction in the tendency to think in terms of immanent justice. It would seem that a certain level of mental age may be a necessary but not a sufficient condition for advance beyond this kind of thinking. Much must depend upon the social reality which people have to face.

Boehm[40, 41] found that 'academically gifted children' matured earlier than children of lower intelligence in moral judgment as assessed by the tendency to judge actions in terms of intentions rather than results, i.e. the more intelligent children tended to move away from moral realism at an earlier age. Whiteman and Kosier[273] support Boehm in finding that *both* chronological age and IQ within age groups are related to the tendency to 'subjective' as against 'objective' blame (i.e. judging in terms of intentions instead of results). Boehm also observed that there was a greater difference between gifted and average children of upper middle class parents than between gifted and average children of working class parents,[41] thus indicating an interaction between intelligence and social class.

Porteus and Johnson[229] used two types of material in their study, 'cognitive' material consisting of stories and questions similar to those used by Piaget, and 'affective' material, consisting of incomplete stories like those used by Allinsmith[4] and Aronfreed,[11] which involved wrongdoing on the part of the hero. The children had to complete the stories, and they were then scored for 'maturity of affect'. Porteus and Johnson found that intelligence was significantly related to *both* cognitive and affective measures. This positive finding in respect of the affective measure is interesting, because neither Allinsmith[4] nor Aronfreed[11] found any relationship between intelligence and guilt scores on their story completion material. In our own study, our results tended to confirm those of Allinsmith and Aronfreed rather than those of Porteus and Johnson. Using modified Allinsmith stories scored for 'self-criticism' rather than guilt, we found no relationship between intelligence and self-criticism, although we did find that self-criticism increased with chronological age.

Durkin,[68] with children of seven, ten and thirteen years of age, observed no clear relationship between reciprocity and intelligence, although the *more* intelligent of her children appeared *more likely* to resolve the problem of what to do by telling someone in authority, the less intelligent being more likely to favour reciprocity or some other solution. This was confirmed in a further study.[69] She also found that 'equity', or the expression of 'overt concern for particular circumstances' appeared to be unrelated to intelligence.[70] While one might expect more intelligent children perhaps to favour reciprocity rather than *arbitrary* authority, it seems quite understandable that they should wish to refer a problem to someone in authority whom they may regard as likely to be able to take a more balanced view, rather than settling for relatively crude forms of reciprocity. However, one would certainly have expected more intelligent children to view 'equity' solutions with a more favourable eye.

Kohlberg[163] reports a correlation of +.31 between intelligence and maturity of moral judgment as measured by his own interview technique. In our own investigation, we found a correlation between verbal intelligence and moral judgment (Kohlberg 'global' scoring) of +.53 at the age of 11 years, and +.43 at the age of 14 years, both on a sample of 40 children, the difference between the two coefficients being statistically insignificant. Naturally, one would expect to find some difference in the size of correlations when different tests of intelligence are used, with moral judgment correlating more highly with verbal than with non-verbal tests. But there does also seem to be a tendency in American studies to have a somewhat selected population, which would, of course, have the effect of decreasing the size of the correlation coefficient. Kohlberg also reports a correlation of +.59 between moral judgment and chronological age, with intelligence held constant, arguing that intelligence cannot therefore be the only factor in the age-related developmental sequence. It may well be the case that intelligence is relevant only up to a certain point, beyond which further increases in intelligence are of little significance. In a study of children in a special school for backward children, Henson[136] found that the responses of these children to the Kohlberg material were almost wholly restricted to stages one and two; while Bobroff[39] found 'retarded' children to be about two years behind normal children in 'socialized thinking', his stages of socialized thinking corresponding pretty well to what other writers would regard as stages of moral judgment. Boehm[40] found that retarded adolescents (IQ 50–69) scored relatively low in moral judgment, but not as low as she would have expected on the basis of intelligence alone. It is not altogether clear, however, on what grounds she based her expectation.

The importance of a certain level of ability to handle more abstract concepts is supported by the observations of Edwards[73] that more intelligent pupils, when asked to name 'wicked actions' named more *general* crimes such as bigamy and perjury as opposed to more 'concrete' things like cruelty or stealing, and by the report by Kellmer-Pringle and Edwards[155] that dull children named *fewer* wicked actions, while bright children were more subtle and abstract.

Brennan[48] reported that moral judgments, based on material similar to Piaget's, were related at a high level of significance to both mental age and chronological age up to the age of nine and a half years, but between nine and a half and eleven years, mental age became of less importance and chronological age of no significance. Bull[55] found a general tendency for intelligence to be relevant to his tests, especially for girls, but this association was not consistent over his different tests, and unfortunately Bull does not provide details of which tests are related to intelligence, nor how highly. However, he does offer some support for Brennan's finding of the decreasing importance of mental age with increasing chronological age when he notes that by the age of 17 years, there are no indications whatever of positive relationship between intelligence and moral judgment for either sex. When different authors find intelligence to be relatively important or relatively unimportant at different ages, we must, of course, remember that the findings must depend on the precise nature and 'difficulty' of the material used. It is easy enough to construct moral judgment material which will show that by the age of 15 years, for example, differences in intelligence over a fairly wide range are unimportant. But what matters most is to show that it is impossible, or seems to be extremely difficult, to construct material in which differences of intelligence *are* important. We must be cautious about drawing general conclusions from any one set of material unless this has been designed to provide sufficient 'head-room' at the top. It seems most unlikely that at any age, intelligence is *wholly* irrelevant to any kind of moral judgment.

Finally, Mischel and Metzner[206] observed that preference for a larger but delayed reward over a smaller but immediate reward was associated with higher intelligence, while Mischel[204] found that delay of reward was related to Performance IQ in the Wechsler Intelligence Scale for Children, but *not* to Verbal IQ, for both boys and girls. This may suggest an association of intelligence with self-control, but it is likely to reflect also the fact that intelligence tends to be associated with a more realistic time-perspective.

Intelligence is an ubiquitous kind of quality, associated with many other things which may be relevant to different aspects of morality, and we must always bear it in mind as a possible relevant variable and be cautious about attributing causal significance to other factors where differences in intelligence are not controlled for or demonstrated to be irrelevant. But also, as Unger[269] indicates, caution is called for in interpreting the relations between intelligence and 'moral variables', since measures of the moral variables may themselves be contaminated by an intrusion of intelligence. And finally, intelligence might quite conceivably appear to be of direct importance, whereas it might in reality be important only because of its association with other factors, such as family atmosphere. Nevertheless, when all due caution has been observed, the case for the relation of intelligence to various aspects of morality, especially to moral thinking and judgment, is impressive.

There seem to be two main ways in which intelligence is relevant to moral development. (1) It enables children better to judge what the probable results of their behaviour are likely to be, and therefore should make them less likely to commit offences which will probably be discovered. It should also enable them better to grasp the longer-term consequences of their behaviour for themselves. That is, it should have a mainly 'prudential' value. (2) It enables children to acquire more abstract linguistic and conceptual tools in terms of which to judge behaviour and to assess consequences, both to themselves and to others. In so far as a higher level of moral judgment or thinking involves the use of more abstract concepts, it is hard to see how intelligence could fail to be relevant, though this does not, of course, mean that it is the only thing which matters. It may be that a certain minimum of intelligence is necessary for the higher stages of moral thinking, beyond which further increases in intelligence become less relevant. As far as feelings of guilt and remorse are concerned, it would seem that intelligence is less likely to be directly relevant, although learning theory would suggest that the generalization of guilt feelings along verbal dimensions would be facilitated by relatively high verbal intelligence and capacity for more abstract thinking. Intelligence may also be associated with other factors such as family morale, which may be very relevant to the development of guilt feelings, and also to control of overt behaviour. But, while intelligence tends to be associated with 'moral variables', relatively high intelligence does not guarantee a high level of moral judgment, much less a high level of moral conduct; and, where the moral level is low for other reasons, intelligence may simply operate to enable a rascal to indulge in more sophisticated roguery, with a better chance of succeeding in his evil designs and avoiding the consequences. Moreover, a higher level of verbal skill, in particular, may enable children (and adults) to rationalize their own behaviour more effectively, to produce better excuses to others and to themselves, thus avoiding the impact of the kind of things which might make them change their ways.

Sex

There is little really satisfactory evidence of systematic sex differences in respect of moral behaviour, judgment or attitudes.

Freud had suggested[110] that men had a more severe superego, and a more strongly internalized superego than women because of the greater intensity of the Oedipus complex in boys. Hall[125] claimed to have found 'a modest confirmation' of Freud's suggestion. His method of investigation is interesting because it seems to 'fit' psychoanalytic theory quite well compared with many other attempts to 'test' various aspects of the theory. Hall examined the dreams reported by young men and women, and concentrated upon dreams in which (i) the dreamer was *either* the aggressor or the victim of aggression and (ii) misfortune befell *either* the dreamer or some other person or persons. *Assuming* that dreams of being the victim of aggression indicates an *externalized* superego, and that dreams of being the victim of misfortune indicate an *internalized* superego, Hall found that more young women than young men had dreams of being the victim of aggression, more young men dreaming about being aggressive themselves, while more young men had dreams of being themselves the victim of misfortune, more young women dreaming about misfortune befalling others. Hall concludes from this that Freud's hypothesis is confirmed. The argument, however, depends upon the assumption, which seems quite a considerable one, that 'victim of aggression' dreams indicate externalization and 'victim of misfortune' dreams indicate internalization. If we are not prepared to accept this argument, of course, we have to find some possible explanation of the sex differences reported by Hall. It might, for example, be assumed (not implausibly) that women are more likely in reality to be victims of aggression than to be aggressors, and that they have corresponding dreams; and that, because of their social role, men are relatively more concerned about misfortunes which might befall them, while women are relatively more concerned about misfortunes which might befall others. They are generally, for instance, more concerned about possible accidents to their children. The most that can be said about Hall's study is that the results are not incompatible with psychoanalytic theory, although there may also be other quite plausible explanations. Whether we find them *more* or *less* satisfactory will depend to a considerable extent on our initial sympathies in the matter of theory.

Some writers less sympathetic to the psychoanalytic view have tended, if anything, to find women more 'conscience controlled' than men. There is, of course, the well-known fact that for most crimes, there are many more male criminals than female; and Kohlberg,[161] on the basis of a survey of the relevant literature, concludes that girls conform more to rules and authority than boys. This no doubt reflects the expectations associated with the female role, but may also be associated with constitutional differences in aggressiveness; after all, one may ask how the female role came to be defined as it is. In any case, however, Kohlberg's conclusion is quite compatible with the notion that women have a more externalized superego.

At a less general level, Blum[38] found indications that females experience more guilt, and males tend to be more concerned with fears of external harm. This, of course, is incompatible with the idea that males have a more severe and more internalized superego. Rempel and Signori[233,] refer to three studies[32, 203, 204] all of which found women to be more inhibited and controlled by conscience than men. Rempel and Signori themselves use a seven point self-rating scale on the influence of conscience in determining behaviour, and report that their results supported the finding of the three authors mentioned. It should, however, be pointed out that Rempel and Signori's method of self-rating lays their results open to the common objection to such methods—that what people *say* of themselves is not necessarily true, and may reflect what they *think* they ought to say. In the present case, if women are more sensitive to what others think, they might well tend to answer in such a way as to give the impression that they are more dominated by conscience than in fact they are.

Sears, Maccoby and Levin[248] also found young girls to show a higher level of 'conscience' (e.g. signs of guilt, asking pardon and the like) than boys, but in this case, since findings were mainly based on mothers' reports, it is possible that they reflect at least in some degree the kind of expectations mothers have for their children. Bronfenbrenner[51] is another who reports females to have stronger internal controls than males.

Rebelsky, Allinsmith and Grinder[232] find that in story-completion studies, girls more frequently use confession, and Lee[174] that girls more frequently use confession, apology and reparation. Rebelsky *et al.* suggest that confession may be a form of affiliative, dependent behaviour, regarded as more appropriate for girls in our society and thus encouraged and rewarded, and also that girls may have easier command of language for such social purposes. Sears, Maccoby and Levin,[248] however, suggest that there are no appreciable general sex differences in dependency. They propose, in fact, that there may be a number of different kinds of dependency behaviour, more or less unrelated. Lee[171] suggests that, although her findings may reflect current expectations and specific encouragement, in girls' schools, of confession and apology, they may also reflect a greater degree of internalization of standards. Aronfreed, however,[11] distinguishing between 'externally oriented responses' (for example, being found out, suffering an accident) and 'internally oriented responses' (for example, self-criticism, spontaneous action to correct the consequences of wrongdoing) found that boys gave fewer externally oriented responses than girls. The use of confession and apology, therefore, does not necessarily indicate a high level of internal control or of feelings of guilt, but may represent either one kind of technique for dealing with or avoiding guilt, or even a form of response alternative to feelings of guilt. In our own study, we found no significant sex differences in number of self-critical responses. Rebelsky et al., Lee, Aronfreed and we ourselves, all used the projective story-completion technique of telling children a story involving an act of wrongdoing and asking them to complete the story. In the absence of convincing evidence of the validity of this technique, results based upon it should probably be regarded with caution, but it is interesting to see that different people using the technique have obtained rather similar results, suggesting that girls do tend to use more externally oriented reactions to transgression, and thus lending some support to the idea that females tend to have a more externalized attitude.

With regard to cheating or 'resistance to temptation', Hartshorne and May[130] found that boys showed rather more resistance to temptation and were rather more consistent across different test-situations. Sears, Maccoby and Levin,[248] however, found that *girls* showed greater resistance to temptation and slightly more emotional reactions to transgressions. Medinnus[198] found no sex difference for nine year old children on a 'ray-gun test' in which the children could increase their scores by cheating, but did find that among twelve year olds, girls were rather *less* likely to cheat than boys. In our own investigation, we found sex differences in cheating to be statistically insignificant, but did find boys tending rather more frequently to make very high cheating scores. Since cheating is the sort of thing in respect of which expectations are likely to be more or less the same for both boys and girls, and since there seems to be no reason to suppose that, in general, boys and girls should be differentially motivated to do well in all kinds of situations, it seems likely that any difference found in a particular study may be due either to the particular situations or measures used, or to the selection of the populations. In some tasks, e.g. the ray-gun test used by Medinnus, boys may be more strongly motivated to succeed, while in other tasks, the reverse may be true.

Though Piaget himself does not mention sex differences, a number of those who have based their work directly or indirectly on his, have done so. Whiteman and Kosier[273] in a study of 'objective judgments' (moral realism) and 'subjective judgments' (in terms of intentions), and Magowan[197] in a study of immanent justice, found no sex differences. Porteus and Johnson[229] found girls to be more mature on Piaget-type moral judgment items, and also in 'affective' items of a story completion kind. In support of Porteus and Johnson, Bull[55] found girls in advance of boys in each of four areas of moral judgment studied—value of life, stealing, lying and cheating, though his boys had almost, but not quite caught up with the girls by the age of 17 years. Bull thinks that girls have an *innate* advantage over boys, which gives them a greater initial sympathy, stronger feelings for others, and hence a deeper 'natural' sensitivity to personal and social attitudes. Bull observes that in his 'value of life' test, girls show more 'sympathy and reciprocity' in regard to saving someone from drowning, and considers McDougall's claim that '. . . all altruistic conduct has its root and origin in the maternal instinct'[187] (p. 175) probably justified. However, he observes that such an 'instinct' could hardly be the basis of the girls' superiority in the other three moral tests as well. Bull's results are somewhat complicated by the fact that his girls tended to be more intelligent than his boys, especially those of 11 and 13 years of age, at which ages his girls showed the greatest superiority over the boys in the stealing and cheating situations, though not in the life-saving and lying situations. Bull suggests that, while the differences in intelligence cannot be the *whole* story, these differences themselves reflect a constitutional difference in rate of development between boys and girls, the girls developing more rapidly about 11 to 13 years of age. It is further possible that, in general, an innate difference in aggressiveness might be relevant. However, it is also possible that sex-role expectations are involved. In fact, in some of his tests, Bull found that his girls showed a 'peak' at the age of 13 years. Without further evidence, however, we should probably regard this with caution. It is often tempting but always dangerous to invoke innate factors without compelling and consistent evidence. In our own investigation, we found no such sex differences in intelligence at the age of 11 and 14 years as those reported by Bull; moreover, we found the boys to be slightly superior to the girls in moral judgment based on Kohlberg's material.

In social values, such differences as are reported seem to reflect quite accurately the differential expectations of the male and female social roles. Bray[47] and Kelmer-Pringle and Edwards[155] both find that in choosing their 'most admired person', boys give preference to 'ideal persons' associated with war, politics, adventure and sport, while girls name more figures associated with humanitarian and religious activities, and with royalty. Both also report that more male figures were named by boys than female figures by girls, reflecting the differential status of the sexes. Bray also found that more girls than boys valued receiving help and affection. Very similar results were reported by Bradburn[46] who found that more boys valued personal success, more girls kindness to animals and the aged, although in general, sex differences in moral values were slight.

It must be admitted that many, if not all the studies referred to have been at a more or less superficial level. Freud was led to the view that part of the superego must be *unconscious* by his observations on the 'resistance' of certain patients to treatment, which he felt could be explained only by an unconscious need for punishment as opposed to the patient's conscious wish to recover and get rid of his distressing symptoms. If such behaviour as apology, confession and even verbal self-criticism represent little more than social techniques, then studies of such behaviour at an overt level are really scarcely relevant to Freud's notion. On the other hand, the very fact that girls appear to be, if anything, more responsive to social demands for conformity and thus more responsive to situational pressures, would tend to support Freud's view. Men do, certainly, appear from history to have got much more worked up about matters of conscience than women. This really seems to be the kind of problem to which situational experimental techniques, including self-rating scales, questionnaires and the like, are not very relevant, and which call for more complex and deeper-reaching techniques. A further point perhaps worth mentioning is how far Freud intended his hypothesis to cover *everybody*. In the *New Introductory Lectures*,[113] he suggests that as far as conscience is concerned, many people have very little beyond the basic human prohibitions against incest and murder, being kept in order by fear of external sanctions much more than by any internalized controls. Thus perhaps it is only for the few who have genuine superegos that we should expect to find any real difference between the sexes.

Religion

It has been a common practice to associate morality with religion, and many still maintain that religion is the essential basis for the achievement of a healthy morality. Others, like Bull,[56] see a danger in making religion the basis of morality because they fear that if the two are too closely associated, a decline in religious belief must be associated with a corresponding decline in the level of morality. There is an important distinction to be made here between the social function of religion in the community in promoting morality by its concern with moral questions which are thereby kept alive as issues, and the personal or individual function of religion in promoting a higher level of morality in the believer. If we believe that religion is a necessary basis of, or even that it promotes, personal morality, then we should expect to find that the religiously inclined show a higher general level of morality. This does not necessarily follow from assuming that religion may tend to promote morality in the community. The question of the social function of religion in this and other senses is not one with which we shall be concerned here, but it is an extremely difficult question to which to find an answer. We shall be concerned here with the more individual or psychological question of whether there are any grounds for supposing that religious beliefs are related to the level of personal morality.

Hartshorne and May[130] found that, in general, children who went to Sunday school were more honest than those who did not. As they allow, however, this is probably because of associated factors of family background rather than because of the particular effect of religious teaching as such. Although clear evidence is lacking, it is reasonable to suppose that, on the whole, the parents of the children in Hartshorne and May's study who saw that their children went to Sunday school also provided them with a general background of experience more likely to further such things as honesty. There may also have been a relevant social class selective factor involved. Maller,[193] however, found that the honesty of a group of Jewish children improved while they were attending religious schools, suggesting that for these children, at any rate, religious teaching did tend to promote honesty. One cannot, however, know here whether the *religious basis* of the teaching was important as such, or whether the children became more honest simply because they were encouraged to be so. Moreover, the increased honesty might be a rather specific thing, specific either in the sense that the improvement was confined to certain situations, or that other aspects of behaviour besides honesty were not affected. A further but important point is that Hartshorne and May's work was carried out forty or more years ago, and their findings should not be taken automatically to hold today.

Bull[55] used a measure of frequency of church attendance, which he called 'religious class', but, arguing that children may go to church for various different reasons, also included a test of religious 'attitude' based on a sentence completion technique, with each item scored on a five point scale ranging from 'very positive' at one end to 'very negative' at the other. The two measures (attendance and attitude) correlated consistently on average about +.50 in several samples of boys and girls ranging from nine years to 17 years of age. Although these correlations are not very high, Bull concluded that church attendance is 'not so crude a yardstick of religious influence and conviction as might be supposed' (pp. 274–275), and felt justified in using his 'religious class' measure to relate to measures of 'moral' variables. (It is not clear why he should have used 'religious class' rather than 'religious attitude', nor, indeed, why he did not use both). His findings are very tentative. There were no consistent relationships between religious class and moral judgment on his interview tests, although religious class did tend to be related to judgment in his 'Lying' situation and in his 'Value of Life' situation. 'Both tests involved respect and concern for others', Bull comments, 'so that religious influence may be seen as a factor in shaping such attitudes' (p. 284). However, the results scarcely seem to justify much confidence in this conclusion. In his written tests, the association of religion and moral judgment seemed rather more marked for children of 13 and 15 years of age; and the test showing the highest relationship of judgment to religious class was one concerned with the concept of justice. Bull's findings are therefore very tenuous and do not provide much support for the importance of religion in individual moral development. Stephenson[259] found little difference in scores on his three measures of conscience (Intropunitive Guilt, Other-Directed Anxiety and Conscience Motive) between middle class church-goers and middle class non church-goers. For working class subjects, those who attend church scored rather higher than those who did not, especially on 'Conscience Motive', but again, the differences were slight; and there may very well have been related intrusive variables such as home atmosphere at work.

A number of studies have been concerned with the religious habits of delinquents. Sheldon and Eleanor Glueck[118] found that a smaller proportion of delinquents were in the habit of attending church every week. Wattenberg[271] in his study of delinquent boys, found fewer recidivists among those who were regular church attenders. Wattenberg suggests that church-going is part of a general mode of living which reduces the tendency to delinquency. Similarly, Ferguson[82] in Glasgow found that delinquents showed a relatively low rate of church attendance, probably for similar reasons. It is also true, however, that there are many church-goers and many professedly religious people to be found among delinquents and prisoners. As far as professions of religious belief are concerned, it may well be the case that prisoners tend to report themselves as more religious than they are. Nevertheless, religious conviction is a different thing from church attendance, although, as Bull[55] showed, the two are related. We would, I think, scarcely expect mere church attendance to be related to morality except to a rather limited extent; fear of what other church members might think might sometimes be a relevant motive for keeping out of trouble. Nor would we expect relatively superficially held beliefs to be important. However, genuine, strongly held religious convictions involving real commitment might very well be associated with a more moral attitude as revealed both in the avoidance of wrongdoing and in the positive aspect of regard and sympathetic consideration for others. The positive aspect has not yet received very much attention, but Shoben[251] reports a study by Siegman of prisoners in Israel. Siegman developed a scale of religious observance which classified subjects into three categories—(i) those with a firm religious commitment, including strict observance of orthodox Jewish dietary laws, abstention from work on the sabbath and regular attendance at the synagogue, (ii) those who failed to meet these three criteria consistently but who nevertheless professed sincere belief, and (iii) those who performed no acts of religious observance or professed no belief at all. Siegman compared a group of 125 prisoners in Israeli gaols with a control group matched in respect of national origin, social class membership and intelligence. Only 41 per cent of the prisoners fell into categories one and two, as compared with 67 per cent of the non-delinquent control group. Siegman points out that 92 per cent of the prisoners and 90 per cent of the control group had had some kind of religious training, and concludes that mere religious training does not provide a safeguard against anti-social behaviour. Shoben's conclusion is that when religious training, along with other factors, leads to 'a relatively intense and enduring religious commitment, then the chances of succumbing to illegality are significantly reduced' (p. 139).

Argyle[8] indicates that most European studies have found Catholics to have a relatively high delinquency rate, while Jewish and non-religious groups have the lowest rate. Here, findings are almost certainly affected by the important associated variable of social class position. However, Trenaman,[265] in his study of delinquency in the army, found the delinquent soldiers to contain a relatively high proportion of Catholics and a relatively small proportion of non-conformists compared with non-delinquent soldiers, and is satisfied that in this case, Catholics and non-conformists were from very similar social backgrounds. Argyle observes that there is some evidence that Protestants tend to have a higher level of guilt than Catholics. (This has frequently been maintained, e.g. George Simpson's *Editor's Introduction* to the English version of Durkheim's *Suicide*.[67] In a later paper[9] Argyle also provides some empirical evidence of his own, based on sentence completion material, that Protestants have a more strongly internalized superego than Catholics (though it is possible that this also is affected by social class and other possible biases.) Boehm[41] comes to the aid of the Catholics. In a study of children in American semi-rural and urban public (state) schools and Catholic parochial schools, she found that, in responding to Piaget-type situations, in terms of intention rather than outcome of action, 'Catholic parochial school children, regardless of socio-economic class and intelligence level, score higher at an earlier age than public school children' (p. 601), and also tend to show earlier development of independence of adults and peer reciprocity. We must, however, be cautious here. While it seems that Catholic concern with 'responsibility' does advance children's judgments where it is relevant, the evidence from a few questions is slight; the superiority of the Catholic children may be relatively superficial, may represent little more than a better trained verbal habit, and may, in the absence of follow-up studies, be relatively transient. As I have remarked elsewhere, 'It seems likely not only that these differences reflect the somewhat different experience of Protestants and Catholics, but that their importance also depends upon the more general social context within which the two religious groups function'[119] (p. 110). It has frequently been observed, for example, that in Eire, with a population mainly of Catholics, the rate of crime is low, but that among Irish populations in urban centres outside Eire, it is disproportionately high.

A significant distinction is made by Middleton and Putney[200] between 'anti-ascetic' and 'anti-social' behaviour. They found that students in Florida and California who believed in a personal God gambled less, and less frequently had pre-marital intercourse than agnostics, but that there was no difference between believers and non-believers in such anti-social things as shoplifting, cheating on examinations or striking another person in anger. Kinsey[154] also reports less sexual activity among the religious. Like Middleton and Putney, Wright and Cox[281] distinguish between 'ascetic' questions, where the consequences of an individual's action primarily involve the individual himself, and 'social' questions, where the consequences of an individual's action may cause distress to others. Wright and Cox asked sixth-form pupils in maintained grammar schools questions about gambling, drunkenness, smoking, lying, stealing, pre-marital intercourse, suicide and the colour bar. They found that the more religious pupils strongly tended to be more severe in their judgments *particularly* over the more 'ascetic' questions. Non-religious pupils were inclined to argue that if behaviour does not harm others, it should not be subject to moral judgment by other people, while the religious subjects tended to say that *all* behaviour is of concern to God and may properly be subjected to evaluation. Wright and Cox observe that moral beliefs seem in some measure to fulfil a defensive function for some religious pupils while they are regarded by other religious pupils as conditions for the development of self-respect and responsibility. Moreton[209] found some tendency for adolescents and adults to view religion as a necessary prerequisite for a 'good life', while Forrester[88] found the same for adolescents. This, of course, provides no evidence that religion *is* thus necessary; and in fact, one half of Forrester's subjects regarded religion as *unessential* to leading a good life, while Hilliard[138] reports similar findings in his study of college and university students.

The evidence on the whole suggests that there does tend to be *some* association between religious belief and morality, though this is complicated by other factors. But it seems quite likely that religion is *personally* relevant and important when it is believed and accepted with real commitment, as Shoben[251] suggests. At the same time, we have many outstanding cases of non-believers who offer splendid examples of the application of the highest moral principles in the conduct of their lives. It seems to me that the more important function of religion is the social one, a view which Shoben expresses well when he writes that religion is important, not as the 'institutionalized embodiment of command-ments or rules, but as the carrier of great traditions of moral conduct, great models of responsible manhood. It is in these great religious traditions that one finds the material about which a rational man can most profitably learn to think, and by engaging in such thought, to learn, unlearn and learn anew the styles of the moral life that enable him to participate in the human community and to confront, with courage and even a little gaiety, the poignant but distinctively human inevitability of the moral dilemma' (p. 145).

Social Class

Piaget was careful to say that the children with whom he carried out his study of moral development were 'children from the poorer parts of Geneva. In different surroundings the age aver-ages would certainly have been different'[227] (p. 37n). Others have suggested that more than simply the age averages would have been different.

It seems reasonable to suppose that the surroundings in which children of parents of different socio-economic levels are brought up might be sufficiently different in a variety of ways, for differen-ces in moral orientation to be associated with socio-economic differences, and there is quite a lot of evidence to support this. In one of the first relevant studies, Harrower[127] used a slightly modi-fied version of Piaget's technique to study children's attitude to punishment. Her subjects were children of two age groups, five to seven years and eight to ten years, taken from two different kinds of school, one a London County Council school with predominantly working class children and the other a private school whose children came mainly from upper middle class families. Among the LCC children, nearly all the younger children favoured 'retributive' punishment, while appreciably more of the older children favoured 'reciprocity' punishment, just as Piaget had found. Among the middle class children, however, quite an

I

appreciable number of the younger children favoured reciprocity, and this proportion failed to increase with age. Harrower
considers the possibility that the middle class children had passed
through Piaget's earlier stage by the time they took part in her
investigation, but she regards this as unlikely, and prefers to view
her results as reflecting alternative kinds of orientation, depending
on the child's experience and the way in which he has been
encouraged to think of such things as punishment, from a very
early age. In other words, like the learning theorists, Harrower
conceives of differences in orientation as reflecting different kinds
of experience and demands, rather than as representing different
sequential stages of development.

Harrower did not control for possible differences in intelligence
between her working class and her middle class children, but a
few years later, Lerner[76] in American found that even when he
controlled for both intelligence and age, children of higher socio-
economic status showed an earlier decline in moral realism.
Unlike Harrower, Lerner interpreted his findings as indicating that
the middle class children passed through the earlier stage more
quickly. Lerner thought that the class difference he observed was
probably due to the fact that working class parents were more
authoritarian and gave their children fewer opportunities to learn
more autonomous attitudes. Macrae,[191] however, while confirming Lerner's finding of a class difference, thought that the explanation was more likely to be that lower-status parents probably gave
only a superficial impression of exercising more authority because
they used more direct punishment, but in fact, exercised *less*
influence in the direction of inculcating norms.

Boehm and Nass,[43] using children of from six to twelve
years of age, report little by way of social class differences. They
found no significant difference between working class and middle
class children in tendency to judge in terms of intentions rather
than consequences, although they did find a slight and insignificant tendency for the working class children to be more
concerned with 'material value' than intention. There were no
class differences with respect to motives for aggressive behaviour,
no differences in attitude to lying and no difference in regard for
peers as opposed to regard for authority. However, Boehm[40] did

find, with children of six to nine years of age, that upper class children showed more regard for intentions compared with consequences at an earlier age than working class children. This might be explained by assuming that *both* a higher degree of intelligence *and* proper encouragement are necessary to develop a high level of 'intentionality'. However, Boehm also reports that working class children showed an earlier development of reciprocity in relation to peers, and an earlier independence of adult authority figures. These findings strongly suggest that peer reciprocity and independence are a different kind of thing from intentionality. In a further article, Boehm[41] reports academically gifted upper middle class children in both Catholic and State schools to score higher on intentionality than academically gifted working class children, and working class children to score higher in peer reciprocity and independence of adults.

Boehm's finding that working class children reach earlier independence of adults does not seem to fit with Lerner's[76] view quoted above, nor with the finding of Kohn[168] that working class parents stressed obedience to parental authority while middle class parents tended to lay more emphasis on internal standards of conduct. It may be that, while working class parents tend to stress obedience, they do not exercise such close control, and do not achieve as much *acceptance* of their authority as middle class parents.

Aronfreed[11] found that, in story completion tests, middle class children more often showed self-criticism, while working class children were more frequently oriented toward punitive consequences from without, and more often sought external sources of justification for transgressions. We ourselves also found that working class children of 11 and 12 years of age made fewer self-critical responses in story completions than middle class children, but that there was no significant difference for children of 14 and 15 years. Aronfreed also found that middle class *girls* more often made responses involving confession, working class girls more often responses involving discovery and punishment. His results were supported by Maureen Lee[174] working with English children.

Aronfreed further claims[14] that parents of higher socio-economic status usually exercise closer control, more frequently withdraw affection or threaten to withdraw affection, and make wider use of explanation in dealing with their children, all of which he very reasonably considers likely to contribute to the development of a more 'internal' orientation. Moreover, people of higher status generally have more freedom to make decisions and to evaluate their actions, and this will tend to permeate the atmosphere of a home where in any case, 'induction' techniques of discipline are likely to be much in use. Tuma and Livson,[266] using various techniques, collected information on the tendency of children to *conform to* pressures from parents, school and peers, and found that higher status children were less conforming, and that conforming was inversely related to the education of the parents, especially the mother. Again, middle class parents, in general, are more likely to set an example of control for their children by the fact that they themselves use more 'rational' methods in dealing with their children. Sears, Maccoby and Levin,[248] indeed, while they found middle class parents more permissive and less likely to use physical punishment, found little class difference in the tendency to withhold affection. But their data, collected by interview from mothers, may not be wholly trustworthy. In any case, if one distinguishes between 'induction' and 'love-withdrawal', with Hoffman and Saltzstein,[142] it may be the 'induction' rather than the 'withdrawal of love' which is the main operative factor. In support of his claim that middle (and upper) class people tend to have a more internal orientation, Aronfreed[14] refers to the findings of Henry and Short in their book *Suicide and Homicide*[135] where it is claimed that the middle and upper classes are more likely to commit suicide, the working classes to commit homicide. In the former case, Henry and Short argue, following Freudian theory, aggression is turned inward, in the latter case, it is turned outward. This is, however, a rather tenuous argument.

Kohlberg[162] reports a direct relationship between social class and level of moral judgment as established by his interview technique. We ourselves also found class differences in moral judgment on Kohlberg's material but found these to be rather small when intelligence was controlled by matching. In fact, we found the same effect with cheating on an academic task—a marked class difference almost disappeared when intelligence was controlled. It is therefore important, when interpreting class differences, to be sure that they do not simply reflect differences in intelligence. The situation is, of course, complex, since middle class children may do better on intelligence tests because their parents provide a higher level of verbal and intellectual stimulation and this, especially when coupled with a more 'responsibility-oriented' attitude on the part of the parents, is likely also to raise the moral level. As Kohlberg[166] observes, social classes (and other groups) differ crucially in the amount of social and cognitive stimulation which they provide for their children. He finds, in particular, that middle class, 13 year old children tend to have more mature judgment if their parents encourage the discussion of moral issues. Moreover, middle class children have, for various reasons, more opportunity for role-taking, and thus for developing the capacity to take the perspective of other people. In England, the children of middle class, especially upper middle class, and upper class parents are more likely to go to private fee-paying schools ('Public' Schools), and this is also likely to have an effect, although there is so far no satisfactory evidence of this.

But, although Kohlberg observes that middle class children move faster and further along this developmental progression, he also holds that, in general, social classes do not differ in the major basic values they hold. Attitudes towards specific issues or institutions may differ between classes—for example, attitude to law and police—but the main basic values are much the same. This view is shared by John and Elizabeth Newson,[222] who point out that parents of all classes show warmth and love, and share many values, but that the middle class parents are more likely to use verbal reasoning, more likely to give weight to the child's *own* reasons, and also to encourage habits of verbal self-justification. They are more concerned with showing the nature and general applicability of moral principles, and are more likely to emphasize fairness and reciprocity. Bernstein[36] has emphasized the importance of class differences in the use of language. Middle class children are likely to hear, to be introduced to and to use more abstract language. This is bound to be reflected in their moral thinking and orientation, as in other spheres.

Stephenson[259] found 'conscience motive' (factors 'directly concerned with personal evaluation and direction of conduct') to be related to all measures of social status and education. This relationship seemed to hold throughout all the six social class groupings which he used, but he suggests that the greatest difference is between class III manual and class III non-manual. In other words, there is a critical difference between white-collar and blue-collar. Stephenson's middle class children also scored higher on 'other-directed anxiety' ('the individual's susceptibility to external moral sanctions, reflected in the tendency to anticipate and avoid disapproval') but there were no class differences in 'intropunitive guilt' ('the self-inflicted remorse and unhappiness which may follow wrongdoing'). Stephenson mentions that McCord and McCord[185] found a slight indication (statistically insignificant) that their other-directed type of conscience occurred more frequently in middle class subjects (young adults), and also that their 'integral' conscience was more frequent in middle class subjects. It is interesting that Stephenson found no class differences in intropunitive guilt, because, according to Aronfreed's analysis, we should have expected to find a greater tendency to feelings of guilt among middle class children than among working class children. However, Stephenson's children were 15 years of age, and according to him, we might expect the more morally mature to have 'replaced' some of their 'intropunitive guilt' by 'conscience motive'. Some slight support is given to this view by our own finding that middle class children of 11 years of age but not of 14 gave more self-critical responses than working class children of the same age. This is, however, a complex question and we certainly are not yet in a position to give an answer with confidence.

Finally, Havighurst and Taba[132] found the moral 'reputation' of adolescents as judged by ratings made by teachers, employers, peers and others, to be directly related to social class position. This was so for ratings of honesty, loyalty, responsibility, moral courage and friendliness, especially the first four. 'Friendliness' is clearly a rather different kind of thing from the others. Nora Weckler, who wrote the chapter on *Social class and school adjustment in relation to character reputation,* in this book, thinks that 'the character reputation of subjects is determined primarily by the degree to which their actual behaviour conforms to the middle-class standards of the school' (p. 52). 'Upper middle class boys and girls may conform to school expectations because of the consistent reinforcement of middle class standards and goals by all the character-building agencies with which they come in contact—their homes, their play groups, their schools, their churches and so on' (p. 53). Reputation scores were found to be more homogeneous in upper middle class children, and to show a wider range in lower class children. Weckler reasonably thought that this might be because *some* of the lower class families were upwardly oriented, whereas probably the majority were not.

There is therefore, considerable and rather convincing evidence of the association of moral level with social class. It is probable that this is mediated by wider use of 'reasoning' techniques in discipline, together with a higher general level of intelligence and subtler use of language.

Those cases frequently referred to as 'psychopaths' are of particular interest to a study of moral development and learning, since they are often described as 'amoral' or completely devoid of 'conscience'. The term 'psychopathy' has been used in various senses, sometimes to refer to more or less any form of mental disorder. Here, however, we use it specifically to refer to those apparently 'conscienceless' cases. As McCord and McCord remind us, J. C. Pritchard, an English doctor, produced the phrase, which was to become so widely used, 'moral insanity'. He used it to refer to cases in which 'the power of self-government is lost or greatly impaired and the individual is found to be incapable, not of talking or reasoning upon any subject proposed to him, but of conducting himself with decency and propriety in the business of life'[184] (*qu.* p. 21). In 1888, Koch proposed the term 'psychopathic inferiority', which later became modified to 'constitutional psychopathy'. This term, implying that psychopathy was due to a constitutional tendency or predisposition, enjoyed a long popularity. It was, however, often used in a more general sense than is our present concern.*

McCord and McCord propose six criteria by which psychopaths can be distinguished. (1) They are asocial, i.e. do not seem to be at all responsive to the kind of social factors which exercise at least some restraint or influence on most people. They are, for example, not concerned with the implications of their behaviour for the happiness or well-being of others. (2) They are driven by 'primitive desires'. The emphasis here seems to be on the word

* For a compact review of literature on psychopathy and the meaning of the term, see M. Craft[63]

'driven'. Psychopaths want the same kind of things as other people, but don't seem able to tolerate even temporary frustration. McCord and McCord suggest, however, that in particular, psychopaths may have an exceptionally high need or desire for excitement and variety. (3) They are highly impulsive, with little or no capacity for sustained application in pursuit of long-term goals. This seems to be very much the same kind of thing as the second criterion. (4) They are aggressive. However, this aggressiveness is due more to the absence of inhibitions than to an excessively high level of aggressive drive. 'The normal man has learned to control aggression. . . . The psychopath, on the other hand, characteristically reacts to frustration with fury' (p. 9). (5) They show little or no guilt or remorse. This may, indeed be taken as the most important and crucial criterion. It is frequently accompanied, as might be expected and is almost implied by the term 'absence of guilt', by evidence of callous heartlessness and indifference to the sufferings of others. This absence of guilt, as McCord and McCord remark, distinguishes the psychopath not only from normal people, but also from non-psychopathic criminals who generally have *some* feelings of obligation to at least *some* others, though not all those which most members of society would like them to have. Absence of guilt and remorse, however, do not prevent them from talking of their sorrow and regrets for what they have done. 'Some psychopaths exhibit a deceptive shell of remorse, but the shell is empty. They talk of morality but inside they feel none, and their words do not hinder their actions' (p. 11). (6) They have a warped capacity for love. They tend to have only fleeting attachments, and no sense of the mutual obligations normally recognized in genuine emotional attachments. This criterion seems to follow from (2) and (5). Since anyone driven by primitive desires, aggressive and showing no guilt and no sense of social or personal obligation can certainly be called 'asocial', one might conveniently telescope these criteria into three—driven by desires, free from guilt or remorse, aggressive. D. J. West[272] also poses three main criteria. (1) Behaviour disturbance in the absence of severe neurotic or psychotic illness. This specifically states that true 'psychopaths' are *not* neurotic or psychotic in the usual sense, i.e. that the presence of symptoms recognized as neurotic or psychotic is incompatible with a diagnosis of 'psychopathic'. (2) Liability to unrestrained aggression. (3) Anti-social behaviour which suggests indifference. The implication so far has been that the various aspects or criteria of psychopathy form a unified syndrome, and one should expect to find them generally, or at least commonly, together. No doubt cases can be found where all the 'stigmata' do occur; but West, in a study of 19 repeated offenders from whom all showing neurotic or psychotic trends had been excluded, found *no case* in which all his three criteria were applicable, and in general, found that the three 'constitutents of psychopathy' were unrelated. His cases were rated for emotional indifference, lying, absence of guilt, shallowness of feelings and impulsive aggressiveness. However, it might be argued that people might show in some degree one or other 'sign' of psychopathy without properly being regarded as 'psychopathic', and that, in fact, West had no genuine psychopaths in his sample. Whereas West had *excluded* all cases with neurotic or psychotic symptoms, Jenkins[147] found severe neurotic symptoms and psychopathic behaviour *not* to be mutually incompatible, though actively anti-social prisoners tended to show emotional indifference. However, Jenkins reported that, in general, violence and emotional indifference tended to be independent. Other writers have also held that there may be neurotic elements in the psychopathic makeup. Robert Lindner, for example,[178] thinks that the psychopath's aggressiveness represents an attempt to overcome anxiety and fearfulness. Most observers report psychopaths to be singularly free from anxiety, but of course, if one admits the possibility of 'unconscious anxiety' it becomes possible to argue for the presence of anxiety purely as an intervening variable which need not be observable by the generally accepted signs. It will appear from this that there is not complete agreement as to what should be included under and excluded from the definition of psychopathy, but we shall adopt impulsivity and apparent absence of guilt and remorse as our main criterion, with the added proviso that any possible neurotic or psychotic trends should appear only as minor rather than as dominating aspects of the picture. The great problem is, what are the possible factors underlying the development of such a 'conscienceless' character? Or, putting it the other way round (which may make better sense), what are the factors which may be associated with the *failure* of psychopaths to develop anything like a normal conscience or normal personal responsiveness?

There are three main possibilities which must be considered by way of explanation. Psychopathy or 'consciencelessness' might conceivably be due to hereditary or genetic factors, to physiological effects of trauma or illness, or to particular kinds of experience. As McCord and McCord indicate, many people since Pritchard have held that psychopathy is a hereditary disease and have tried to support their view by pointing to family resemblances. For example, many psychopaths have been reported as coming from families with a history of mental abnormality of one kind or another. However, some relevant comments may be made here. (a) Such studies often seem to have selected their psychopaths by rather vague general criteria, and we can have no great confidence that they may not have included *other* forms of abnormality as well. (b) Many normal people also have family histories of abnormality. This in itself is not evidence against a hypothesis of genetic causality, but the case for the genetic hypothesis would be strengthened if it were clearly shown that there was more abnormality in the family histories of psychopaths than of normal people. (c) We find psychopaths where there seems to be no family history of abnormality. (d) If psychopathy is to be regarded as a hereditary disorder, we should have evidence, not only that abnormality is more frequent in the families of psychopaths, but that specifically *psychopathic* abnormality is more frequent. Even so, it would be difficult to dispose wholly of the argument that psychopathy might tend to run in families because of the way in which psychopathic parents treat their children. Adequate twin studies specifically of psychopaths do not seem to have been carried out, perhaps because of practical difficulties.

It is important to distinguish between the presumed psychopath and the criminal and delinquent population as a whole. Psychopaths represent only a small proportion of criminals, and not all psychopaths are necessarily criminals. The Gluecks[118] have maintained that violent criminals tend to be 'endomorphic' in build, i.e. big and strong, and suggest a constitutional tendency in the endomorphic constitution as an explanation. It seems just as reasonable, however, if not more reasonable, to suppose that big strong men are more likely to have learned that violence may pay.

An important aspect of the heredity argument is whether we think of psychopathy as inherited in a unitary way, or whether we think of the inheritance of a *tendency* to psychopathy. If the former, we should be inclined to look for evidence of some hereditary basis for specific physical defect associated with excessive impulsiveness and inability to learn to *inhibit* behaviour. Quite recently, Price and Whatmore[230, 231] have reported findings in support of the view that individuals with an extra 'Y' sex chromosome show severe personality disturbance and tend strongly to a history of crime. If further supporting evidence is found, this is obviously an important factor. If we think of a more general hereditary *tendency toward* psychopathy, then we need not think of the psychopath as being 'qualitatively' different, but as representing the extreme end of the distribution of a 'predisposing' variable which might depend upon the accumulation of a number of different hereditary factors. Even if the case for the importance of the extra 'Y' chromosome were to be established exclusively, in the sense that all people with this defect are psychopathic, there may be other cases of psychopathy which do not have this particular defect. Price and Whatmore, after all, report only nine cases though all showed the same pattern.

Many attempts have also been made to link psychopathy with physical abnormality due to accident or illness. Alpers (reported in ref. 184), for example, found that lesions in the hypothalamus part of the brain were associated with an increase in aggressiveness, anti-social tendencies and partial or complete loss of insight. Only a relatively small proportion of psychopaths have a history of hypothalamic injury, however, although it is possible that others may have undiagnosed hypothalamic abnormalities of some kind. At present the evidence, although indicating that hypothalamic defect may well be important in some cases, is insufficient for us to be able to say that such defect can be assumed to be present in *all* cases. Henderson[133] and Lauretta Bender[29] suggested that encephalitis might be a possible cause, and André Berge, who distinguished between cases of inability to control impulsiveness and cases lacking in the capacity to be moved by the distress they caused to others, reports[33] (p. 53) that Dr. Combes-Hamelle found *both* these forms of behavioural disturbance to be possible sequelae of encephalitis in children, the intellectual functions remaining unimpaired. And Stafford-Clark *et al.*[256] found that almost one half of their population of criminal psychopaths had a history of either epilepsy or head injuries. Unfortunately, McCord and McCord[184] (p. 57) report a German study of 154 cases of encephalitis where there seemed to be no signs of psychopathic or delinquent tendencies as an aftermath. Encephalographs have been reported to show abnormal patterns of brain activity, particularly in aggressive psychopaths, but not all research has confirmed these reports. Ostrow and Ostrow (reported by McCord and McCord,[184]) found the incidence of abnormal patterns of encephalograph no more frequent in psychopaths than in other 'abnormal' groups. As McCord and McCord comment, 'Failing to differentiate psychopathy from other disorders, the research nevertheless indicates the strong probability of a greater proportion of abnormal EEG patterns among psychopaths than among the normal population'[184] (p. 54). However, this does not establish brain defect as the cause of, or even a primary factor in, psychopathy, although it is suggestive.

According to McCord and McCord, Lindner[178] reported that all eight of a sample of criminal psychopaths investigated under hypnosis had suffered cruel treatment from their parents. In particular, Lindner thought that the basis of psychopathy lay in rejection of rather than identification with the father. He felt that as a result, psychopaths suffered from an inadequate superego and also from (unconscious) feelings of guilt for parricidal fantasies. The extent to which *absence* of manifest signs of guilt seem characteristic of psychopaths would only be incompatible with Lindner's idea if we do not accept the notion of unconscious guilt. If we do, and if we think of unconscious guilt as something which is repressed and has to be defended against, then it is clear enough that we should expect relatively little by way of manifest guilt. Only the fairly strongly psychoanalytically-minded have accepted the notion of unconscious guilt unreservedly, as we have seen. But Lindner's view that psychopaths suffer from rejection as children has received a substantial amount of support. Bowlby, in 1946[44] reported early and severe or repeated *separation* from the mother to be common in his cases of 'delinquent character formation' (affectionless, psychopathic character). Bowlby[45] considered that the critical age for 'maternal deprivation' to have its most adverse effect on the child's character development was between the ages of six and 18 months, although some effects, decreasing with increasing age, might be expected up to the age of eight years or so. Ainsworth,[3] after a careful review, concludes that early and severe deprivation (including insufficient maternal care as well as physical separation from the mother or mother-substitute) is likely to be a significant antecedent of affectionless characters, though the number of 'deprived children' in this sense who grow into affectionless or psychopathic characters is likely to be relatively small. Like Lindner, Andry[7] suggests that a faulty relationship with the father may also be a significant factor. Some supporting evidence comes from Glueck and Glueck[118] who found that the loss of *either* parent before the age of five years was twice as frequent in delinquents (not, however, necessarily affectionless or psychopathic) than in non-delinquents. Ainsworth[3] suggests that 'a multiplicity' of people looking after children is likely to reduce the amount of adult-child interaction, and if this kind of 'deprivation' is severe and prolonged, it may tend to have a generally 'depressing' and retarding effect, while if we have many caretakers supplying lots of 'care', but discontinuously so that the active caretaker is constantly changing, this might be expected to produce *indiscriminate* social responsiveness which if prolonged would tend to inhibit the development of the capacity for genuine involvement in interpersonal relations which might lead to the emergence of an 'affectionless character'. There is, however, no evidence directly supporting this hunch. Bender[30] found that defects in language, abstract thinking and concept formation as well as impaired capacity for forming emotional attachments formed a part of a syndrome which she called 'psychopathic behaviour disorder', and concluded that this syndrome frequently followed severe maternal deprivation in the first few years of life. It is interesting to find Bender including deficiency in such intellectual functions, clearly identifiable as 'ego functions'. There thus seems to be a fair amount of support for thinking that deprivation or rejection may be an important factor, although perhaps not quite for McCord and McCord's conclusion that rejection is a *necessary* prerequisite for the development of a psychopathic personality. They believe that factors like brain damage, especially to the hypothalamus, may be relevant in cases of *mild* rejection, but that severe rejection by itself may be sufficient. In other words, the role of brain damage is to sensitise the victim to the effects of deprivation, and it is *not* a sufficient cause of psychopathy in the absence of rejection. 'The psychopathic syndrome can be traced to early deficiency in affectional relations. Extreme emotional deprivation, or moderate rejection coupled with neural damage to inhibitive centres does account for the development of psychopathy. The theory reconciles the two major discoveries: that all psychopaths are, in some degree, rejected, and that many psychopaths have a neural disorder'[184] (p. 71). By the inclusion of deprivation and rejection together, it seems to be implied that it is the *lack* of 'emotional sustenance' which is crucial. However, it may be rash to assume that relative lack of affection (such as has been reported of some institutions) has the same kind of effects as, though less severe than, more positive rejection by 'bad' parents. McCord and McCord may well have over-stated their claims; but the emphasis on affection fits in well with the more general findings on the importance of affection and attention from others in the development of the normal and 'excessive' conscience. The non-brain damaged psychopath, according to this view, should be the *extremely* deprived. However, the evidence seems to suggest several cautions. (a) It may not in fact be the case that *all* psychopaths suffer from a higher-than-normal degree of deprivation or rejection, even among the non-brain-damaged. (b) Only a relatively small number of even severely deprived children may develop into psychopaths. Are there not severely deprived children who nevertheless are not psychopathic? (c) It is very much easier to conduct *retrospective* studies of psychopaths than to conduct *pro*-spective studies of deprived children, and it may be only too easy to find retrospective evidence of deprivation —after all, nobody is entirely 'undeprived'. (d) It may be difficult to know what is the chicken and what is the egg. When one finds evidence of rejection in childhood, one is very much tempted to argue that initially rejection sets up a vicious circle in which rejection leads to behaviour which produces further rejection. However, unless the evidence of rejection is from infancy or very early childhood, it is also possible, in the absence of other evidence, to argue the case the other way round. The behaviour of the child may be what in the first instance induces the rejecting behaviour on the part of the parents and starts off the vicious circle.

As we have already indicated, the influence of psychoanalytic
theory on research in moral development and learning has been
indirect rather than direct. The wide and general nature of the
theory and the way in which it is stated have served to draw
attention to particular areas and to suggest general kinds of questions rather than to provide directly derived hypotheses capable
of empirical testing. Investigators also influenced by learning
theory have directed their attention to such areas. Psychoanalytic
theory has suggested the interest in the nature of the relations
between children and their parents, especially in the earlier years
of life. Indeed, it might perhaps be said that the influence of
psychoanalytic theory has induced people to pay rather too
much attention to both parent-child relations and early experience. The results of research so far have scarcely been commen-
surate with the amount of effort expended. Psychoanalytic theory
is, like conditioning and reinforcement theory, basically a hedonistic theory, and has tended to stimulate interest, perhaps disproportionate, in the affective or 'feeling' aspects of moral development and in less 'rational' aspects of conscience. In other words,
the influence of psychoanalytic theory has been via superego
notions rather than via ego notions, although to some extent, the
more recent development of psychoanalytic ego theory has
suggested that this imbalance should be righted. Psychoanalytic
theory has also tended to emphasize the negative, restrictive
aspects of moral control rather than the more positive prescriptive
aspects, although in this respect, we must remember that, if Freud
seemed to pay special attention to the restrictive aspects of the
superego, he did also include the prescriptive aspects, although

still emphasizing the unconscious basis of these prescriptions. It may also be held, with some justification, that psychoanalytic theory has overemphasized the importance of guilt and the avoidance of guilt as a basis of morality, in which it has perhaps been followed by some brands of learning theory. On the positive side, psychoanalytic theory performed a service by emphasizing that there may indeed be an important basis of morality in non-rational factors, and that these need to be taken into account by any wholly adequate theory. Psychoanalytic theory was, of course, largely responsible for the widespread use of the concept of identification. We have suggested that we may be well advised to stop trying to use identification as an explanatory concept, though we may still continue to use it in a general descriptive sense. The concept of identification has, however, drawn attention to the importance of being able to 'put oneself in another's place' (also known as empathy) which, as we have seen, is an important factor particularly in the development of altruism and unselfishness, and cannot be overlooked by any comprehensive approach to moral development.

It seems, indeed, as if Freud himself had been more concerned with providing a theoretical edifice to explain why people behave in some way *at variance with* what might reasonably be expected of them by way of moral behaviour, rather than in explaining why people in general do tend to think and act in conformity with generally accepted norms. Thus, Freud seems to have been especially concerned with the machinations of the superego as a way of explaining why some people seem to carry their 'morality', their ascetic tendencies, their self-critical, self-defeating, self-aggressive and masochistic impulses to such extremes. But to the extent that this is true, it comes near to implying an acceptance of *normal* or 'reasonable' conformity as natural and in need of no special explanation. This, indeed is what we had in mind when we observed that Freud often seemed to take the activities of the ego more or less for granted.

Learning theory, including both conditioning and reinforcement theory, has, on the other hand, generated a lot of empirical research, although much of it may be criticized on the grounds that the experimental demonstrations with which this kind of research abounds are in effect limited to showing how things *might* work, rather than providing convincing evidence that this is how moral learning in real life really does proceed. It may be suggested that conditioning theory, as expounded by Eysenck, attempts to explain in other (in some ways, perhaps more acceptable) terms, the kind of irrational basis of 'moral' behaviour which Freud's superego was also primarily designed to explain. Conditioning theory may be criticized on rather similar grounds to psychoanalytic theory, that it does not allow sufficiently for more rational or 'ego' factors. Conditioning is, of course, a different 'kind of thing' from the establishment of the superego, in the sense that conditioning and counter-conditioning can go on during a person's whole life, whereas the development of the superego is something which takes place basically during early childhood (although Freud did allow for some later modification). There is, however, a certain similarity in Freudian and Eysenckian theory. For both, the development of the basis of conscience was essentially an unthinking and unquestioning process. For Freud, the superego was laid down by instinct and experience with one's parents, and once the critical early period was passed, deficiencies could, generally speaking, only be made good by specifically psychoanalytic experience, including the analytic experience with the therapist or parent-substitute. For Eysenck, an underdeveloped conscience was due to insufficient social conditioning in conjunction with a given constitution, and could best be put right by a specifically designed programme of appropriate conditioning. Again, both Freud and Eysenck concerned themselves mainly with the negative aspects of conscience—the restrictive superego, and avoidance conditioning.

For pure reinforcement theory, a defective conscience reflects experience of an inappropriate pattern of rewards and punishments. The role of punishment is not altogether clear, although both conditioning and reinforcement theory are agreed that punishment is not the opposite of reward, and therefore should not be expected to produce the opposite kind of results. As far as conditioning theory is concerned, one of its difficulties seems to be that it is not clear how far conditioned avoidance responses may generalize, and thus how far they may be applied in situations differing from those in which they were learned. As far as positive reinforcement is concerned, a similar objection could be made. It is not known how far the effects of positive reinforcement may generalize. Considering both these aspects together, we may fairly safely make the general observation that, the more and the more rapidly environmental factors change, the less appropriate any generalized habits which may be formed are likely to be. Social learning theory, with its emphasis on imitation or 'modelling' indicates the importance of the adult 'models' to whom a child is exposed, and whom he may come to imitate. If, however, the environment is changing rapidly, models may quite quickly come to appear irrelevant, and thus to be discounted and lose their influence, or come to *be* irrelevant and thus to become *inadequate* as models.

More extremely behaviouristic varieties of learning theory tend to ignore the cognitive and subjective aspects of morality, and although they have an attractively simple and positive approach, are probably too narrow. The concern of many more recent learning theorists with mediating processes tends to support this view. Of reinforcement theory as advocated by Skinner, it may be said that this is basically no more than a version of the old utilitarian hedonistic theory. But it is a more thoroughly developed theory in detail, as in its development of the notion of 'schedules of reinforcement', and is of interest particularly for its emphasis on positive reward, as distinct from the negative emphasis of the superego and avoidance conditioning. The more subjective aspects of experience are difficult to define and perhaps to talk about intelligibly, and yet we all know perfectly well that they exist. Aronfreed, in his cognitively oriented version of learning theory, has tried to introduce some aspects of this experience, and thus to provide a bridge between behaviouristic theory and the more fundamentally cognitive theories of people like Piaget and Kohlberg (although the attempt to do so has been severely criticized by behaviouristic fundamentalists like Gewirtz).

By developmental theories, we mean theories which have considered moral development primarily in terms of a developmental process through a series of clearly differentiated stages without, however, any necessary implication that development need be discontinuous, or proceed in 'jumps' from one stage to the next. As we have seen, there has been a fair measure of agreement among a number of exponents of the developmental point of view, from McDougall on, as to the nature of such stages. Although one may take a purely empirical view of stages of development, regarding them simply as a convenient way in which to divide up the sequential process of change which takes place in characteristic patterns of moral behaviour and orientation with increasing age, there is an underlying implication of developmental theory that the process of development follows the course it does at least in part because of tendencies 'built into' the human being. This is particularly so, perhaps, in the case of the cognitive-developmental theory associated mainly with the names of Piaget and Kohlberg. As compared with psychoanalytic theory, cognitive developmental theory emphasizes *cognitive* aspects or factors. It is not implied that affective or emotional aspects or purely behavioural aspects are not important, but that in man, to a very large extent, those aspects are mediated by cognitive, organizing factors. In other words, our 'definition of the moral situation' is crucial, although indeed this cognitive definition of the situation may be influenced to a greater or lesser extent by affective and motivational factors, just as our feelings depend in part upon our definition of the situation. But cognitive schemata do not exist in independence of action, and in fact can only be understood in relation to action—in the sphere of social relations as a means of regularizing and 'normalizing' systems of human interaction. Piaget indicates that in general, human psychological development is a process whereby a kind of equilibrium or 'match' is established between the expectations which, as a result of his own organizing tendencies and his experience, a person brings into a situation, and the degree to which such expectations are effective or justified by events. 'Equilibrium' in the social-moral sense is most adequately established (i.e. reaches its most mature form) when the expectations and norms which people bring into their social relations and socially relevant decisions as to action, are such as to maximize the probability that the pattern of social relationships will continue to function smoothly. In the case of rational argument, for example, both parties to an argument must accept the rule that full rational consideration must be given to the opposing arguments. In so far as this is not so, this particular form of interchange is likely to break down. In the case of moral judgment and action based upon it, it must be accepted that the *same* rules apply to everyone with exceptions only as may be agreed in respect of exceptional circumstances.

It would be misleading to imagine that cognitive developmental theory insists exclusively upon the importance of built-in factors, but it certainly does tend to emphasize them. Two of the main difficulties of this approach seem to be the difficulty of defining 'stages' in a non-arbitrary way, and the difficulty of demonstrating that a 'new integration' or new way of seeing things has developed as a result of interaction between the actively structuring individual and external factors, interaction leading naturally to a more mature level of functioning, rather than simply that the individual has learned to respond to social requirements in an appropriate way. Apparent demonstrations of the 'irreversibility' of such reorganizational learning do not provide a wholly satisfying answer, since some forms of conditioning, for example, are also very resistant to extinction. The best kind of evidence would be a demonstration that development proceeds by similar stages in a range of different societies with very different value systems and presuppositions. Kohlberg claims that there is this kind of 'universality' about his stages, but the evidence so far is rather slight.

The recapitulationist theory, as put forward by William Kay,[154] if accepted, does add weight to the developmental point of view. Briefly, the recapitulationist view maintains that in the course of his own moral development, the individual traverses essentially the same course as that traversed by mankind in the course of the history of the human race. The problems associated with recapitulationism are interesting problems, but we cannot go into them here. The present point is simply that, *if* we are prepared to accept recapitulationist arguments, then they do add to the developmentalist case that account must be taken of developmental tendencies characteristic of, or built into, the human being, in addition to his unquestioned capacity for learning and adaptation.

It should also be clear that people who approximate to the more 'moral' types, or who function to an appreciable extent at the more advanced 'stages' of development, must have a well-developed sense of *themselves* as responsible, decision-making individuals with a sense of moral purpose. Since William James, G. H. Mead and McDougall, there has been some literature, especially relatively recently, on the development of the self-picture or self-concept and of self-awareness. Both Maslow[195] and Allport[6] draw attention to the importance of this development. However, psychologists have not, in general, directed much attention to empirical studies of the development of the self-concept specifically in relation to moral learning and development. It looks as if this should now be a profitable line to pursue, particularly in association with cognitive-developmental theory. We should try to study the development of cognitive awareness of oneself as a moral decision-making person, and the kind of experiences which encourage the development of such a 'moral self' picture. If the results of much of the empirical work to which we have referred in previous chapters appears rather disappointing, this may be at least partly because of the relative neglect of the moral aspects of the self-concept.

Moral education

We are not really concerned in this book with questions of moral education, but it may be appropriate to mention this problem briefly. The term 'moral education' has been used in more than one sense, but here we use it to refer to the general role of the educational system in developing a sense of moral values as well as more directly utilitarian skills. The ultimate aim of moral education is to raise the level of moral judgment and consequent behaviour, in such a way that judgment and behaviour are based to as great an extent as possible upon general moral principles. These are principles concerned with the proper consideration of the rights and interests of others, which require that rules or laws which are applicable to some should be applicable to all except for special consideration which it is proper to give to those who may for one reason or another be in special circumstances. For example, special rights may be allowed to those with special responsibilities, or with special handicaps. By the general applicability of moral principles, we mean that no person can claim for himself special privileges *except* in respect of special extenuating circumstances. It is clear that in the long run, we do not aim at producing a generation of well-conditioned or well-trained conformists. Although factors like limitations of intellect mean that by no means everyone can reach the highest levels of development, and constitutional factors and/or early experience may predispose to psychopathy or 'consciencelessness', we must aim at getting everyone to as high a level as possible, and at having as many people as possible capable of thinking about moral problems and principles, and about the ways in which principles should be applied to new and changing circumstances. Moral *principles* are not *rules of behaviour*. They are general guiding statements to which reference should be made when existing rules are questioned, or seem to be inapplicable, or when conflicting possible lines of action appear to be open, both in some sense defensible in terms of existing rules. Nevertheless, as we have suggested, it may be misleading to suggest that conditioning, reward learning and imitation are irrelevant to true moral development. Some degree of conditioning and some training in 'good habits' are probably essential prerequisites of moral learning or moral education properly speaking, and may be more necessary for some people than for others. However, in the course of childhood, we certainly want to encourage children to think in terms of rules and principles at as high a level of generality as the children can understand. We also want, as far as possible, to encourage those 'ego factors' such as capacity for inhibiting selfish or impulse-satisfying behaviour in the interests of later and more ultimately satisfying gain to the actor, and more especially, in the interests of other people; and to encourage the development of a healthy concept of oneself as a moral human being with both rights and obligations. The ability to inhibit impulse in the interests of later personal gain to the actor is probably an important step toward inhibiting selfish impulses for the sake of others. One has not only to be capable of principled judgment, but *able* to act accordingly. The main contribution of psychoanalytic theory here lies in its drawing attention to the fact that very often people are, because of emotional distortions, either unable to reach a judgment essentially undistorted by emotional involvement or unable to put into practice the line of conduct indicated by their principles. Of cognitive factors, one of the most important is to be able to anticipate reasonably accurately the probable consequences, especially for other people, of different possible lines of action.

In the case of a society where values are relatively static, there is in general less distinction between principles and rules. The appropriate conduct in various circumstances tends to be generally agreed, and therefore it is easier for people to learn applicable rules, and to apply them effectively. This is because most people's expectations are more or less the same, and situations involving dilemmas or uncertainty as to how one should behave are less likely to occur. In times when traditional rules have to an appreciable extent ceased to be generally accepted, especially among younger people, the learning of rules prescribing and proscribing behaviour is less likely to be effective and such rules are less likely to be generally accepted as adequate guides for behaviour. Hence in these circumstances, it is more important to try to educate as many people as possible, not in the old rules, but in the capacity for examining principles and weighing up current practice to see how far it is compatible with principles, and in examining new situations with a view to seeing how principles could be properly applied to such new situations.

Cognitive developmental theory seems to provide the most promising guide with respect to moral education directed toward this end. This is because it provides a framework to suggest what kind of procedures should be taken next. There is a clear implication that children should be able to function adequately at any level of moral judgment before an attempt is made to introduce them to more advanced moral thinking. And the 'more advanced' thinking should be that characteristic of the next stage in the developmental sequence. If moral development takes place as a process of reorganization of what one sees as one's 'moral world', conveniently codifiable from the outside, as it were, in terms of Kohlberg's six stages or some similar scheme, then we might expect children to be receptive to discussion of and analysis of problems at a level just one stage above their current stage of functioning, and as we have seen, there is some evidence that this is indeed the case. Frequently, this kind of discussion, in class for example, will have been triggered by some actual incident in which the children have been involved or with which they have had some real contact. However, Kohlberg writes, 'It is not always necessary that these matters be ones of the immediate and real-life issues of the classroom. I have found that my hypothetical and remote but obviously conflict situations are of intense interest to almost all adolescents and lead to lengthy debate among them. They are involving because the adult right answer is not obviously at hand to discourage the child's own moral thought, as so often is the case. The child will listen to what the teacher says about moral matters only if the child first feels a genuine sense of uncertainty as to the right answer to the situation in question. The pat little stories in school readers in which virtue always triumphs or in which everyone is really nice are unlikely to have any value in the stimulation of moral development. Only the presentation of genuine and difficult moral conflicts can have this effect'[165] (pp. 22–3). One is strongly reminded here of William McDougall's view that realization of conflict of values may stimulate movement toward moral maturity. Where there is not experience of conflict, it is likely that, although we may have what many would regard as a satisfactory degree of conformity to established rules, we are not likely to have advance.

Although the presentation of 'hypothetical and remote' problems may have a place, as Kohlberg suggests, it would seem clear that the more immediate 'real-life' issues of classroom and school are likely to be more effective. But these issues must be handled in a way which is both meaningful and stimulating to the children concerned. Discussion must be neither facile nor below the level of the children's capacity, nor too much above it. It is also important, as Kohlberg suggests, for moral discourse to be kept for genuinely moral questions, and not confused with matters of classroom convenience, social habit and so on. For example, tidiness is undoubtedly convenient, and up to a point is something which should be encouraged, but it is not a *moral* virtue, and it is misleading to treat tidiness as the same kind of thing as, for example, stealing or bullying. Again, moral questions should be treated as moral questions, and not as mere matters of convenience or expediency, as soon as children are capable of making this distinction. For example, although with young children one may use the argument that they should not cheat in school examinations because they are likely to be found out, or it is not likely to do them any good in the long run, this treats honesty as a matter of 'policy', and should not be used as the main argument with older children capable of understanding that dishonesty involves a breach of trust. This does not imply that a teacher should not exercise authority in class, but that he should distinguish moral expectations from requirements for conformity in behaviour for practical or expedient reasons. Moreover, by making unrealistic demands in moral terms, a teacher or person in authority may succeed in increasing conformity at the expense of impeding genuine moral development. An attitude of reasoned acceptance of authority for particular purposes is perfectly defensible morally; an attitude of unreasoning acceptance (or rejection) of authority is not. The provision of good moral 'models' by parents and teachers in particular, and also by other adults, is critically important. It is not simply that they provide models for imitation. But if they do not earn respect by their own adherence to basic moral principles, these principles are likely to be discredited and appear as of little importance in the eyes of the children. That children should rebel against adult authority or adult norms is not necessarily a bad thing, though it can sometimes be a great nuisance for the elders. Rebellion can be a healthy sign if it shows a concern for principles which seem to be being betrayed by the adult world. It is a bad thing if it represents a 'contracting out' and a denial of commitment and of the relevance of moral principles to living. Naturally, of course, the teacher's scope will be limited by the experience of the children outside school, and especially at home. There is no doubt about the importance of the home and parents. But at least to some extent, what teachers can achieve will depend upon what they themselves are, how they live and how they encourage their charges to live, not merely on the precepts they pronounce.

Wilson[276] proposes an interesting analysis of the 'components' or dimensions of morality which is primarily but not exclusively cognitive in orientation, and which should prove useful in practice. He distinguishes six components, which can be regarded as indicating six different kinds of conditions which must be met before action can be regarded as genuinely moral in the fullest sense of the word. He gives these components Greek derived names in order to provide compact and distinctive labels.

(1) PHIL 'refers to the degree with which one can identify with other people' (p. 192). If one cannot identify with other people, or put oneself in their place, in any degree at all, then it is hard to see how one can ever be 'moral' in the sense of taking proper account of the feelings and interests of others. People may, of course, differ in the *extent* of their capacity to 'identify' with others, in the *range* of others with whom they identify, and in the particular *kind* of others with whom they identify.

(2) EMP refers to the ability to *judge* what the feelings of other people are, and to describe them correctly. Wilson suggests that one might distinguish between AUTEMP, or awareness of one's own feelings, and ALLEMP, or awareness of others' feelings. Psychoanalytic theory does, of course, stress the importance of self-awareness, and implies that greater self-awareness is likely to increase our appreciation of the feelings of others. Although logically one may be good at identifying and describing the feelings of others without necessarily empathizing with them, we would expect PHIL and EMP to be empirically related. Logically, also, one might be good at judging the feelings of others, without having one's own behaviour in any way influenced for the better by such knowledge—indeed, certain kinds of fraud depend upon just this combination of capacity for accurate recognition of the feelings of others and lack of real fellow feeling.

(3) GIG refers to the fact that to make correct moral decisions, 'one also needs to have a reasonable idea of what consequences one's actions will have' (p. 139). A would-be helper, for example, who gives a man with a head wound a glass of spirits to revive him may both feel for the sufferer and know that he would like a drink, but may be ignorant that his action may prove fatal rather than beneficial. Or, in Wilson's example, Marie Antoinette may

not have been lacking in empathy or understanding of others, but in factual knowledge when she suggested that starving peasants eat cake instead of bread. Obviously, it is sometimes difficult to know whether a person is 'to blame' for his own ignorance, but he can almost certainly be said to be 'to blame' if he has *ignored* or not *bothered* to get available information which is relevant to the consequences of his decisions for others.

(4) DIK refers to the rational formulation of a set of rules or moral principles to which the individual commits himself, on the basis of knowledge of feelings, empathy and knowledge of the probable consequences of different possible lines of action. This requires *moral* decisions and judgments to be based on more or less logically consistent principles of general application and binding force.

(5) PHRON refers to the 'rational formulation of rules and principles . . . relating to one's own life and interests' (p. 193). This implies than an ideally moral person will try to conduct his own life and affairs according to more or less consistent rational standards—in fact, the standards that he takes to be applicable to others.

(6) KRAT refers to 'the ability to translate DIK or PHRON principles into action', i.e. the ability to act upon or live up to one's own principles or standards. This seems to be very much what psychoanalytically inclined writers refer to as 'ego-strength'. It should, however, be clear that the qualities which make up such an ability might also be used in the pursuit of purely selfish, amoral or immoral ends. The model case of a person lacking in KRAT to which Wilson refers is the addict, who wishes to act otherwise and may be by no means devoid of empathy, knowledge and rationally formulated principles, but is unable to act upon such principles. Thus KRAT is essentially a motivational-behavioural component.

To these six components, I would suggest that we add a seventh, ALIT, or the capacity to feel *guilt* when one causes others harm, or in general fails to live up to the requirements of an accepted moral rule. Learning theory suggests that this may sometimes be an important component in motivating behaviour intended to right the wrong done.

It seems that the four components, GIG, DIK, PHRON, and KRAT, and to some extent also EMP refer to what psychoanalysts would regard as predominantly ego rather than superego factors. To include the capacity for feeling guilt (which may indeed be related to PHIL but is clearly not the same thing) would be to include a factor which is predominantly a superego rather than an ego factor, though clearly ego factors may also be relevant to the capacity to feel guilt.

Wilson suggests that a general 'moral education' index might be obtained from some combination of measures of his six components (although of course, this would be arbitrary in the absence of any rationale of how the components, assuming that they could be adequately measured, should be weighted). It might be suggested that a *profile* might be more useful than a single combined score, and that this might more appropriately be called a profile of moral level rather than an index of moral education. It is further clear that Wilson's components can be used as a basis for moral education in the sense that the attention of pupils can be drawn by example, precept, discussion and explanation to these six different aspects of moral development. For example, young children can in particular be encouraged to 'put themselves in other children's places'. Role-playing may sometimes be effective when used for this purpose.

The Farmington Trust in Oxford are at present engaged in research on moral development based upon this analysis, and the Schools Council Moral Education Curriculum Project, on research in moral education based upon an analysis which is rather similar. As these would certainly appear to be the most thorough and most systematic moral development researches to have been carried out in Britain, we may look forward with interest to the results when they appear in due course.

References

1 Abel, Theodora M., 'Moral judgments among subnormals',
  J. abnorm. soc. Psychol., 1941, 36, 378–392

2 Adorno, T. *et al.*, *The Authoritarian Personality*, New York:
  Harper, 1950

3 Ainsworth, Mary D., 'The effects of maternal deprivation:
  a review of findings and controversy in the context of research
  strategy', pp. 97–165 in *Deprivation of Maternal Care, a
  Reassessment of its Effects,* Geneva: World Health Organization, 1962.

4 Allinsmith, W., 'Moral standards: II. The learning of moral
  standards', pp. 141–176 in D. R. Miller and G. E. Swanson,
  Inner Conflict and Defence, New York: Holt, 1960

5 Allinsmith, W. and Greening, T. C., 'Guilt over anger as
  predicted from parental discipline: a study of superego
  development', *Amer. Psychol.*, 1955, 10, 320.

6 Allport, G. W., *Pattern and Growth in Personality*, New
  York: Holt, Rinehart and Winston, 1961

7 Andry, R. G., *Delinquency and Parental Pathology,*
  London: Methuen, 1960

8 Argyle, M., *Religious Behaviour*, London: Routledge and
  Kegan Paul, 1958

9 Argyle, M., 'Introjection, a form of social learning', *Brit. J.
  Psychol.*, 1964, 65, 391–402

10 Argyle, M., 'Eysenck's theory of the conscience: a reply',
   Brit. J. Psychol., 1965, 56, 309–310

11 Aronfreed, J., 'The nature, variety and social patterning of
   internalized responses to transgression', *J. abnorm. soc.
   Psychol.*, 1961, 63, 223–240

12 Aronfreed, J., 'The effects of experimental socialization paradigms upon two moral responses to transgression', *J. abnorm. soc. Psychol.*, 1963, 66, 437–448

13 Aronfreed, J., 'The origin of self-criticism', *Psychol. Rev.*, 1964, 71, 193–218

14 Aronfreed, J., *Conduct and Conscience*, New York and London : Academic Press, 1968

15 Aronfreed, J., 'The concept of internalization', pp. 263–323 in D. Goslin (ed.), *Handbook of Socialization Theory and Research*, Chicago : Rand-McNally, 1969

16 Aronfreed, J. and Reber, A., 'Internalized behavioural suppression and the timing of social punishment', *J. pers. soc. Psychol.*, 1965, 1, 3–16

17 Aronfreed, J., Cutick, R. A. and Fagen, S. A., 'Cognitive structure, punishment and nurturance in the experimental induction of self-criticism', *Child Devpt.*, 1963, 39, 281–294

18 Aronson, E., and Carlsmith, J. M., 'Effect of severity of threat on the devaluation of forbidden behaviour', *J. abnorm. soc. Psychol.*, 1963, 66, 584–588

19 Ausubel, D. P., 'Relationships between shame and guilt in the socializing process', *Psychol. Rev.*, 1955, 62, 378–390

20 Baer, D. M. and Sherman, J. A., 'Reinforcement control of generalised imitation in young children', *J. exp. child Psychol.*, 1964, 1, 37–49

21 Baldwin, A. L., *Theories of Child Development*, New York : Wiley, 1967

22 Bandura, A., 'Social learning theory of identificatory processes', pp. 213–262 in D. Goslin (ed.), *Handbook of Socialization Theory and Research*, Chicago : Rand-McNally, 1969

23 Bandura, A. and Huston, A. C., 'Identification as a process of incidental learning', *J. abnorm. soc. Psychol.*, 1961, 63, 311–318

24 Bandura, A. and McDonald, F. J., 'The influence of social reinforcement and the behaviour of models in shaping children's moral judgments', *J. abnorm. soc. Psychol.*, 1963, 67, 274–281

25 Bandura, A. and Mischel, W., 'Modification of self-imposed delay of reward through exposure to live and symbolic models', *J. pers. soc. Psychol.*, 1965, 2, 698–705

26 Bandura, A. and Walters, R. H., *Adolescent Aggression*, New York: Ronald Press, 1959

27 Bandura, A. and Walters, R. H., *Social Learning and Personality Development*, New York: Holt, Rinehart and Winston, 1964

28 Bandura, A., Ross, Dorothea and Ross, Sheila A., 'A comparative test of the status envy, social power and secondary reinforcement theories of identificatory learning', *J. abnorm. soc. Psychol.*, 1963, 67, 527–534

29 Bender, Lauretta, 'Post-encephalitic behaviour disorders in childhood', Josephine B. Neal (ed)., *Encephalitis*, New York: Grune and Stratton, 1942

30 Bender, Lauretta, 'Psychopathic behaviour disorders in children', R. Lindner and R. Seliger (eds.), *Handbook of Correctional Psychology*, New York: Philosophical Library, 1947

31 Benedict, Ruth, *The Chrysanthemum and the Sword*, Boston: Houghton Mifflin, 1946

32 Bennett, E. M. and Cohen, L. R., 'Men and women: personality patterns and contrasts', *Genet. Psychol. Monogr.*, 1959, 59, 101–155

33 Berge, A., *Les Maladies de la Vertu*, Paris: Grasset, 1960

34 Berkowitz, L., 'Responsibility, reciprocity and social distance in help-giving: an experimental investigation of English social class differences', *J. exp. soc. Psychol.*, 1968, 4, 46–63

35 Berkowitz, L. and Friedman, P., 'Some social class differences in helping behaviour', *J. pers. soc. Psychol.*, 1967, 5, 217–225

36 Bernstein, B., 'Language and social class', *Brit. J. Psychol.*, 1960, 51, 271–276

37 Bloom, L., 'A reappraisal of Piaget's theory of moral judgment', *J. genet. Psychol.*, 1959, 95, 3–12

38 Blum, G. S., 'A study of the psychoanalytic theory of psychosexual development', *Genet. Psychol. Monogr.*, 1949, 39, 3–99

39 Bobroff, A., 'The stages of maturation in socialised thinking

K

and in ego development of two groups of children', *Child Devpt.*, 1960, 31, 321–338

40 Boehm, Leonore, 'The development of conscience: a comparison of American children of different mental and socioeconomic levels', *Child Devpt.*, 1962, 33, 575–590

41 Boehm, Leonore, 'The development of conscience: a comparison between students in Catholic parochial schools and in public schools', *Child Devpt.*, 1962, 591–602

42 Boehm, Leonore, 'Moral judgment: a cultural and subcultural comparison with some of Piaget's research conclusions', *Internat. J. Psychol.*, 1966, 1, 143–150

43 Boehm, Leonore and Nass, M. L., 'Social class differences in conscience development', *Child Devpt.*, 1962, 33, 565–574

44 Bowlby, J., *Forty four Juvenile Thieves*, London: Baillière, Tindall and Cox, 1946

45 Bowlby, J., *Child Care and the Growth of Love*, London: Penguin Books, 1953

46 Bradburn, Elizabeth, 'The teacher's role in the moral development of children in primary schools', unpublished thesis, University of Liverpool, 1964

47 Bray, D. H., 'A study of children's writing on an admired person', *Educ. Res.*, 1962, 15, 44–53

48 Brennan, W. K., 'Relation of social adaptation, emotional adjustment and moral judgment to intelligence in primary school children', *Brit. J. educ. Psychol.*, 1962, 32, 200–204 (Abstract of thesis, University of Manchester)

49 Breznitz, S. and Kugelmass, S., 'Intentionality in moral judgment: developmental stages', *Child Devpt.*, 1967, 38, 469–479

50 Brogden, H. E., 'A factor analysis of 40 character traits', *Psychol. Monogr.*, 1940, 52, no. 3 (Whole no. 234)

51 Bronfenbrenner, U., 'Freudian theories of identification and their derivatives', *Child Devpt.*, 1960, 31, 15–40

52 Bronfenbrenner, U., 'Some familial antecedents of responsibility and leadership in adolescents', pp. 239–271 in L. Petrullo and B. M. Bass (eds.), *Leadership and Interpersonal Behaviour*, New York: Holt, Rinehart and Winston, 1961

53 Bronfenbrenner, U., 'Parsons' theory of identification', pp.

191–213 in M. Black (ed.), *The Social Theories of Talcott Parsons*, Englewood Cliffs, New Jersey: Prentice Hall, 1961

54 Brown, R., *Social Psychology*, New York: Free Press; London: Collier-Macmillan, 1965

55 Bull, N. J., *Moral Judgment from Childhood to Adolescence*, London: Routledge and Kegan Paul, 1969

56 Bull, N. J., *Moral Education*, London: Routledge and Kegan Paul, 1969

57 Burton, R. V., 'The generality of honesty reconsidered', *Psychol. Rev.*, 1963, 70, 481–499

58 Burton, R. V., Maccoby, Eleanor E. and Allinsmith, W., 'Antecedents of resistance to temptation in four year old children', *Child Devpt.*, 1961, 32, 689–710

59 Caruso, I. H., 'La notion de responsibilité et du justice immanente chez l'enfant', *Arch. de Psychol.*, 1943, 29, 114–169

60 Chapanis, Natalie and Chapanis, A., 'Cognitive dissonance: five years later', *Psychol. Bull.*, 1964, 61, 1–22

61 Chassell, C. F., *The Relation between Morality and Intellect*, New York: Columbia University Contributions to Education, No. 607, 1935

62 Child, I. L., 'Socialization', pp. 655–692 in G. Lindzey (ed.), *Handbook of Social Psychology*, vol. II, Reading, Mass. and London: Addison-Wesley, 1954

63 Craft, M. *Ten Studies into Psychopathic Personality*, Bristol, Wright, 1965

64 Crowley, P. M., 'Effect of training upon objectivity of moral judgment in grade-school children', *J. pers. soc. Psychol.*, 1968, 8, 228–232

65 Dennis, W., 'Animism and related tendencies in Hopi children', *J. abnorm. soc. Psychol.*, 1943, 38, 21–37

66 Doland, D. J. and Adelberg, Kathryn, 'The learning of sharing behaviour', *Child Devpt.*, 1967, 38, 695–700

67 Durkheim, E., *Suicide*, English translation with an editor's introduction by G. Simpson, London: Routledge and Kegan Paul, 1952

68 Durkin, Dolores, 'Children's concepts of justice: a comparison with the Piaget data', *Child Devpt.*, 1959, 30, 59–67

69 Durkin, Dolores, 'Children's acceptance of reciprocity as a justice principle', *Child Devpt.*, 1959, 30, 289–296

70 Durkin, Dolores, 'Children's concepts of justice: a further comparison with the Piaget data', *J. educ. Res.*, 1959, 52, 252–257

71 Durkin, Dolores, 'Sex differences in children's concepts of justice', *Child Devpt.*, 1960, 31, 361–368

72 Durkin, Dolores, 'The specificity of children's moral judgments', *J. genet. Psychol.*, 1961, 98, 3–13

73 Edwards, J. B., 'Some moral attitudes of boys in a secondary modern school', part I, *Educ. Rev.*, 1965, 17, 114–127

74 Erikson, E. H., *Childhood and Society*, New York: Norton, 1950

75 Erikson, E. H., 'Identity and the life cycle', selected papers, *Psychol. Issues*, 1959, 1, Monograph 1

76 Estes, W. K., 'An experimental study of punishment', *Psychol. Monogr.*, 1944, 57, no. 3 (Whole no. 263)

77 Eysenck, H. J. 'The contribution of learning theory', *Brit. J. educ. Psychol.*, 1960, 30, 11–21 (Symposium on moral development)

78 Eysenck, H. J., *Crime and Personality*, London: Routledge and Kegan Paul, 1964

79 Eysenck, H. J., 'A note on some criticisms of the Mowrer–Eysenck conditioning theory of conscience', *Brit. J. Psychol.*, 1965, 56, 305–307

80 Eysenck, S. B. G., 'Personality and pain assessment in childbirth of married and unmarried mothers', *J. ment. Sci.*, 1961, 107, 417–430

81 Fenichel, O., *The Psychoanalytic Theory of Neurosis*, 1st ed., London: Routledge and Kegan Paul, 1945

82 Ferguson, T., *The Young Delinquent in his Social Setting*, Oxford University Press, 1952

83 Festinger, L., *A Theory of Cognitive Dissonance*, London: Tavistock Publications, 1957

84 Festinger, L., 'The psychological effects of insufficient reward', *Amer. Psychol.*, 1961, 16, 1–11

85 Festinger, L. and Carlsmith, J. M., 'Cognitive consequences of forced compliance', *J. abnorm. soc. Psychol.*, 1959, 58, 203–210

86 Festinger, L. and Freedman, J.L., 'Dissonance reduction and moral values', pp. 220–247 in P. Worchel and D. Byrne (eds.), *Personality Change*, New York: Wiley, 1964

87 Fine, B.J., 'Introversion-extraversion and motor vehicle drive behaviour', *Percept. mot. Skills*, 1963, 12, 95–100

88 Forrester, J. F. F. 'A study of the attitudes of adolescents toward their own intellectual, social and spiritual development', unpublished thesis, University of London, 1946

89 Freedman, J. L., 'Long term behavioural effects of cognitive dissonance', *J. exp. soc. Psychol.*, 1965, 1, 145–155

90 Freud, Anna, *The Ego and the Mechanisms of Defence*, London: Hogarth Press and Institute of Psychoanalysis, 1936

91 Freud, Anna, *Normality and Pathology in Childhood*, London: Hogarth Press and Institute of Psychoanalysis, 1966

92 Freud, S. (and Breuer, J.), 'Studies in Hysteria', in S. Freud, *Complete Psychological Works*, Standard Edition, 24 volumes, London: Hogarth Press, 1953–1966, Vol. II

93 Freud, S., 'The neuropsychoses of defence', *S.E.*, III, 45–61

94 Freud, S., 'Further remarks on the neuropsychoses of defence', *S.E.*, III, 162–185

95 Freud, S., 'The interpretation of dreams', *S.E.*, IV and V, 339–625

96 Freud, S., 'Three essays on sexuality', *S.E.*, VII, 125–243

97 Freud, S., 'My views on the part played by sexuality in the aetiology of the neuroses', *S.E.*, VII, 271–279

98 Freud, S., 'Character and anal erotism', *S.E.*, IX, 167–175

99 Freud, S., 'Totem and tabu', *S.E.*, XII

100 Freud, S., 'On narcissism', *S.E.*, XIV, 69–102

101 Freud, S., 'Instincts and their vicissitudes', *S.E.*, XIV, 111–158

102 Freud, S., 'Mourning and melancholia', *S.E.*, XIV, 237–258

103 Freud, S., 'Criminals from a sense of guilt', *S.E.*, xiv, 332–333

104 Freud, S., 'Introductory lectures on psychoanalysis', *S.E.*, xv and xvi

105 Freud, S., 'From the history of an infantile neurosis', *S.E.*, xvii, 7–122

106 Freud, S., 'Group psychology and the analysis of the ego', *S.E.*, xviii, 67–143

107 Freud, S., 'The ego and the id', *S.E.*, xix, 3–59

108 Freud, S., Moral responsibility for the control of dreams', *S.E.*, xix, 131–134

109 Freud, S., 'The dissolution of the Oedipus complex', *S.E.*, xix, 173–179

110 Freud, S., 'Some psychological consequences of the anatomical distinctions between the sexes', *S.E.*, xix, 248–258

111 Freud, S., 'Inhibitions, symptoms and anxiety', *S.E.*, xx, 77–175

112 Freud, S., 'Civilization and its discontents', *S.E.*, xxi, 59–145

113 Freud, S., 'New introductory lectures on psychoanalysis', *S.E.*, xxii, 5–182.

114 Freud, S., 'Outline of psychoanalysis', *S.E.*, xxiii, 144–171

115 Freud, S., 'Analysis terminable and interminable', *S.E.*, xxiii, 216–253

116 Gewirtz, J. L., 'Mechanisms of social learning : some roles of stimulation and behaviour in early human development', pp. 57–212 in D. A. Goslin (ed.), *Handbook of Socialization Theory and Research*, Chicago : Rand-McNally, 1969

117 Gewirtz, J. L. and Stingle, K. G., 'Learning of generalised imitation as the basis for identification', *Psychol. Rev.*, 1968, 75, 374–397

118 Glueck, S. and Glueck, Eleanor, *Unravelling Juvenile Delinquency*, New York : Commonwealth Fund, 1950

119 Goldman, R. J., *Religious Thinking from Childhood to Adolescence*, London : Routledge and Kegan Paul, 1964

120 Graham, D., 'Children's moral development', pp. 101–118

in H. J. Butcher (ed.), *Educational Research in Britain*, London : University of London Press, 1968

121 Grinder, R. E., 'Relations between behavioural and cognitive dimensions of conscience in middle childhood', *Child Devpt.*, 1964, 35, 881–891

122 Grinder, R. E. and McMichael, R. E., 'Cultural influence on conscience development : resistance to temptation and guilt among Samoans and American Caucasians', *J. abnorm. soc. Psychol.*, 1963, 66, 503–507

123 Grinker, R. R., 'On identification', *Int. J. Psychoanal.*, 1957, 38, 379–390

124 Grusec, Joan, 'Some antecedents of self-criticism', *J. pers. soc. Psychol.*, 1966, 4, 244–252

125 Hall, C. S., 'A modest confirmation of Freud's theory of a distinction between the superego of men and women', *J. abnorm. soc. Psychol.*, 1964, 69, 440–442

126 Hall, C. S. and Lindzey, G., *Theories of Personality*, New York : Wiley, 1957

127 Harrower, M. R., 'Social status and the moral development of the child', *Brit. J. educ. Psychol.*, 1934, 4, 75–95

128 Hartmann, H., *Ego Psychology and the Problem of Adaptation*, London : Imago Publishing Company, 1958

129 Hartmann, H., *Psychoanalysis and Moral Values*, New York : International Universities Press, 1960

130 Hartshorne, H. and May, M. A., *Studies in the Nature of Character*, 3 vols., New York : Macmillan, 1928–1930

131 Havighurst, R. J. and Neugarten, Bernice L., *American Indian and White Children, a Sociopsychological Investigation*, Chicago : University of Chicago Press, 1955

132 Havighurst, R. J. and Taba, Hilda, *Adolescent Character and Personality*, New York : Wiley, 1949

133 Heilbrun, A. B. Jr., 'The measurement of identification', *Child Devpt.*, 1965, 36, 111–127

134 Henderson, D. K., *Psychopathic States*, New York : Norton, 1939

135 Henry, A. F. and Short, J. F. Jr., *Suicide and Homicide:*

Some Economic, Sociological and Psychological Aspects of Aggression, Glencoe, Ill.: Free Press, 1954

136 Henson, K. G., 'A study of factors thought to be relevant in moral judgment in educationally subnormal children', unpublished thesis, University of Durham, 1968

137 Hill, W. F., 'Learning theory and the acquisition of values', *Psychol. Rev.*, 1960, 67, 317–331

138 Hilliard, F. H., 'The influence of religious education upon the development of children's moral ideas', *Brit. J. educ. Psychol.*, 1959, 29, 50–59

139 Hoffman, M. L., 'The role of the parent in the child's moral growth', *Religious Education*, 1962, 37, Research Supplement S-18–S-33

140 Hoffman, M. L., 'Child rearing practices and moral development: generalizations from empirical research', *Child Devpt.*, 1963, 34, 295–318

141 Hoffman, M. L., 'Parent discipline and the child's consideration for others', *Child Devpt.*, 1963, 34, 573–588

142 Hoffman, M. L. and Saltzstein, H. D., 'Parent discipline and the child's moral development', *J. pers. soc. Psychol.*, 1967, 5, 45–57

143 Hollander, E. P., *Social Psychology*, New York: Wiley, 1967

144 Howe, Louisa P., 'Some sociological aspects of identification', pp. 61–79 in W. Muensterberger and S. Axelrad, *Psychoanalysis and the Social Sciences*, vol. IV, New York: International Universities Press, 1955

145 Jacobson, Edith, *The Self and the Object World*, London: Hogarth Press and Institute of Psychoanalysis, 1965

146 Jahoda, G., 'Immanent justice among West African children', *J. soc. Psychol.*, 1958, 47, 241–248

147 Jenkins, R. L., 'The psychopathic or anti-social personality', *J. nerv. ment. Dis.*, 1960, 131, 318–334

148 Johnson, R. C., 'A study of children's moral judgments', *Child Devpt.*, 1962, 33, 327–354

149 Johnson, R. C., 'Early studies of children's moral judgments', *Child Devpt.*, 1962, 33, 603–606

150 Jones, E., *Papers on Psychoanalysis*, 5th ed., London: Baillière, Tindall and Cox, 1948

151 Kagan, J., 'The concept of identification', *Psychol. Rev.*, 1958, 65, 296–305
152 Kagan, J., 'Personality development', pp. 117–173 in P. London and D. Rosenhan, *Foundations of Abnormal Psychology*, New York: Holt, Rinehart and Winston, 1968
153 Kagan, J. and Phillips, W., 'Measurement of identification: a methodological note', *J. abnorm. soc. Psychol.*, 1964, 69, 442–444
154 Kay, W., *Moral Development*, London: Allen and Unwin, 1968
155 Kellmer-Pringle, M. L. and Edwards, J. B., 'Some moral concepts and judgments of junior school children', *J. soc. clin. Psychol.*, 1964, 3, 196–215
156 Kennedy-Frazer, D., *The Psychology of Education*, London: Methuen, 1944
157 Kinsey, A. C., Pomeroy, W. B. and Martin, C. E., *Sexual Behaviour in the Human Male*, Philadelphia: Saunders, 1948
158 Klein, Melanie, 'The early development of conscience in the child', pp. 267–277 in *Contributions to Psychoanalysis*, London: Hogarth Press and Institute of Psychoanalysis, 1948
159 Klein, Melanie, 'On criminality', pp. 278–281 in *Contributions to Psychoanalysis*, London: Hogarth Press and Institute of Psychoanalysis, 1948
160 Klein, Melanie, *The Psychoanalysis of Children*, London: Hogarth Press and Institute of Psychoanalysis, 1949
161 Kohlberg, L., 'Moral development and identification', pp. 277–332 in H. W. Stevenson (ed.), *Child Psychology. Yearbook of the National Society for the Study of Education 1963*, Part I, Chicago: University of Chicago Press, 1963
162 Kohlberg, L., 'The development of children's orientations toward a moral order. 1. Sequence in the development of moral thought', *Vita Humana*, 1963, 6, 11–33
163 Kohlberg, L., 'The development of moral character', pp.

383–431 in M. L. Hoffman and Lois W. Hoffman (eds.), *Review of Child Development Research*, 1, New York: Russell Sage Foundation, 1964

164 Kohlberg, L., 'A cognitive-developmental analysis of children's sex-role concepts and attitudes', pp. 82–173 in Eleanor E. Maccoby (ed.), *The Development of Sex Differences*, Stanford, California: Stanford University Press, 1966

165 Kohlberg, L., 'Moral education in the schools: a developmental view', *School Rev.*, 1966, 74, 1–30

166 Kohlberg, L., 'Stage and sequence: the cognitive-developmental approach to socialization', pp. 347–480 in D. A. Goslin (ed.), *Handbook of Socialization Theory and Research*, Chicago: Rand-McNally, 1969

167 Kohlberg, L. and Kramer, R., 'Continuities and discontinuities in childhood and adult moral development', *Human Development*, 1969, 12, 93–120

168 Kohn, M. L., 'Social class and the exercise of parental authority', *Amer. sociol. Rev.*, 1959, 24, 352–366

169 Kugelmass, S. and Breznitz, S., 'The developments of intentionality in moral judgment in city and Kibbutz children', *J. genet. Psychol.*, 1967, 111, 103–111.

170 Kugelmass, S. and Breznitz, S., 'Intentionality in moral judgment: adolescent development', *Child Devpt.*, 1968, 39, 249–256

171 Kuhn, Deanna Z., Madsen, C. H. Jr. and Becker, W. C., 'Effects of exposure to an aggressive model and "frustration" on children's aggressive behaviour', *Child Devpt.*, 1967, 38, 739–745

172 Lana, R., *Assumptions of Social Psychology*, New York: Appleton-Century-Crofts, 1969

173 Lazowick, L. M., 'On the nature of identification', *J. abnorm. soc. Psychol.*, 1955, 51, 175–183

174 Lee, Maureen, 'Children's reactions to moral transgressions', unpublished thesis, University of Durham, 1965

175 Le Furgy, W. G. and Woloshin, G. W., 'Immediate and long-term effects of experimentally induced social influence

in the modification of adolescents' moral judgments', *J. pers. soc. Psychol.*, 1969, 12, 104–110

176 Lenrow, P. B., 'Studies of sympathy', pp. 264–294 in S. S. Tomkins and C. E. Izard (eds), *Affect, Cognition and Personality: Empirical Studies*, New York: Springer, 1965

177 Lerner, E., *Constraint Areas and Moral Judgment in Children*, Manasha, Wisconsin: Banta Publishing Co., 1937

178 Lindner, R., *Rebel without a Cause—The Hypnoanalysis of a Criminal Psychopath*, New York: Grune and Stratton, 1944

179 Loughran, R., 'A pattern of development in moral judgments made by adolescents derived from Piaget's schema of its development in childhood', *Educ. Rev.*, 1967, 19, 79–98

180 Lunzer, E. A. and Morris, J. F., 'Problems of motivation', pp. 304–361 in E. A. Lunzer, *The Regulation of Behaviour*, London: Staples Press, 1968

181 Lykken, D. T., 'A study of anxiety in the sociopathic personality', *J. abnorm. soc. Psychol.*, 1957, 55, 6–10

182 McCord, Joan and Clemes, S., 'Conscience orientation and dimensions of personality', *Behav. Science*, 1964, 9, 19–29

183 McCord, Joan, McCord, W. and Howard, A., 'Family interaction as antecedent to the direction of male aggressiveness', *J. abnorm. soc. Psychol.*, 1963, 66, 239–242

184 McCord, W. and McCord, Joan, *Psychopathy and Delinquency*, New York: Grune and Stratton, 1956

185 McCord, W. and McCord, Joan, 'A tentative theory of the structure of conscience', pp. 108–134 in Dorothy Wilner (ed.), *Decisions, Values and Groups*, 1, Oxford: Pergamon Press, 1960

186 McCord, W., McCord, Joan and Howard, A., 'Familial correlates of aggression in nondelinquent male children', *J. abnorm. soc. Psychol.*, 1961, 62, 79–93

187 McDougall, W., *An Introduction to Social Psychology*, 23rd ed., London: Methuen, 1960

188 McKenzie, J. G., *Guilt: its Meaning and Significance*, London: Allen and Unwin, 1962

300 References

189 McKnight, R. K., 'The moral sanctions of the child', unpublished thesis, University of Glasgow, 1950

190 Mackinnon, D. W., 'Violation of prohibition', pp. 491–501 in H. A. Murray *et al.*, *Explorations in Personality*, New York: Oxford University Press, 1938

191 Macrae, D. Jr., 'A test of Piaget's theories of moral development', *J. abnorm. soc. Psychol.*, 1954, 49, 14–18

192 Magowan, S. A., 'A study of immanent justice in the moral development of the child', unpublished thesis, University of Glasgow, 1966

193 Maller, J. B., 'General and specific factors in character', *J. soc. Psychol.*, 1934, 5, 97–102

194 Martin, W. E., 'Learning theory and identification: III The development of values in children', *J. genet. Psychol.*, 1954, 84, 211–217

195 Maslow, A. H., *Motivation and Personality*, New York: Harper, 1954

196 Medinnus, G. R., 'Immanent justice in children: a review of the literature and additional data', *J. genet. Psychol.*, 1959, 90, 253–262

197 Medinnus, G. R., 'Objective responsibility in children: a comparison with the Piaget data', *J. genet. Psychol.*, 1962, 101, 127–133

198 Medinnus, G. R., 'Age and sex differences in conscience development', *J. genet. Psychol.*, 1966, 109, 117–118

199 Medinnus, G. R., 'Behavioural and cognitive measures of conscience development', *J. genet. Psychol.*, 1966, 109, 147–150

200 Middleton, R. and Putney, S., 'Religion, normative standards and behaviour', *Sociometry*, 1962, 25, 141–152

201 Midlarsky, Elizabeth and Bryan, J. H., 'Training charity in children', *J. pers. soc. Psychol.*, 1967, 5, 408–415

202 Mills, J., 'Changes in moral attitudes following temptation', *J. Pers.*, 1958, 26, 517–531

203 Milner, E., 'Effects of sex role and social status on the early adolescent personality', *Genet. Psychol. Monogr.*, 1949, 40, 231–325

204 Mischel, W., 'Theory and research on the antecedents of self-

imposed delay of reward', pp. 85–132 in B. A. Maher (ed.), *Progress in Experimental Personality Research*, New York and London: Academic Press, 1966

205 Mischel, W. and Grusec, Joan, 'Determinants of the rehearsal and transmission of neutral and aversive behaviours', *J. pers. soc. Psychol.*, 1966, 3, 197–205

206 Mischel, W. and Metzner, R., 'Preference for delayed reward as a function of age, intelligence and length of delay interval', *J. abnorm. soc. Psychol.*, 1962, 64, 425–431

207 Money-Kyrle, R. E., 'Psychoanalysis and ethics', in Melanie Klein and Paula Heimann (eds.), *New Directions in Psychoanalysis*, Oxford: Blackwell, 1955

208 Monroe, Ruth, *Schools of Psychoanalytic Thought*, London: Hutchinson, 1957

209 Moreton, F. E., 'Attitudes to religion among adolescents and adults', *Brit. J. educ. Psychol.*, 1944, 14, 69–79

210 Morris, J. F., 'The development of adolescent value judgments', *Brit. J. educ. Psychol.*, 1958, 28, 1–14

211 Mowrer, O. H., *Learning Theory and Personality Dynamics*, New York: Ronald Press, 1950

212 Mowrer, O. H., *Learning Theory and the Symbolic Processes*, New York: Wiley, 1960

213 Mowrer, O. H., *The New Group Therapy*, Princeton, New Jersey: Van Nostrand, 1964

214 Murdock, G. P. and Whiting, J. W. M., 'Cultural determination of parental attitudes: the relationship between the social structure, particularly family structure, and parental behaviour', pp. 13–34 in M. J. Senn (ed.), *Problems of Infancy and Childhood*, New York: Josiah Macy Jr. Foundation, 1951

215 Mussen, P. H., 'Early socialization: learning and identification', pp. 51–110 in G. Mandler *et al* (eds.), *New Directions in Psychology*, III, New York: Holt, Rinehart and Winston, 1967

216 Mussen, P. H. and Distler, L., 'Masculinity, identification and father–son relationships', *J. abnorm. soc. Psychol.*, 1959, 59, 350–356

217 Mussen, P. H. and Distler, L., 'Child-rearing antecedents

of masculine identification in kindergarten boys', *Child Devpt.*, 1960, 31, 89–100

218 Mussen, P. H. and Parker, Ann L., 'Mother nurturance and girls' incidental imitative learning', *J. pers. soc. Psychol.*, 1965, 2, 94–97

219 Najarian-Svajian, P. H., 'The idea of immanent justice among Lebanese children and adults', *J. genet. Psychol.*, 1966, 109, 57–66

220 Nesbitt, J. E., 'The development of character integration in children from nine to 14 years', unpublished thesis, University of Manchester, 1962

221 Newcomb, T. M., Turner, R. H. and Converse, P. E., *Social Psychology*, New York: Holt, Rinehart and Winston, 1965

222 Newson, J. and Newson, Elizabeth, *Patterns of Infant Care in an Urban Community*, London: Penguin Books, 1965

223 Parsons, T. and Bales, R. F., *Family Socialization and Interaction Process*, London: Routledge and Kegan Paul, 1956

224 Peck, R. H. and Havighurst, R. J., *The Psychology of Character Development*, New York: Wiley, 1960

225 Peters, R. S., *Authority, Responsibility and Education*, London: Allen and Unwin, 1959

226 Piaget, J., *The Child's Conception of the World*, London: Kegan Paul, 1929

227 Piaget, J., *The Moral Judgment of the Child*, London: Routledge and Kegan Paul, 1932

228 Piers, G. and Singer, M. B., *Shame and Guilt, a Psychoanalytic and a Cultural Study*, Springfield, Ill.: Charles C. Thomas, 1953

229 Porteus, Barbara D. and Johnson, R. C., 'Children's responses to two measures of conscience development and their relation to sociometric nomination', *Child Devpt.*, 1965, 36, 703–711

230 Price, W. H. and Whatmore, P. B., 'Criminal behaviour and the XYY male', *Nature*, 25 February 1967, 213, 815

231 Price, W. H. and Whatmore, P. B., 'Behaviour disorders and pattern of crime among XYY males identified at a

maximum security hospital', *Brit. med. J.*, 4 March 1967, 533–536

232 Rebelsky, F. G., Allinsmith, W. and Grinder, R. E., 'Resistance to temptation and sex differences in children's use of fantasy confession', *Child Devpt.*, 1963, 34, 955–961

233 Rempel, H. and Signori, E. I., 'Sex differences in self-rating of conscience as a determinant of behaviour', *Psychol. Rev.*, 1964, 15, 277–278

234 Rest, J., Turiel, E. and Kohlberg, L., 'Level of moral development as a determinant of preference and comprehension of moral judgments made by others', *J. Pers.*, 1969, 37, 225–252

235 Rickman, J., 'The development of the moral function', pp. 67–86 in J. A. Lauwerys and N. Hans (eds.), *Yearbook of Education, 1951*, London: Evans Bros., 1951

236 Rosenhan, D., 'Some origins of concern for others', pp. 491–507 in D. Rosenhan and P. London (eds.), *Theory and Research in Abnormal Psychology*, New York: Holt, Rinehart and Winston, 1969

237 Rosenhan, D. and London, P., 'Character', pp. 251–289 in P. London and D. Rosenhan, *Foundations of Abnormal Psychology*, New York: Holt, Rinehart and Winston, 1968

238 Ross, Dorothea, 'Relationship between dependency, intentional learning and incidental learning in preschool children', *J. pers. soc. Psychol.*, 1966, 4, 374–381

239 Ruma, E. and Mosher, P., 'Relationship between moral judgment and guilt in delinquent boys', *J. abnorm. soc. Psychol.*, 1967, 72, 122–127

240 Sandler, J., 'On the concept of superego', pp. 128–162 in *The Psychoanalytic Study of the Child*, 1960, 15, New York: International Universities Press, 1960

241 Sanford, N., 'The dynamics of identification', *Psychol. Rev.*, 1955, 62, 106–118

242 Schafer, R. 'The loving and beloved superego in Freud's structural theory', *Psychoanal. Study of the Child*, 1960, 15, 163–188

243 Schafer, R., 'Ideals, the ego ideal and the self', pp. 129–176 in R. R. Holt (ed.), *Motives and Thought: Psychoanalytic Essays in Honour of David Rapaport. Psychol. Issues*, 1967, 5, Monogr. 18/19

244 Schoeppe, A. 'Sex differences in adolescent socialization', *J. soc. Psychol.*, 1953, 38, 175–185

245 Schwartz, S. H., Feldman, K. A., Brown, M. E. and Heingartner, A., 'Some personality correlates of conduct in two situations of moral conflict', *J. Pers.*, 37, 41–57

246 Sears, R. R., 'The growth of conscience', pp. 92–111 in Ira Iscoe and H. W. Stevenson (eds.), *Personality Development in Children*, Austin, Texas: University of Texas Press, 1960

247 Sears, R. R., 'Relation of early socialization experiences to aggression in middle childhood', *J. abnorm. soc. Psychol.*, 1961, 63, 466–492

248 Sears, R. R., Maccoby, Eleanor E. and Levin, H. *Patterns of Child Rearing*, Evanston, Ill.: Row Peterson, 1957

249 Sears, R. R., Rau, Lucy and Alpert, R., *Identification and Child Rearing*, Stanford, Cal.: Stanford University Press, 1965

250 Shaffer, H. R. and Emerson, Peggy E., 'The development of social attachments in infancy', *Monogr. of the Society for Research in Child Development*, 1964, 29, No. 3 (Serial No. 94)

251 Shoben, E. J., 'Moral behaviour and moral learning', *Religious Educ.*, 1963, 58, 137–145

252 Skinner, B. F., *Walden Two*, New York: Macmillan, 1948 (Paperback, 1962)

253 Skinner, B. F., *Science and Human Behaviour*, New York: Macmillan 1953 (Paperback, New York: Free Press, and London: Collier-Macmillan, 1965)

254 Skinner, B. F., *Verbal Behaviour*, London: Methuen, 1959

255 Solomon, R. L., Turner, L. H. and Lessac, M. S., 'Some effects of delay of punishment on resistance to temptation in dogs', *J. pers. soc. Psychol.*, 1968, 8, 233–238

256 Stafford-Clark, D., Bond, D. and Doust, J. W. L., 'The psychopath in prison: a preliminary report of cooperative research', *Brit. J. Delinquency*, 1951, 2, 117–129

257 Stein, E. V., *Guilt: Theory and Therapy*, London : Allen and Unwin, 1969

258 Stein, M. H., 'Self-observation, reality and the superego', pp. 275–297 in R. M. Loewenstein *et al.*, *Psychoanalysis, a General Psychology (Essays in Honour of Heinz Hartmann)*, New York : International Universities Press, 1966

259 Stephenson, G. M., *The Development of Conscience*, London : Routledge and Kegan Paul, 1966

260 Stoke, S. M., 'An inquiry into the concept of identification', *J. genet. Psychol.*, 1950, 76, 163–189

261 Stuart, R. B., 'Decentration in the development of children's concepts of moral and causal judgment', *J. genet. Psychol.*, 1967, 111, 59–68

262 Swainson, Beatrice M., 'The development of moral ideas in children and adolescents', unpublished thesis, University of Oxford, 1949

263 Terman, L. M. and Oden, Melita H., *The Gifted Child Grows Up*, Stanford, Cal.: Stanford University Press, 1947

264 Tran-Thong, *Stades et Concept de Stade de Développement de l'Enfant dans la Psychologie Contemporaine*, Paris: Librairie Philosophique J. Vrin, 1967

265 Trenaman, J., *Out of Step*, London : Methuen, 1952

266 Tuma, E. and Livson, N., 'Family socioeconomic status and adolescent attitudes to authority', *Child Devpt.*, 1960, 31, 387–399

267 Turiel, E., 'Developmental processes in the child's moral thinking', pp. 92–133 in P. H. Mussen *et al* (eds.), *Trends and Issues in Developmental Psychology*, New York : Holt, Rinehart and Winston, 1969

268 Turner, G. N. H., 'A re-examination of certain of Piaget's inquiries on children's moral judgments in the light of his later theory', unpublished thesis, University of Manchester, 1966

269 Unger, S. M., 'Antecedents of personality differences in guilt responsibility', *Psychol. Rep.*, 1962, 10, 357–358

270 Walters, R. H. and Amoroso, D. M., 'Cognitive and emotional determinants of the occurrence of imitative behaviour', *Brit. J. soc. clin. Psychol.*, 1967, 6, 174–185

271 Wattenberg, W. W., 'Church attendance and juvenile misconduct', *Sociol. soc. Res.*, 1950, 34, 195–202

272 West, D. J., *The Habitual Prisoner*, London : Macmillan, 1963

273 Whiteman, P. H. and Kosier, K. P., 'Development of children's moralistic judgments—age, sex, IQ and certain personal-experiential variables', *Child Devpt.*, 1964, 35, 843–850

274 Whiting, J. M., 'Resource mediation and learning in identification', pp. 112–126 in Ira Iscoe and H. W. Stevenson, *Personality Development in Children*, Austin, Texas : University of Texas Press, 1960

275 Whiting, J. W. M. and Child, I. L., *Child Training and Personality*, New Haven : Yale University Press, 1953

276 Wilson, J., 'What is moral education?' Part 1, pp. 39–220 in J. Wilson, N. Williams and B. Sugarman, *Introduction to Moral Education*, London : Penguin Books, 1967

277 Winch, R. F., *Identification and its Familial Determinants*, Indianapolis : Bobbs-Merrill, 1962

278 Winnicott, D. W., 'Psychoanalysis and the sense of guilt', pp. 15–28 in *The Maturational Processes and the Facilitating Environment*, London : Hogarth Press and Institute of Psychoanalysis, 1965

279 Wright, D., 'Does "conscience" exist?', *New Society*, 21 November 1968, no. 321, 751–754

280 Wright, D. S., 'Moral development', pp. 588–615 in D. S. Wright *et al.*, *Introducing Psychology. An Experimental Approach*, London : Penguin Books, 1970

281 Wright, D. and Cox, E., 'A study of the relationship between moral judgment and religious belief in a sample of English adolescents', *J. soc. Psychol.*, 1967, 72, 135–144

282 Zarncke, Lilly, *Enfance et Conscience Morale*, (translated from German), Paris : Editions du Cerf, 1955

Indexes

Author Index

Subject Index

Abnormality 267
Accommodation 19, 212
Achievement, need for 16
Affect, maturity of 241
Affection 146, 231
Aggressiveness 35f., 41, 44, 46, 247,
    250, 265, 268
Aggression 35f, 39, 45, 57, 81f, 87,
    89, 115, 134, 139, 140, 146, 147,
    149, 150, 151, 215, 218, 246, 258,
    260, 266
Altruism 16, 56, 159–171, 183,
    249, 274
Altruistic surrender 56
Anomy 183, 185, 204
Anxiety 32, 40, 43, 44, 45, 55, 82f,
    86, 99, 100, 103, 120, 123, 125,
    126, 129, 132, 139, 140, 154, 155,
    156, 164, 174, 176, 186, 266
Anxiety, other-directed 178–187,
    253, 262
Apology 247, 250
Arousal, vicarious 164
Assimilation 19, 212, 214
Authority 10, 37, 64, 187, 201, 202,
    203, 204, 219, 228, 246, 258, 259,
    283
Autonomy 155, 184, 192, 195, 202,
    203, 204, 205, 220
Autonomy *versus* doubt and shame
    58

Behaviour, anti-ascetic 255
Behaviour, anti-social 255

Behaviour disorder, psychopathic
    270
Beliefs, moral 240
Bullying 283

Castration fears 29, 33
Censorship 21, 22
Centration 226
Character, affectionless 270
Character, moral 13, 25, 240
Character types 172–180, 188
Cheating 14, 15, 16, 131, 134, 136,
    152, 205, 219, 239f, 248f, 260
Child-rearing methods 139ff
Class, social 105, 237, 255, 257–263
Cognitive template 117–120
Cognitive theories 17, 18, 20, 276,
    279, 281f
Conditioning 95, 100ff, 112, 167,
    168, 273, 274, 280
Conditioning, vicarious 164
Confession 13, 14, 122, 123, 126,
    127, 148, 156, 247, 250, 259
Conflict, moral 176, 205, 235, 282
Conformity, conventional role 227
Conscience 13, 26, 32, 34, 35, 36,
    38, 43, 46, 54, 58, 77, 84, 103, 106,
    107, 108, 129, 144, 145, 174, 175,
    177, 178, 180, 202, 216, 228, 246,
    247, 251, 264, 267, 271, 273, 275
Conscience, dimensions of 179f
Conscience, levels of 175
Conscience, types of 179
Conscience motive 178, 186, 187,
    253, 262